The Monastic World
1000-1300

The Monastic World
1000-1300

Christopher Brooke
Photographs by Wim Swaan

Random House ⌂ New York

TO
FATHER DAVID

Library of Congress Cataloging in Publication Data
Brooke, Christopher Nugent Lawrence.
The monastic world, 1000-1300.
1. Monasticism and religious orders — Middle Ages,
600-1500. I. Title.
BX2470.B76   1974   271′.009′02   74-5368
ISBN 0-394-47478-3

Designed by Harold Bartram

Filmset in England by Photocomp Limited, Birmingham
I.G.D.A., Officine Grafiche, Novara 1974 Printed in Italy

1 *'Andate là, quivi è la porta.'* 'Pass that way: here the gate is.' Dante
Purgatorio, ix.90. Durham Cathedral, England, twelfth-century bronze door
knocker.

Contents

Preface

I embarked on this book in the conviction that the dialogue between the literature and the buildings of medieval monastic communities was a theme too little developed by historians. What a presumptuous idea! I know how rich is the literature on monastic architecture and monastic life and letters, how frequently they have been brought into relation one with another. Yet I still feel that there is a large gap. I have seen it often when discussing monastic buildings with students; I have seen it when reading or listening to historians and art historians discussing similar themes. Monastic buildings can be the material for an inquiry at once very searching and very agreeable. If they are set in relation to the other evidence for monastic history they stretch our minds and constantly urge us to ask questions. They also lead us to many pleasant and beautiful places; and sometimes the beauty of the buildings or the setting gives us a clue we could hardly otherwise discover. Above all, they show us a vital part of the artistic creation of Romanesque and early Gothic art and architecture. Thus I accepted the publishers' invitation to collaborate with Wim Swaan, not only to have a share in a beautiful book, but in one in which his sharp eye for architectural and artistic form and detail could provide historical evidence otherwise unobtainable. It is a work of collaboration: we have both tried to see in the visible remains of medieval monasteries the history, culture, way of life and religious sentiment which they reveal, especially in the period 1000-1300; and to describe in our different media the history of the medieval monastic world.

The book is chiefly about monks and monasteries. But the religious life has always been open to people who were not monks: in our period especially to those who followed the Rule of St Augustine and are known as canons regular, to those who followed the inspiration of St Francis or St Dominic and are called friars, to those who became entangled in the military adventures of the Crusades, and so were knights; and, above all, to women, to the nuns, who may well have been first in the field and in recent generations have far outnumbered the men. Monks, canons, friars—it is convenient to use these words distinctly, though they have been often and honourably confused. The communities they lived in, according to medieval usage, may all be called convents, for the word at root simply means communities; but we may distinguish monasteries, the homes of monks, from the houses of friars and canons, and also distinguish abbeys, religious houses ruled by abbots, from priories ruled by priors. The rich variety of medieval religion means that a book on this scale must be extremely selective—but not narrow, for our

examples are drawn from all over western Europe and from many orders and settings.

So far as possible, the plates and text march together; but it was in the nature of the case that this would not happen in the early chapters; and here are gathered plates to illustrate the geographical range and the variety of the monastic houses of western Europe—a monastery of the mountains; a hill-top shrine turned abbey; two artistic centres, one Romanesque, one Gothic, the second set in an ancient city; and a new Cistercian house of the twelfth century, plain and puritanical.

The eleventh century saw the heyday of traditional monasticism, that is, of the monastic life lived according to the Rule of St Benedict and a body of customs which had grown up over the centuries: it was a great and traditional ritual aimed to provide a fitting setting for communal life. In the late eleventh century new ideas began to foster the greatly increased variety characteristic of the twelfth and thirteenth centuries. Hence part I treats the formation and nature of the traditional monastic life, part II sketches the physiognomy and inspiration of the new. In part III we draw the threads together, especially in chapter 13, and look briefly at the destiny of these movements.

My chief debt is to Wim Swaan, for it was his skill which first inspired and then sustained the enterprise; and his friendship and co-operation have enhanced the privilege of working with such a master of his craft. It has not been an easy book to write; without him it would never have been written; nor would it have come to fruition without the sustained help and encouragement and shrewd criticism of Professor Donald Bullough, Dr Robert Markus, and, above all, my wife, Dr Rosalind Brooke. The early stages of its writing were clouded by misunderstanding, but in the final phase I have been grateful to Mr Paul Elek and his colleagues for their friendly co-operation, and especially to Miss Moira Johnston for her generous help; I am also very grateful to Miss Julia Twigg and Miss Mary Turner. I greatly appreciate the skill and expertise of Mr Harold Bartram in the maps and plans and in the design of the book.

I am deeply grateful for help, in numerous different ways, to the Reverend N. Backmund, O. Praem., Miss Brenda Bolton, Professor the Reverend Owen Chadwick, Mr John Chancellor, Professor K. J. Conant (see p. 8), Professor G. Constable, Professor C. R. Dodwell, Brother Christopher Mannion, M. Pierre Quarré, Dr R. W. Southern, Professor George Zarnecki and Professor Monsignore Don Piero Zerbi. Mr and Mrs P. B. Clark, Professor and Mrs Manfred Hesse, and

Mr and Mrs Charles Robertson have helped me on my visits to a number of monastic sites: by Mrs Robertson's kindness I was able to join the Courtauld Institute Summer School in Provence in 1971 and visit a number of houses under the expert guidance of Dr Alan Borg, Dr Peter Kidson and Mr Christopher Hohler. I am particularly indebted to Mrs Gillian Bateman and Miss Claire McCue for help in typing the manuscript.

In the choice of examples and the revision of the captions Mr Neil Stratford gave expert and invaluable guidance. The dates of many of the monuments illustrated are disputed: we have had particular help in pursuit of the best current views from Mr Stratford and Professor Zarnecki; for errors and aberrations neither they nor any other of my helpers can claim any credit.

To Professor Dom David Knowles, once my teacher—and always the master of those who study monastic history—I dedicate the book in affection and gratitude.

Christopher Brooke
1974

Acknowledgements

The author and publishers wish first to acknowledge five acts of personal kindness in the search for additional illustrations. Professor K. J. Conant has been very generous in providing material and advice from the rich store of his learning; in particular he has provided us with plate 87, and with permission to reproduce both the plan of Cluny and this plate; we are also indebted to the Mediaeval Academy of America and its Secretary, Dr Paul Meyvaert, for copyright permission. Professor Conant's researches have modified his plan of Cluny from time to time, and the most recent plan involves minor changes in the infirmary and guest-house not shown in fig. 6.

The engraving of Reichenau, pl. 68, was obtained for us by the kindness of Frau Barbara Hesse from the Staatsarchiv in Zürich; it is 'nach einem grossen Ölgemälde aus der Münster-kirche auf Reichenau aus: *"Die Insel Reichenau im Untersee (Bodensee, bei Constanz) mit ihrer ehemaligen berühmten Reichsabtei"*, urkundlich beschrieben von F. X. C. Staiger, Constanz, 1860, Druck und Verlag v. J. Stalder, Commissions-verlag von J. T. Stettner in Lindau.'

For plate 384 we are very grateful to Professor Dr Brigitte Kürbis. Dom Norbert Backmund, O. Praem., among other acts of kindness, provided us, with the help of Dr U. Lange, with the photocopy from A. Kamphausen, *Der Dom zu Ratzeburg*, 2nd edn., Heide, 1966, p. 7, on which fig. 21 is based. Prof. Mgr Don Piero Zerbi and Mgr Can. Theodolindo Brivio took particular trouble to arrange permission for Wim Swaan to photograph the Basilica of Sant'Ambrogio.

To them, and to all the other individuals and organisations in many parts of western Europe who permitted Wim Swaan to photograph their buildings, books and treasures, the author, photographer and publishers would like to offer their thanks for their co-operation and courtesy.

Acknowledgement is made to the following for photographs not taken by Wim Swaan and for their permission for

reproduction: The Trustees of the British Museum, plates 30, 50, 51, 74, 78, 90-7, 141-3, 179-80, 190, 216-17, 289-90, 323; the Bibliothèque Nationale, Paris, 83, 192, 349; the Kunsthalle, Hamburg, 390; the Mansell Collection, 321; Photographie Giraudon, 44; the Stiftsbibliothek, Sankt Gallen, 39. Dr K. H. Esser and the editor and publishers of *Archiv für mittel-rheinische Kirchengeschichte* gave permission for the repro-duction of pl. 252, from a copy in the Bodleian Library.

For the extracts quoted in the text the author and publishers would like to acknowledge permission to reproduce from the following: Professor the Reverend Owen Chadwick and the SCM Press for O. Chadwick's *Western Asceticism*; Professor C. R. Dodwell and Thomas Nelson & Sons for Theophilus, *De diversis artibus;* Dr Decima Douie and the Delegates of the Oxford University Press for the extract from *Magna Vita Sancti Hugonis*; Sir Maurice Powicke's literary executor and Thomas Nelson & Sons for Walter Daniel's *Life of Ailred of Rievaulx*; and the Longman Group for Christopher Brooke's *Europe in the Central Middle Ages*.

The maps and plans were drawn by Harold Bartram from material supplied by the author, who was much helped in his work by numerous historical atlases etc. especially the classic Spruner-Menke, *Hand-Atlas für die Geschichte des Mittlelalters und der neueren Zeit* (3rd edn., Gotha, 1880); the Elsevier-Nelson, *Atlas of the Early Christian World*, ed. F. Van der Meer and C. Mohrmann (London, 1959) esp. map 6; and the Elsevier, *Atlas de l'ordre cistercien*, ed. F. Van der Meer (Amsterdam-Brussels, 1965).

The author and publishers would like to acknowledge the sources of the maps and plans and to thank the publishers and the authors for permission to use them.

Alcobaça: ed. M.-A. Dimier, *L'art cistercien hors de France*, Zodiaque (1971), p. 298; Alvastra: Dimier (1971), p. 30; Bologna, San Stefano: G. Aprato, *Tesori d'arte cristiana*, 11, p. 281; Buildwas: Dimier (1971), p. 180; Cluny: see above; Dryburgh: Dept. of the Environment Guide, HMSO (2nd edn., 1948); Eberbach: Dimier (1971), p. 104, compared with W. Braunfels, *Monasteries of Western Europe*, Eng. trans. Thames & Hudson (1972), p. 78; Fossanova: Dimier (1971), p. 197; Fountains: Dept. of the Environment Guide, HMSO (1970), Sir W. St John Hope in *Yorks. Arch. Journ.*, XV (1900), D. Knowles and J. K. S. St Joseph, *Monastic Sites from the Air*, Cambridge University Press (1952), p. xxi, Fontevrault: M. Melot, *Fontevrault*, Petites Monographies des Grands Édifices de la France, Librairie Henri Laurens, Paris, Editions Jacques Lanore Succ., (1971), pp. 8-9; Heiligenkreuz: Dimier (1971), p. 34; Hovedö: Dimier (1971), p. 34; Jumièges: A. W. Clapham, *English Romanesque Architecture after the Conquest*, Clarendon Press, Oxford (1934), p. 10; (after G. Lanfry); Lacock: H. Brakespear, *Archaeologia*, LVII (1901); Maul-bronn: Braunfels (1972), p. 78; Milan, Sant'Ambrogio: F. Reggiori, *La Basilica di Sant'Ambrogio*, Cassa di Risparmio delle Provincie Lombarde, Milan (1966), p. 42; Mont Saint-Michel: P. Gout, *Le Mont Saint-Michel*, II, Librairie Armand Colin, Paris (1910), planches XXVI-XXVIII; Mount Grace: St John Hope in *Yorks. Arch. Journ.*, XVIII (1905); Much Wenlock: Dept. of the Environment Guide, HMSO (1948, repr. 1967); Poblet: Dimier (1971), p. 135; Ratzeburg: see above; Rievaulx: Dept. of the Environment Guide, HMSO (1967); Rome, Santi Quattro Coronati: A. Carletti, *Basilica dei SS. Quattro Coronati*, Foto-Fano-Vitturini Rome (n.d.), p. 44; Sénanque: from an old plan publ. by Clement St Just, Avignon, reproduced in *Abbaye de Sénanque*, Lyon, Helio-gravure Lescuyer; Le Thoronet: P. Colas, *L'abbaye du Thoronet*, Caisse Nationale des Monuments Historiques (1971).

Note on the plans of monastic buildings

Where possible, photographs of each monastic complex have been grouped together so as to make them more comprehensible; and for twenty-one houses plans are also provided. To make these as intelligible as possible to English and non-English readers alike, abbreviated names for the various parts of the building have been given in standard form; this saves us from an elaborate numerical code, though numbers are used in a few cases to explain special features of a plan. No attempt is made to identify every part of the buildings—indeed, the identifications which appear on some modern plans are sometimes very conjectural—but to clarify the normal and fundamental elements in the monastic plan.

A typical arrangement in a monastery of the mid or late Middle Ages comprised a large church, cruciform in shape, with a cloister garth nestling against its nave and south transept—a square courtyard, that is, with the main domestic buildings beside the remaining walks: chapter house and parlour(s), with dormitory above, on the east walk, kitchen and refectory on the south, offices and storehouses on the west—or, in a Cistercian house, the quarters of the lay brothers. Outside this central group lay the guest-house, commonly to the west, and the abbot's lodging and infirmary, sometimes round a subsidiary cloister further east. This plan was subject to numerous modifications; even the most uniform order, the Cistercian, adapted their plans to the sites in a certain degree. In particular, they were comparatively indifferent whether the cloister lay south or north of the church: no doubt they shared the general preference for a sunny cloister, but essentially they looked for a site where they could lay a church on solid ground and the domestic buildings towards a river, for water supply and drainage. See especially pp. 139, 204.

The following abbreviations are used in the plans:
Abb = Abbatia, abbot's lodging
Arm = Armarium, book cupboard or room
Atr = Atrium, narthex, courtyard to west of church
Cal = Calefactorium, calefactory, warming room, monks' parlour
Cap = Capitulum, chapter house
Cla = Claustrum, cloister (at Sant'Ambrogio, Milan, 'Mon', monachorum, and 'Can', canonicorum, monks' and canons' cloisters: see p. 220
Conv = Conversi, lay brothers (quarters of)
Coq = Coquina, kitchen
Dor = Dormitorium, dormitory

Eccl = Ecclesia, church
Gal = Galilaea, galilee, paradise, western porch
Hosp = Hospitium, guest house
Inf = Infirmaria, infirmary
Lat = Latrina, latrine(s)
Lav = Lavatorium, lavabo, ceremonial wash-place in cloister, near refectory
Nov = Noviciorum cella, novices' room
Pr = Prioratus, prior's lodging (and Priorissatus, prioress's)
Ref = Refectorium, refectory

A few minor features are only noted occasionally: thus the night stair from dormitory to church, normal in Cistercian houses and not uncommon e.g. in Augustinian, is marked on the plan of Maulbronn and noted on that of Buildwas, figs. 13, 12.

Fig.1 *Overleaf* Map of Europe showing the monastic sites used as examples in the text and plates.

Falkenau

Lyse

Hovedö

Alvastra

Dünamünde

Nydala

Iona

Esrom

Melrose Kelso
Dryburgh Jedburgh
Hexham Jarrow
Carlisle Monkwearmouth
Blanchland Durham
Finchale
Bangor Mount Grace Whitby
Ripon Rievaulx
Fountains York
Pontefract

Odensee

Ratzeburg

Mellifont

Durrow

Sulejow

Kirkstead
Buildwas Sempringham
Much Wenlock Leicester
Northampton
Worcester Bury St Edmunds
Llanthony I Evesham Markyate Colchester
Llanthony II St Albans
Kingswood London
Lacock Abingdon Reading
Glastonbury Witham Canterbury
Sherborne Winchester

Vreden Gandersheim Quedlinburg
Xanten Helmarshausen Gernrode
Essen
Essen-Werden
Altenberg Tyniec

Brogne
Villers-la-Ville Prague
Arrouaise
Maria Laach Fulda
Paraclet Eberbach
Trier Rupertsberg bei Bingen
Laon
Jumièges Prémontré
Caen Bec Maulbronn Heidenheim Niederaltaich
Saint-Évroult Bernay Gorze Hirsau
Séez Saint-Denis Saint-Odilien Tegernsee Reichersberg Heiligenkreuz
La Trappe
Mont Saint-Michel Savigny Clairvaux Ottobeuren Salzburg
Tiron Morimond
Solesmes Molesme Reichenau
Fleury Luxeuil St Gallen
Vézelay Dijon Einsiedeln
Fontevrault Cîteaux
Poitiers Saint-Savin-sur-Gartempe (Taizé)
Grandmont Cluny
Marcigny

Milan Verona
Fruttuaria Chiaravalle
La Grande Chartreuse Sagra di San Michele Turin
Conques Mazan Bobbio
Bologna
Moissac Florence Camaldoli
Saint-Ruf Senanque Lucca Vallombrosa
Apt Pisa Fonte Avellana
Saint-Gilles Silvacane
Toulouse Arles Le Thoronet Assisi
Saint-Guilhem- Marseille Spoleto
Santiago de Compostela Lézat le-Desert
Farfa
San Juan de la Peña Cuxa Rome Subiaco
Sahagún Las Huelgas Casamari
Saint-Martin-du-Canigou Tre Fontane Monte Cassino
Silos Ripoll Fossanova
Osma La Cava dei Tirreni
Montserrat
Poblet Santes Creus

Tomar Toledo
Alcobaça

Vivarium

Monreale Cefalù

0   50   100   200   300 miles
0   100   200   300   400km

part 1
The monastic tradition

Fig. 1

1 Prelude

Origins

From the very beginnings of Christianity the question has been asked: can the good life, the Christian life, be led in the world, is it compatible with earthly joys and pleasures?—or must it, in its highest and truest forms, involve renunciation, stern discipline, an ascetic life, and celibacy? There is a single chapter in St Matthew's Gospel[1] in which the claims of family life, and of children, are bewilderingly juxtaposed with the call to renounce both family and the resources to support it.

'And they twain shall be one flesh. . . . What therefore God hath joined together, let not man put asunder. . . . [To refrain from marriage] is something which not everyone can accept, but only those for whom God has appointed it. For while some are incapable of marriage because they were born so, or were made so by men, there are others who have themselves renounced marriage for the sake of the kingdom of Heaven. Let those accept it who can. . . .

'Let the children come to me; do not try to stop them; for the kingdom of Heaven belongs to such as these. . . .

'If you wish to go the whole way, go, sell your possessions, and give to the poor, and then you will have riches in heaven; and come, follow me. . . . It is easier for a camel to pass through the eye of a needle than for a rich man to enter the kingdom of God.

'Then who can be saved? . . . For men this is impossible; but everything is possible for God. . . . Anyone who has left brothers or sisters, father, mother or children [and in a similar context St Luke demands renunciation of one's wife as well], land or houses for the sake of my name will be repaid many times over, and gain eternal life.'

There is clear justification in this chapter for many varieties of personal and religious experience; it is impossible to convert the moral teaching of Jesus into a code. One can only cut out the apparent inconsistencies by surgery so extreme as to be fatal. The reason is clear enough: Our Lord's teaching was addressed to actual human situations; it was *ad personam*; if it was to have any depth, subtlety, truth to human experience, it could not be at the superficial level consistent. In a similar way the married and the ascetic have over the centuries both derived some comfort from St Paul. 'It is a good thing for a man to have nothing to do with women' is an unpromising start to his account of marriage and its problems in I Corinthians, and he clearly prefers his own state of celibacy and thinks women something of an encumbrance on men and on the Church. In the Epistle to the Ephesians[2] the union of husband and wife in marriage is likened to the relation of

2 Maria Laach, Germany, a model of the church in the founder's hands, in wood, from the thirteenth-century effigy of the eleventh-century Count Henry.

Christ and the Church. It is clear that Paul had to deal with a bemusing variety of views and practices, and that in I Corinthians he was trying to save marriage from total disrepute, while not condemning celibacy, in the comparatively brief space before the world came to an end. As it became clearer that the world would survive awhile, and the Church had to come to such terms as it could with society, a clearer, and, one is bound to say loftier, doctrine of marriage was propounded. In the Pastoral Epistles, especially in I Timothy, there is a warm domesticity.

But coming to terms with society could not involve renunciation of the standards and ideals of Jesus and Paul. The austere ascetic life which the author of I Timothy had authorised for older widows remained a feature of many churches; and beside chastity a moderate poverty was from the first natural to many in a community largely made up of the poor. In a passage of the Acts quoted in almost every monastic Rule which has ever been written, St Luke described how 'The whole body of believers was united in heart and soul. Not a man of them claimed any of his possessions as his own, but everything was held in common. . . .'[3] And all the Synoptic Gospels described the poverty and simplicity in which the disciples had been sent to preach, taking nothing for the way.[4] Whenever we are allowed a real insight into early Christian communities, we find a variety of experience and approach, some rejoicing in family life and in the world as God's creation, others looking to the austerer words of the New Testament for their inspiration. But while variety seems to most modern readers of the New Testament to have been the practice and expectation from the first, there seem always too to have been voices raised which proclaimed a single element in the Christian tradition as the only true path. Many a monastic founder of early and medieval times read the Gospels and Acts and concluded that he alone was imitating the apostles; the *vita apostolica*—the apostolic way of life—was a rallying cry for all manner of religious reformers.[5] Out of the early ascetic groups, scattered all over the Roman Empire, developed the movement which has since been specifically known as 'monastic'.

In its original, etymological sense, a monk was one who dwelt alone (μόνος in Greek), and the first monks of the Egyptian desert were hermits or anchorites. But from very early days there came to be communities of monks living in monasteries, *coenobia* (from the Greek κοινός or common) and most of the monks who are the subject of this book have lived in communities and hence were called coenobites. The

3-6, 9 Saint-Martin-du-Canigou, France. Built on a lofty, lonely site chosen by the count of Cerdagne and the monk and priest Selva; one of many abbeys founded about 1000. It was settled by monks from Ripoll *c.*1009, completed in the early or mid eleventh century, and little altered before its substantial restoration early in the twentieth century.

3 The southern gallery, looking across the gorge; mostly of the twelfth and twentieth centuries.

4 The main church looking east, eleventh century.

monastic ideal, however, is commonly reckoned to owe its formation to St Antony (*c.* 251-356), and he was the first great anchorite and leader in the Egyptian desert at the turn of the third and fourth centuries; it is beyond doubt that it was in the deserts of Egypt in the early fourth century that monasticism, as a large-scale movement, was born. Three men conspired to create the tradition of orthodox monasticism: Athanasius the bishop and theologian, Antony the hermit, and Pachomius the coenobite.[6] They hardly knew one another; but they seem to have known that on their co-operation the survival and success of much of what each stood for depended. Antony and Pachomius were the founders; Athanasius, bishop of Alexandria, helped to give their work fame and res-

pectability. He is generally reckoned the author of the first Life of Antony, and so the man primarily responsible for recording and disseminating knowledge of his life and ideals. Beside Antony, in early tradition was set a colleague and rival called Paul; but Paul is a shadowy figure and it is evident that Antony, if not precisely the first hermit in time, was the true founder of the movement. We cannot be sure of all the reasons for the primacy of Egypt, but two are particularly clear. First, though many early monks were very simple men and Antony himself no theologian, monasticism was partly inspired by a powerful intellectual stimulus. The Christian Platonists of Alexandria—perhaps the most remarkable group of theologians of the day—had brought together, in a unique world of learning and devotion, the known deposits of Greek philosophy and religious practice with the traditions of early Christianity; and the greatest of them, Origen, made himself a eunuch for the Kingdom's sake and preached an extreme asceticism; celibacy was to him as holy as martyrdom. Yet for the rank and file of the Egyptian Church martyrdom was the highest aspiration of the Christian; and as Christianity ceased to be the religion of a few devout souls and became a popular religion, the contrast between heroic Christians ready

4

Fig. 2

Fig.2 Centres of monastic life, c.250-735. Only major centres mentioned in early chapters are named; the areas of work and influence of a few of the major leaders of the fourth and fifth centuries are also indicated.

5 Saint-Martin-du-Canigou. Winged rams and a bird; twelfth-century capital from the gallery.

6 Saint-Martin-du-Canigou, from the south.

to face martyrdom and fairweather Christians who came and went with the crowd became increasingly evident. It seems that it was in Egypt that large masses of people first joined the Church, and by a paradox Antony and his colleagues and followers fled into the desert to escape both popular religion and persecution. In the late third century the crowd must have seemed the greater menace; in the opening years of the fourth century came persecution by the colleagues of Diocletian; then peace for the Church, first tolerance, then favour, then—at the end of the fourth century—the era in which Christianity was the official religion, and all others were frowned on and suppressed.

'. . . After the death of the apostles,' wrote John Cassian in the brief summary of monastic history contained in his *Collations* (c. 400) 'crowds of strangers and men of different races flowed into the Church. . . . And as day by day the number of converts at home and abroad grew, and the primitive Christians lost their fervour . . . the Christians who were still fervent . . . and remembered the original and perfect way of life, left their cities and the company of those who thought that they could live negligently and comfortably in God's Church,' and formed communities apart from the

world.[7] A long stretch of history is here considerably fore-shortened. Yet is evidently true that it was when Christianity, for long the sect of a minority, officially proscribed and sometimes persecuted, became a popular religion, that the need for a separate way of life for the more fervent, vigorous and ascetic, was first seriously felt.

Cassian held that all the early fervent, ascetic Christians were 'coenobites', and so he could say: the 'coenobites . . . were . . . a stem from which grew many flowers and fruit—the hermits. Everyone knows the founders of this way . . ., Paul and Antony. Their motive for choosing the solitary life was not cowardice nor intolerance of community living, but a wish to advance further in the contemplation of God, though Paul is said to have been driven into the desert to escape arrest during the persecution.' The followers of this way 'are called anchorites. . . . They have not remained satisfied with defeating the attack which the devils secretly plan in human society, but have been ready to meet them in open war.' In the first instance, and in some cases, the flight to the desert may have been an escape from worldly entanglements and even temporal embarrassment and persecution; but the monks of the desert rapidly found that psychological warfare became more and not less acute in the desert, that it was there (as they characteristically put it) that the devil's onslaught was most fierce. We have stressed that the monastic movement was in its origin—as all the great ascetic movements of Christian history have in some measure been—a reaction by men of fervour to the laxer standards of the Church in the world. But it was much else besides; and so it rapidly became a popular movement, and a widely recognised way of life of much variety, with causes and inspiration which are too rich and complex for brief analysis. Crucial for the direction it was to take was the personal influence of a small group of early ascetics who showed that the life was possible and who inspired men of varied talent to imitate them; among these the central figure was Antony himself. Equally important was the deep influence of the Christian Platonists of Alexandria; and in interpreting their ascetic teaching, and the segments of Greek philosophical

5

tradition congenial to ascetics, the central figure was Evagrius of Pontus (*c.* 346-99). He developed the familiar Greek theme of *telos*, the aim towards which the human soul tended or strove; and he first analysed the 'eight principal temptations' which stand between the soul and purity of heart: greed, lust, avarice, anger, melancholy, accidie (see p. 21), vanity and pride. Their conquest, their stripping, leads to freedom from passion, *apatheia*—a word often misunderstood to mean a negative, passive state—in which charity is born; and hence the soul may advance to *gnosis*, knowledge of God.[8]

The combination of powerful personal influences and teaching with the reaction against worldly prosperity takes us a fair way to understanding the success of early monasticism. But there is much still to ponder and to puzzle us; for we shall presently witness a similar movement in the Celtic west, in a country which had never felt either the Roman peace or Greco-Roman wealth (see pp. 42-3).

How can one begin to characterise a movement of the human spirit so distant and so strange? There are indeed many monks today. Nonetheless, to most of us the rigour and asceticism of the desert seem utterly alien. It grew from a conviction that the world and man's body, though created by God, were terribly corrupted by the fall; and that even if redemption came by God's free gift, intense human striving was needed if God's will was to be in any adequate sense fulfilled; that a life of rigour and renunciation was pleasing to God, that it was possible for humans to strive, by intense mortification and ceaseless fight against the devil, to something approaching 'the perfect life'. In the fourth century the monastic call drew large numbers into the desert; this, and the rich and varied intellectual milieu from which many of them came, gave great variety as well as intensity to the movement. Hence the ideal, not only of the hermit Antony, but of the coenobite Pachomius; hence too the 'Sarabaites', Cassian's third variety of monks,[9] those who have abandoned discipline and obedience and live in wickedness—for, as we should expect, as soon as there were monks there were bad monks: it is in the nature of great human experiments that they lead to failure as well as success, and no human adventure can be kept within safe paths. This the founders of monasticism themselves clearly understood. The lives of the fathers of the desert, as recorded in their own and later generations, were full of the marvellous and extraordinary: incredible feats of endurance, marvellous battles with demons, encounters with fantastic monsters. But the recorded sayings of the really eminent directors of the desert are full of inspired common sense, psychological wisdom and experience, and above all, pleas for moderation. This remains an outstanding characteristic of early ascetic literature. However strange their way of life, it is abundantly clear that their teaching was based on accumulated insight and psychological subtlety which make the writings of Cassian and others, who enshrine the teaching of the desert, more sophisticated reading than anything of the kind which we shall meet again before the twelfth century. The variety and the nature of this teaching will become clearer if we observe how monasticism spread through the Christian

8

9

7 Canterbury Cathedral Priory, England, the fourteenth-century cloister.

8 La Sagra di San Michele, Italy, see next page.

9 Saint-Martin-du-Canigou, the church.

10

8,10-17 La Sagra di San Michele or Chiusa. Near Turin, Italy, the original chapel of *c.*1000 and the slightly later monastery reflect both the popular religious movement which inspired much monastic patronage, and the crusading movement of the eleventh century: for the cult of St Michael flourished on many hilltops as a symbol of the military aspirations of the age. The crusading era was also a golden age of pilgrimages and offerings, and the church, perilously balanced on the summit of the hill above a long flight of stairs (11, 13), was built about 1150, though some of it is later. Its architect may have been Master Nicolo, the sculptor of the memorial door jamb (12) recording his work and probably of the capital showing Cain killing Abel (15). Cf. pls.154-5.

Roman Empire, north and west until it came to Gaul and Britain, and yet in how pure a form the basic ideals of the desert fathers were preserved in Cassian's *Collations*.

St Basil

In the mid fourth century, as monastic communities and groups of hermits grew up in many parts of Egypt, similar communities, under a very similar inspiration, were formed in Palestine and Syria. In Cappadocia in eastern Asia Minor an essentially coenobitic way of life developed out of the old communities of pious Christians into specifically monastic institutes under the leadership of St Basil (died 379). St Basil's teaching, advice and instructions, enshrined in the Rule which passed under his name after his death, have played the part in Greek Orthodox monastic life that the Rule of St Benedict has played in the west.[10] Yet it is not easy for Benedict's disciples, or students accustomed to the terse clarity of the best of western Rules, to appreciate the quality of Basil's Rule, even though they may recognize the common inspiration. St Basil's Rule is a continuous flowing exposition by a great leader to assorted groups of monks; it is a series of brief sermons dealing with a host of different situations; it is descriptive rather than mandatory, though it lays emphasis enough on discipline and obedience. Above all, it contains a series of meditations by a man who set particular store on meditation based on the Scriptures. No disciple of Calvin ever

attempted to set the Bible in the centre of his life more fully than St Basil.

Basil knew the Egyptian hermits and cared little for them; he was uncompromisingly coenobitic. His view is inward-looking, but not individualistic. 'The solitary life has one aim, the service of the needs of the individual. But this is plainly in conflict with the law of love. . . . The Lord for the greatness of His love of men was not content with teaching the word only, but that accurately and clearly he might give us a pattern of humility in the perfection of love He girded himself and washed the feet of the disciples in person. Whose feet then wilt thou wash? Whom wilt thou care for? In comparison with whom wilt thou be last if thou livest by thyself? How will that good and pleasant thing, the dwelling of brethren together, . . . be accomplished by dwelling solitary?'[11] Though western readers are not entirely wrong in thinking that Benedict had a clearer idea of legislation and of organisation than Basil, even a hasty glance at Basil's Rule gives some understanding of the enormous influence he had throughout the Greek and Byzantine world, and the admiration Benedict himself felt for his eminent predecessor.

St Augustine

Like Basil, the great African father St Augustine of Hippo (354-430) cared greatly for the monastic life and little for the desert. Augustine's later life as bishop of Hippo was spent, so far as he could arrange it, surrounded by a group of devout, intellectual and hard-working fellow ascetics. Their asceticism was not of heroic stature, but a natural expression of what he and they considered the best Christian tradition of good living.

11

The essential purpose of such groups was practical: to provide for Augustine's need of human company and intelligent conversation, and for the need of his see to have hard-working, dedicated men to manage its spiritual life and temporal welfare. He naturally lent encouragement to other such groups, both of men and of women; and in a famous letter, probably but not certainly by him, a community of women whose holiness had been called in question were told how such a life should be led. From this letter stemmed the later developments to which the name 'The Rule of St Augustine' came to be attached.[12] Whatever its true connection with the African father, it reflects his interest in monasticism. The description of the interior life of the monastery is practical but vague; it is only the foundation for useful work in the world. Augustine was himself the most introspective of men, as he reveals in every page of his *Confessions*; but his view of the monastic life was outward looking. The monastery was a centre in which one could meditate, and converse with men of like mind, and lead one's own spiritual life, then go out into the city and the diocese to do one's work. Some monks in a neighbouring diocese quoted to their bishop the Gospel saying, 'Behold the fowls of the air: for they sow not, neither do they reap, nor gather into barns; yet your heavenly Father feedeth them.'[13] This, they argued, was an instruction to those leading the good life not to work. Augustine, called in by the bishop to help, was not amused, and wrote a treatise explaining the place of work in God's scheme, and how he wished he could set aside the endless chores of his bishopric, especially the law-suits he had to settle, and work with his hands. The idea that work was essential to human dignity, or a divine gift, was entirely alien to the teaching of the early Church and the fathers. St Antony and his successors had taught that manual work was an essential of the monastic life, since it prevented idleness, and the listlessness which could lead to depression and *accidie*, commonest of monastic vices—the sense of emptiness, uselessness and futility which naturally afflicts the lonely and the idle. Augustine went further, and although accepting that work was no part of the life of Adam and Eve before the fall of the blessed in heaven, taught that work was always an essential part of the good life on earth.[14]

Thus Augustine's view of monasticism had a strong outward-looking element and was essentially coenobitic; but he had a mind so capacious that hardly any element in the religious and philosophical tradition of the Greco-Roman world failed to find a corner somewhere in it; and he tells us in his *Confessions* that a talk about the Life of St Antony played a crucial part in his conversion.[15] His monasticism was a macrocosm of his own mind and spirit: in its centre lay intense introspection, meditation and contemplation.

The communities which Augustine supervised included some for women, and these were important in the formation of the monastic tradition. Some of the very earliest ascetic communities had been those of widows described in I Timothy; and in the late fourth century Augustine's eccentric contemporary St Jerome was inspiring small groups of wealthy women to lead a life of renunciation, celibacy and good works. A small coterie of holy ladies followed him from Rome to Bethlehem, adapting their lives to his harsh, unsympathetic counsels; and he rewarded their heroic dedication to the ascetic life with a flood of pamphlets, widely read and imitated in the Middle Ages, in which he inveighed against the fickleness of women and the danger of female company. In his own extraordinary

12

13

14

way, he inspired in the widow Paula and her family, and in countless successors who read his works, a sense of the possible dignity of the ascetic life for women; in combining this with passionate statements of the contribution of Eve and her descendants to the world's evils, he revealed attitudes and influences which make him a kind of parody of St Paul. There was an absurd, perverse, theatrical element in Jerome; yet he greatly influenced the development of the religious life and helped to ensure that women played a distinguished role in it in the early centuries of the Church's history (see pp. 167 ff.).

John Cassian

In the late fourth and early fifth centuries the monastic movement was spreading to many provinces of the Roman Empire.

including Italy and Gaul. In the very early days, this monasticism was in touch with the eastern sources from which it sprang: the eccentric, ascetic, learned, cantankerous St Jerome passed between Rome and Bethlehem, and John Cassian himself, one of the most acute observers of the monks of the desert and their most profound interpreter, was born near the

14 San Michele, the church looking east.

15 San Michele, Cain killing Abel.

16 San Michele. Round the east window is a group of figures, late twelfth century: detail of the Madonna.

17 San Michele, the apse, towering over the substructure.

15

16

17

19

20

Black Sea, brought up in Syria and Palestine, served his monastic apprenticeship in Egypt, and settled in the south of Gaul just before the barbarian hordes broke across the Rhine and began the destruction of the western Empire. These invasions were to lead in due course to the separation of Greek and Latin, of eastern and western. Before Cassian there were already monks in France; most famous was St Martin, first leader of a group of recluses near Poitiers, then bishop of Tours. Thus Cassian, when he arrived in Provence about 400 came to a land ready to receive the message of the desert; and he came just in time.

Cassian had sat at the feet of the leading abbots and spiritual directors of Syria and Egypt, and he ended his days head of a monastic community in Marseille. From his home in Provence he spread about the west a knowledge of the way of life he had studied in the east, first the framework of monastic, coenobitic discipline and spiritual life in his *Institutes*, written for a community recently formed at Apt about forty miles from Marseille; then a deep and searching inquiry into the teaching on the personal life, contemplation and prayer of the great eastern fathers in the *Conferences*, the *Conlationes*, *Collations*.

The *Institutes* describe the framework of monastic life, and also the more elementary stages of the individual's progress on the ladder to knowledge of God. The novice is told that:

> 'The fear of the Lord: leads to
> compunction of heart: leads to
> renunciation of all that is the soul's own: leads to
> humility: leads to
> mortification of the will: leads to
> driving out of the vices: leads to
> flowering of virtue: leads to
> purity of heart: leads to
> perfect charity.'[16]

The earlier stages form the 'active life'—active in pursuit of virtue—the later the contemplative. The active life witnesses the destruction of the eight sins, that is, the eight temptations

18-22 Santo Domingo de Silos. One of the chief centres of monasticism in Spain after its refoundation by St Domingo in the mid eleventh century. The cloister, late eleventh or early twelfth century, is rich in sculpture of exceptional beauty (see p.95).

18 Bas relief at the corner showing deposition from the cross.

19 Most of the early capitals have grotesque animals and foliage (see also plate 22).

21

22

of Evagrius translated into Latin—and later in western tradition reduced to seven by the amalgamation of pride and vanity. The *Institutes* were in due course replaced by the Rule of St Benedict as the fundamental description of the coenobitic life in the west. The contemplative life is the theme of the *Collations*. They were the most elaborate and sophisticated statement of fourth-century teaching on the spiritual life, and one of the supreme masterpieces of early Christian literature, rarely surpassed for subtlety, depth and insight.[17] Thus it was right and natural that the book should become a classic very widely read; and every monastic library of any pretensions in the mid or late Middle Ages possessed at least one copy. It became the normal practice for a chapter of the *Collations* to be read before the service of Compline in the evening in

many monasteries; when this became an hour of refreshment, the collation, from referring to a monastic conference—the heart and centre of the ascetic life—became also a meal.

The *Collations* take the form of dialogues between Cassian and another young monk and the great leaders of the Egyptian monastic life of his youth. They bear much the same relation to the actual words of the hermits as did Plato's *Dialogues* to the teaching of Socrates. They reflect the immense respect Cassian had for his teachers, and the fact that he still felt the inspiration of the desert and the call to the solitary life of

22 Santo Domingo, capitals.

23 Maria Laach, Germany, the abbey church from the west (see pp.57-8).

24

AMILI BEATI
iob nequaq̃ puersi eē potuerint

25

26

DICTIS

27

IN PROLIXO OPERE ESSE

28

YSTORŨ EST

29

VERITATIS VERBA

to face with an ascetic ideal of great power and depth.

This is all the more striking because a modern reader, however remote he may feel Cassian's ideas and ideals to be, cannot fail to be struck by his psychological insight and understanding of human nature. His analysis of temptation avoids the contortions of an over-anxious conscience, but cuts like a sharp knife through flourishing roots of self-deception. 'It is no proof that our hearts are not plagued with ambition, if we abstain from worldly occupations in which we could not engage even if we wanted . . . but only if we eschew everything which ministers to our own power, even when it seems to be clothed in a garment of right.' And in his study of the approach to purity of heart, he takes special note 'why some people, who have given away worldly wealth in gold or silver or lands, are afterwards agitated about a knife, a pencil, a pin or a pen'.[18]

Purity of heart is the immediate aim; the kingdom of heaven the ultimate goal. 'It is for this end—to keep our hearts continually pure— that we do and endure everything, that we spurn parents and home and position and wealth and comfort and every earthly pleasure. . . . To this end everything is to be done. Solitude, watches in the night, manual labour, nakedness, reading and the other disciplines—we know that

Initials from Cîteaux, France, early twelfth century. 24 Q: two monks in brown habits split a log. 25 R: fighting a dragon (scale approx. 1:2). 26 Q: laymen sorting cloth and wool. 27 Q: an angel blesses a monk in white habit. 28 M: two monks with a scroll. Note the variety in the colour of the habit. 29 Q: a monk in brown cutting corn. Dijon, Bibliothèque Municipale, MSS 170, f.59, 168, f.4v, 170, ff.92v, 6v, 20, 75v (Gregory the Great, *Moralia in Job*). All except 25 are approx. original size.

30 Martha and Mary: the active and the contemplative life. An allegorical picture from the twelfth-century Bible from Floreffe, a Premonstratensian abbey (see p. 181), in the style called 'Mosan', i.e. from the Meuse valley, whose *scriptoria* influenced painting over a wide area of the Low Countries, western Germany and northern France. The caption, bottom left, reads: *Signum vitarum sunt hec depicta duarum* . . . these pictures are the image (or sign) of the two lives. London, British Museum, Add. MS 17, 738, f.3v.

31-8 Canterbury Cathedral, England. Becket's murder gave the monks the opportunity to rebuild the choir, and the pilgrims to his tomb provided the funds.

31 The murder of Thomas Becket in 1170, from the cloister vault, fourteenth century.

contemplation. But they are all interpreted according to his own mature thought, and set in a literary form of his devising. The highest life, the life of perfection, is still that of the contemplative alone in his cell; yet for all a preparation in a community is now prescribed, and for most this is the true vocation. Thus he writes for coenobites; and he takes pains to emphasise the elements of moderation and common sense in the teaching of the fathers. He had no use for the exaggerated gymnastics of Symeon Stylites and the other saints who made their homes on pillars. And yet a hot wind from the Egyptian desert blows through his writings, and we are brought face

33

34

35

32 Canterbury Cathedral. The nave, Norman in porportions, remodelled to the design of Henry Yevele in the late fourteenth century.

33-4 South-east transept.

35 The east end, from the site of the martyrdom.

82

36 Stone seats in the cloister, c.1300, with late fourteenth-century vault.

36

their purpose is to free the heart from injury by bodily passions and to keep it free; they are to be the rungs of a ladder up which it may climb to perfect charity.'[19] The *Collations* as a whole are a powerful exposition of the methods of climbing this ladder, culminating in the heights of perfection, and in contemplative prayer. In the Gospel story, Martha had been engaged in good works, and reasonably asked for help; but the Lord told her that Mary had chosen the good part: 'The Lord, you see, placed the chief good in divine contemplation.'[20] Here is an uncompromising statement that the monastic life is interior, first within the community, then within the individual soul; the outside world is mere distraction. Yet Cassian's ideal was neither so individualistic nor so egotistical as could easily be thought. The monastic life is led within, not apart from, the sacramental life of the Church. He does not expect his monks to be priests, but he insists on frequent communion; he has no use for the desert hermits who never communicated at all. Further, he follows a New Testament scheme in dividing prayer into four elements or states: first, supplication, that is a cry of penance, then an act of dedication, next intercession, finally thanksgiving.[21] By intercession he means prayer 'in moments of fervour, for other men and women—our family, the peace of the world. To use St Paul's words, we pray "for all men, for kings, and all in authority".... From each of these four kinds rise other opportunities of richer prayer.' He goes on to explore the heights of mystical experience, with a richness and clarity never equalled in the Middle Ages, save perhaps in the mystical doctrine and experience of the twelfth and fourteenth centuries. Cassian never lost sight of the fact that monks were limbs of Christ's body, members one of another and of the whole body of Christian people, of the Church on earth and in heaven. Though he reckoned himself a teacher of moderation, there is often an uncompromising note in his asceticism, and he declared war on distraction of every kind. The Abba Isaac is made to recall how he had heard St Antony grumble at the sunrise: 'Why do you hinder me? The rising of your light draws my mind away from the true light!'—a saying we shall remember when we meet St Bernard in the twelfth century driving every distraction out of his order's churches, especially the glitter of jewelled shrines and painted glass.[22] Yet the attack on worldly distraction in Cassian, or Bernard's puritanism, was not coupled with distrust of all human emotions and values; in the most fundamental sense of the term, in their interest and belief in human capacity and human emotions, both were humanists. Cassian indeed had indicated in one of his writings the possibility that the first step on the path to perfection might be taken without God's free gift of grace, and for this he was execrated as a heretic in some quarters after his death. But it was in truth a small lapse, for he and Bernard both saw the whole process of man's perfectibility within the economy of divine grace; yet, granted this premise, Cassian laid before the monks who followed him a programme of heroic effort, an intensely strenuous, yet feasible, attempt to answer the appalling challenge: 'Be ye ... perfect.'[23]

37 Canterbury Cathedral Priory. The Norman staircase leading to the almoner's hall. At the foot of the stairs, no doubt, the poor were fed, a reminder that this monastery was the centre of an ancient city.

38 Canterbury Cathedral Priory. The water tower: the centre of an elaborate system of conduits, twelfth century, though altered later.

2 The Rule of St Benedict

The sixth century saw the final separation of Greek east from Latin west, the collapse in the west of all semblance of Roman Empire. But it also witnessed two notable additions to the literature of the cloister. The first of these was probably written somewhere to the south-east of Rome soon after 500, and is usually known as the Rule of the Master.[1] It is a long rambling document, full of striking phrases and ascetic wisdom, lacking the form and refinement and clarity of Cassian's *Collations* and yet in its way more of a rule than Cassian's *Institutes*. The Master's monk was subjected to a discipline of personal poverty, and chastity, and total obedience; he was ruled by an abbot who had all the powers of a Roman pater-familias—that is, a discretion virtually absolute, an authority dissolved only by his death; an abbot whose business it was to guide his monk and also, on occasion, to fuss over him, to see that he blew his 'nose in a way likely to give least offence to the attendant angels'.[2]

Soon after, perhaps about 530, and certainly in Italy south of Rome, at Monte Cassino, the second and more famous of these Rules was written by Benedict of Nursia. The opening chapters of St Benedict's Rule consist of an abbreviated and adapted version of the opening of the Master's, and there are echoes and borrowings throughout. But the result is something much more than a second edition, for in numerous points of principle and practice the Master's teaching is modified; and the whole structure is tightened and clarified. In former generations it was assumed indeed that Benedict's was the earlier document, the Master's derivative; and the Master was generally undervalued. It came as a great shock to the monastic world when in 1937 the doctrine was first propounded that the Master was the earlier, and Benedict the copyist. The result was a controversy. In the words of Dom David Knowles, 'the heather had been set alight and fire-fighters and fire-raisers alike hastened to the spot'.[3] Now the fire is quenched, peace has returned to the scene, and a majority of the scholarly world, Benedictine and non-Benedictine alike, is agreed that the new doctrine is correct. If Benedict was a modern author, publishing under modern laws of copyright, he would be convicted of plagiarism on a large scale. In his own world, he stands convicted of an act of extraordinary humility; and it remains a curious and intriguing fact that his Rule should be so far superior to the document from which it was adapted.

'We must form a school of the Lord's service,' said the Master in his prologue; 'We must form a school of the Lord's service', said Benedict, 'in which nothing too harsh, nothing too heavy,

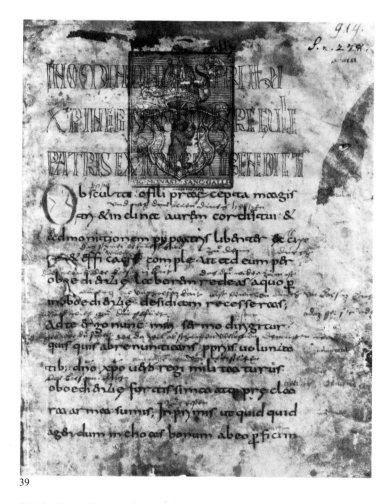

39

39 The Rule of St Benedict. The first leaf of the St Gallen manuscript: 'Listen my son to the master's commands . . .' *Cod. Sangallensis* 914 f.1, early ninth century.

do we hope to see established. . . . As we lead our life in the faith, when our heart has been enlarged, the path of God's commands is run in a sweetness of love beyond words.'[4] Though for the most part much more succinct than the Master, and commonly content to use his words, Benedict takes pains to draw out essential points and everywhere to clarify the message. Moderation, common sense and a measure of organisation are qualities much in evidence. He recognised that there were two kinds of monks, coenobites, 'those living in a monastery under a rule and [or] an abbot'; and anchorites,

40

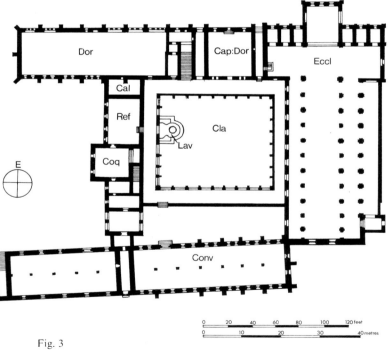

Fig. 3

Dor

Cap:Dor

Eccl

Cal

Ref

Cla

Lav

Coq

Conv

E

0 20 40 60 80 100 120 feet
0 10 20 30 40 metres

Fig.3 Plan of Eberbach as it was in the late Middle Ages. A very characteristic plan, see pp.140ff., save for the small refectory, which was, however, larger at the end of the Middle Ages. Most orders preferred to have their cloisters to the south of the church; here, as often, the shape of the site forced the Cistercians to put it on the north side.

41

'that is the kind of hermits who have learned, not in their first prentice fervour, but by long trial in a monastery, having studied many men's example, can fight against the devil, and can go out from the ranks of the brothers fully instructed to the single combat of the hermitage'. Here Benedict is not only following the Master: he shows himself, as so often, faithful to the tradition and teaching of Cassian.[5]

'We have laid out this Rule so that we may show that those who observe it in their monasteries have in a measure soundness of character or the beginnings of the good life. For anyone who hastens on to the perfect way of life, there are the teachings of the Holy Fathers, the keeping of which leads a man to the peak of perfection. For what page or what sentence of the divine authority of Old and New Testament but is a rule of human life of the most precise? Or what book of the holy catholic Fathers but echoes this word, that by a straight course we may come to our Creator? What else are the *Collations* and the *Institutes* of the Fathers and their *Lives*, and the Rule of our holy father Basil,[6] but instruments of the virtues of monks who lead the good life in obedience? But to us who are idle or live bad or negligent lives every page is shame and confusion.

'Whoever you are, therefore, who hastens to the heavenly country, fulfil completely with Christ's help this little rule written for beginners—and then at last, with God's protection, you may come to the greater heights of teaching and virtue which we have listed above. Amen.'

40-3 Eberbach, Germany

40 In contrast to Silos and Canterbury, a plain bare church of the new Cistercian Order, built *c*.1170-86 (see p.254, chap.9, n.11).

41 The east end with the late medieval tombs of three archbishops of Mainz.

42 The cloister, west and south. On the west the lay brothers' quarters of *c*.1200, separated from the cloister walk by the passage of the lay brothers and a modern building of which the octagon is part. The old lavabo lay under the tree (see fig. 3) at the refectory door.

42

43

44

43 Eberbach, the chapter house, twelfth century, with a vault of the mid fourteenth.

44 Fouquet's painting of St Bernard preaching (fifteenth century) shows how such a chapter house could be used. No doubt the stone benches were the basic furniture of the twelfth century; in later times wooden furniture was added. Detail from *Livre d'Heures d'Étienne Chevalier*, Chantilly, Musée Condé.

The little rule for beginners describes a life of great earnestness and severity; to those of us who lead the life of ordinary mortals in the late twentieth century, a life of dedication and monotony beyond our dreams. Yet the historical record shows that there is far more to it than that; and there are many thousands still obeying St Benedict's precepts today. What is the secret of its astonishing success? To this there is no single or simple answer; the historian who asserts that he understands the problem and can give a crisp and clear answer has failed to take the measure of two of Benedict's most notable qualities—his humility and his practical good sense. Unless we have grappled personally with this problem, the excitement

45-9 Rome, the Santi Quattro Coronati

45 The early basilica, fifth to ninth centuries, was burnt in the late eleventh and rebuilt in the early twelfth century; earlier materials, especially columns, were reused; the paintings are mostly of the sixteenth century. Thus this ancient parish church turned monastery, and now a convent of nuns, is a symbol of architectural continuity in Rome.

46 Outer court: the ninth-century tower—towers were very unusual in southern Europe as early as this—seen from the fifteenth-century arcade.

47 The chapel of St Silvester, with mosaic floor and wall-paintings of the early thirteenth century, is a reminder of the links between the cloister and the world.

Fig.4 Plan of the Santi Quattro Coronati, Rome. The church is mostly early twelfth century, but the first atrium incorporates arches from the atrium of the fifth/sixth-century basilica; the second is fifteenth century. 1.Chapel of St Barbara, ninth century. 2.Chapel of St Nicholas, ninth century. 3.Chapel of St Silvester, with thirteenth-century frescoes. 4.Campanile, ninth century.

45

46

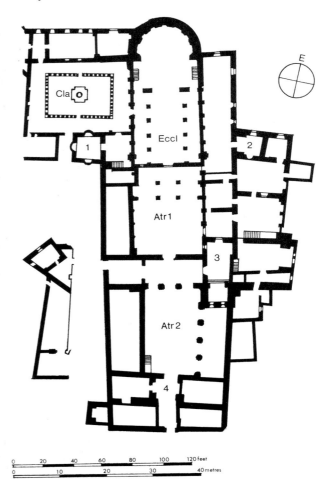

Fig. 4

of exploring a medieval monastery or of monastic life will not begin to unfold.

In a curious way Benedict seems almost to anticipate his own achievement. 'Whoever you are . . .' has a universal ring about it;[7] and so definite and precise and concrete are all his instructions that it is easy, when under the impress of his book, to feel that he knew it would have a large, long-lasting and universal impact. Nothing is less probable. He spoke from a comparatively narrow experience, and never strayed outside it; he legislated for the type of monastery he knew. But the doors of his mind, like the doors of his monastery, were not closed to strangers.

The 'rule written for beginners' is homely, devout and

practical; it shows shrewd and subtle insight into human nature; it combines unyielding demands for obedience and stability with moderation and humanity. It is no masterpiece of coherent legislation, yet it combines something of the genius of Roman Law and of the spiritual teaching of Cassian, legacies of an intellectual world more sophisticated than Benedict's. Nor is its elementary nature to be taken to mean that it was easy. At its heart lie the precepts of complete obedience (a precept to be sternly maintained), personal poverty and chastity; and the life it describes is frugal and severe and monotonous. Later generations of monks often found it impossible to maintain in every syllable, and it had to be reinterpreted to suit conditions other than those of the sixth century and harsher climates than that of Italy. It is a difficult rule to keep; but not impossible, and therein lies its genius. It was the fruit of a lifetime spent in trying to control an intractable body of monks often inspired with genuine devotion, rarely well equipped with native staying power. Externally, what was needed was a set of regulations sufficiently rigid and clear to command unquestioning acceptance from all members of a community. The monk in Benedict's Rule spends most of the day in silence: he is occupied either

48 Rome, the Santi Quattro Coronati. Detail of St Silvester's chapel. Here St Silvester, the pope, welcomes and blesses the Emperor Constantine, and receives the tiara as symbol of Constantine's gift of the city of Rome. This is the legend. The gifts the emperor made in the early fourth century, though lavish, were far less extensive than the 'forged donation' devised in the eighth century. Note the liturgical umbrella.

49 The twelfth/thirteenth-century cloister is one of the most peaceful in Rome.

49

in the communal worship in church (eight services or offices and the mass are spread over various hours of the day) or in private meditation and spiritual reading, or in manual labour for the support of the community, or in eating and sleeping. The principal psychological dangers of such a life are neurotic extremes of depression and exaltation; and the answer to these, humanly speaking, is to maintain regularity and devotion. The regularity of the Rule is as inexorable as a doctor's prescription, and it has proved very effective.

Benedict was deeply influenced by Cassian, and most of the lineaments of his ideal can be found in the *Institutes* or the *Collations*. This is particularly evident in the mixture of sternness and mercy on which Benedict lays such emphasis. The abbot is owed complete obedience, and in the end the monk must obey him—after a pause for proper inquiry—even if he thinks the order wrong. Yet Benedict emphasises at the outset that the abbot's business is to help the monks; and the spirit of the passages in which obedience and authority are discussed has far more to say of the abbot's responsibility, of help and co-operation, than of his ultimately dictatorial power. The idea of obedience comes from Cassian, and most of the chapter on the abbot from the Master—including the famous adjuration to remember the day of judgement, and the abbot's responsibility for his flock in the judge's presence.[8] In Benedict's Rule, however, this is immediately followed by a chapter on taking counsel which has only the vaguest counterpart in the Master's Rule. On crucial matters the abbot is to take counsel of the whole community, 'for often the Lord reveals to a young man [or the young] what is best' (c. 3); on lesser matters he consults the seniors only, following the

50 51

Scenes of Monastic Life

50 A scribe writes the Life, from a twelfth-century manuscript of Bede's Life of St Cuthbert, British Museum Add. MS 39,943 = Yates Thompson 26, f.2.

51 Sitting up in bed: Boisil, Cuthbert's prior at Melrose, on his death bed, from the same manuscript, f.21.

counsel of Ecclesiasticus: 'Do nothing without advice'.[9] After taking counsel, the abbot makes up his own mind; for this the Rule binds him in the end to do. He cannot evade his responsibility, nor pass it to others: much of the strength, and weakness, of the Rule, lie in this vision of the abbot, who is assumed to be both a notable spiritual director and a master

in handling human relations. Such men are rare.

Benedict followed Cassian in making the communal life a necessary foundation for all kinds of monks; whether he thought that the anchorite ideal was in the end higher than the coenobite is far from clear. His opening, in which he claims that the coenobites are the strongest or best of monks, seems to deny it; his epilogue—which is probably a later addition, representing his final view—seems to allow that the anchorite's may be a higher call for a minority, and commends the reading of Cassian in the strongest terms.

This reveals the ambiguity, the tension between the coenobite and the hermit ideal which was to remain a characteristic of western monasticism. As for the other common tension in monastic history, that between the inward and the outward view, Benedict's monastery was clearly a little world, an oasis of sanity in a barbarian kingdom. Yet the outer world was not excluded. 'All guests who arrive should be received as Christ himself would be received . . .' (c. 53), and precise instructions are given for their entertainment in a modest but becoming fashion; a special duty of hospitality is laid upon the abbot. The outer world is not to be entirely ignored or neglected; its presence is to be accepted in a practical way as well as in a spiritual sense, in the monks' prayers. Yet the monastery of the Rule is presumed to be a place in which the essential aim is the good life and the salvation of its own inmates. Social work, pastoral work, are not included; nor are they specifically mentioned in order to be rejected. From this silence many consequences have flowed.

It is also assumed that the buildings of the monastery are much more modest than they later became in many communities in western Christendom. The church is called the oratory—it is simply a place of prayer, where the community can gather for mass and offices or the individual can go to say his prayers. It is the place where God's work is done, just as the kitchen and outhouses are the place where the necessary tasks of the monastery are conducted. The monks' life was passed in God's work and their own, which was to include some of the chores of the monastery and the monastic garden, though Benedict evidently regarded agricultural labour as exceptional. There emerges a vivid picture of a small and compact and almost self-contained community in the heart of barbarian Italy. But Benedict's vision is more than that; it is a link between the early Middle Ages and our own. For in every part of the world today there are communities of monks calling themselves after his name, living by his Rule and constantly studying it and reciting it.

3 The formation of the monastic tradition

From St Benedict of Nursia to St Benedict of Aniane

Benedict prescribed spiritual reading for his monks, and he called their common worship 'God's work'—*opus Dei*. But he assumes no great learning, nor a large library; and the liturgy lacked elaborate ritual or music. Learning never became a normal characteristic of any medieval religious order or of any large group of monasteries; none the less the monastic library, along with the cathedral library, became the repository which ensured the survival of some part of the legacy of ancient literature; and when men of a scholarly turn of mind grew up in the cloister, they could thus sometimes find the food they needed to hand. In a similar way, the growth of liturgical elaboration was at first sporadic and occasional; but in the end it became a normal and inescapable feature of all monasteries of the ninth, tenth and eleventh centuries.

The intellectual tradition began with Cassiodorus, a retired civil servant who spent his declining years in a monastery called Vivarium even further south in Italy than Monte Cassino. He was the last of the great scholars of the ancient world seriously to engage in transmitting Greek thought and literature to the west. His library was the last really massive collection of books which the ancient world produced. Both monastery and library disappeared soon after his death; but a few books were carried to Rome, and it is probably to this that we owe the survival of more than one of the masterpieces of ancient literature. Even before his death his own *Institutes*, a treatise on the principles and techniques of the study of divine scripture, had reached the eternal city. The second part is a complete system of education in the chief Roman disciplines—grammar, rhetoric and the rest—which as a cultivated man he regarded as a necessary preliminary to the study of the Bible; the first part outlines the approach to the Bible itself. This remarkable enterprise was too much for all but a handful of the scholars of the centuries which followed, and it is a symptom of the failure of Cassiodorus' intention that the two parts circulated for several hundred years quite separately; in the eleventh and twelfth centuries, when learning revived for good and all, his scheme provided one of the chief foundations for the reintegration of learning, sacred and profane, of Roman literary science and Christian theological science based on the study of the Bible.

Cassiodorus was one of the most distinguished of a group of men who tried to gather in encyclopedic form the best of ancient learning before the failure of education and the barbarian onslaught destroyed it. One of the liveliest and ablest minds in this tradition was Pope Gregory the Great

(590-604), not so cultivated as Cassiodorus, nor so modest as Benedict, and more the man of affairs than either: there was scarcely a department of ecclesiastical life which his comprehensive genius and organising ability did not stamp. His liturgical reforms were first implemented in the churches and monasteries of Rome, and so entered the monastic tradition alongside the books of Cassiodorus. He conceived an immense admiration for St Benedict, whose praises he sang while chronicling his miracles in the Second Book of his *Dialogues*. He commends the Rule for its penetrating wisdom and clarity (*discretione praecipuam, sermone luculentam*); it seems to have impinged curiously little on his own writings and teaching, but the phrase stuck and helped to make the Rule's fame. In particular, the Rule was taken to England

52

52-8, 62-4 Fleury, Saint-Benoît-sur-Loire

52 Fleury, Saint-Benoît-sur-Loire. The body of St Benedict was brought here in the seventh century. The abbey was reformed in the tenth, and rose to the height of its fame in the eleventh. Its focus is the shrine of St Benedict in the crypt, eleventh century.

in the course of the seventh century, and some of the monks of the second generation in England, notably St Wilfred of Ripon, York and Hexham, and St Benedict Biscop, founder of Bede's monasteries at Monkwearmouth and Jarrow, paid it particular respect. The characteristic monastic rule-book of these early centuries contains an anthology, sometimes even half a dozen rules; even in the ninth century St Benedict of Aniane, from whose work the unique place of the Rule in later monasticism sprang, was the author of just such an anthology. Undoubtedly there were monasteries in various parts of Europe much earlier than this dedicated to following his Rule and honouring the first Benedict's memory. The earliest surviving manuscript of the Rule, now in the Bodleian Library at Oxford, may possibly reflect the special devotion of St Wilfred to it.[2] Another centre of the cult of Benedict was established in the seventh century at Fleury. After Benedict's death the Lombards had come and destroyed Monte Cassino; the remains of his community gathered up his bones and fled. After many wanderings, and the passing of several generations, they came to rest in the late seventh century at Fleury on the Loire, where they have been honoured to the present day and where the great abbey church of Saint-

Benoît-sur-Loire still stands, with massive westwork, aisles and ambulatory to provide space for the pilgrims to his tomb.

In the Britain of St Wilfred and St Benedict Biscop there flourished another monastic tradition uninfluenced by Benedict of Nursia. Columcille (Columba) and Aidan were the most famous representatives in sixth- and seventh-century Scotland and England of the monastic movement which had captured the Irish Church in the generations following the death of St Patrick (probably late fifth century).[3] The heart of this movement lay in sixth-century Ireland in such places as Durrow and Bangor; and although it owed much to continental influence and inspiration, it was also a powerful native growth. Here we have an ascetic movement entirely different in its origin from that of fourth-century Egypt. It flourished in a barbarian society hardly or partly converted; it had from the first a strong missionary element within it. It also bred stern ascetics and the most ruthless denunciation of the human body recorded in western Catholic ascetic literature before the eleventh century; and yet it could not in the nature of the case be a protest against lax standards in the church, for the Irish were poor (compared with the Egyptians) and recently converted. But in truth the Irish monastic experience was

52-8, 62-4

53

54

55

exceedingly varied, and in this it was not so different from the continental monastic scene of the sixth and seventh centuries; and the Irish monks, like the Roman monks of Gregory the Great, became fervent missionaries. Their sternest leader was Columban, who went from Bangor to found Luxeuil in Gaul and Bobbio in Italy; his disciples spread Celtic monastic influence as far as St Gallen in what is now Switzerland. Less fierce, and more ready to compromise with native social customs, were Columcille, founder of Durrow and Iona, and Iona's most celebrated son of the next generation, St Aidan, a man of a gentler nature still than Columcille, the subject of one of the most attractive pen-portraits of the Venerable Bede.[4] Columban despised the body; yet among Irish hermits and monks an exceptional devotion to the beauty of nature can be discerned. A similar variety appears in the Irish monks' treatment of native society, from those who rejected it root and branch to those (especially of the seventh and eighth centuries) who melted into their Celtic background so as to become indistinguishable from it. To accommodate Irish society and the Christian faith had been in the first instance a notable achievement. But in course of time it seems that whole families became monastic in name; and while some members might lead a fervent religious life, others married and gave in marriage and ruled the monastery as if it were a secular community. A similar process of assimilation can be detected in England in the age of Bede, and the disappearance of specifically monastic features from communities of monks has

53 Fleury. The relics of St Benedict are carried from his original tomb to Fleury: bas relief of *c.*1200 from the north door. Figures and drapery show the antique flavour characteristic of some early Gothic sculpture. Above, Christ is surrounded by the four evangelists, angels and prophets.

54-5 A massive shelter for pilgrims and for processions, the porch or west work is commonly thought to be the only surviving remnant of the mid eleventh-century church. 54 In the interior: on the left, Daniel in the lion's den; on the right, St Martin divides his cloak with the beggar.

56 Detail from the porch, the flight into Egypt.

56

been common in many ages. The attempt to check such decadence, and to establish a clear framework of monastic discipline, was to bring the Rule of St Benedict to a new peak of fame in the ninth and tenth centuries. Meanwhile this movement was most obviously prepared for in the intervening centuries in the Northumbria of Bede (died 735) and the

57

58

German monasteries founded by the missionaries of the early and mid eighth century, many of whom were also English. Most influential of these was St Boniface, who started in Friesland in 716, transferred to Germany soon after and was consecrated bishop for Germany by the pope in person in 722; before his martyrdom in 754 he laid the foundations of the German church, in organisation and spiritual life, and inaugurated the reform of the church in West Francia (France and the Rhineland) too. For an English monk it was natural to make a group of monasteries the centre of his work and life, and to set them in close relation with the pope and under a discipline owing much to St Benedict. Some of his colleagues studied the monastic life in Monte Cassino, recently revived, and elsewhere in Italy. From Spain or southern Gaul came St Pirmin, founder of what soon became the chief centre of monastic life in southern Europe, the Reichenau, securely placed on its small island just to the west of Constance. Reichenau performed in the south of Germany the role of Boniface's abbeys farther north; and the chief of these was Fulda, which remained a centre of monastic observance and of pilgrimage after Boniface had been buried there.

It was natural too for an English monk to look for female helpers in his work. Of the many great English abbesses of the previous generation the best known is St Hilda of Whitby, of whom Bede spoke at length and with admiration, and who dominated a large community of both nuns and monks. One such double monastery appeared in Germany in the time of Boniface, at Heidenheim in Thuringia, first under the rule of Boniface's cousin Wynnebald, then of Wynnebald's sister Walpurgis or Waldburg. Other Anglo-Saxon ladies, notably Leoba and Thecla, founded abbeys for nuns in Franconia; and they founded a tradition of female involvement in the monastic life which was to survive and flourish in Germany more abundantly than in England (see pp. 167-8).

In the remains of Bede's monasteries in Northumbria we may still gain something of the impression of the tiny monastic oratories characteristic of the eighth century. Fleury is of the eleventh; and it reflects the new fashions of the Romanesque period (see pp. 99 ff.). There is a dramatic contrast in scale; and this reflects two movements, the liturgical movement which began in the Roman basilicas about 600 and became a general feature of western monastic life in the ninth and tenth centuries, and the popular religious movement which brought throngs of pilgrims to churches like Saint-Benoît from the early eleventh century on. Behind these movements lay the work of Benedict of Aniane in the ninth century and the monastic revival of the tenth.

It has been implicit in what we have said of the influence of Cassian and Benedict and Cassiodorus that the survival and

Fleury

57 Choir and transepts are of *c*.1100 (consecrated 1107), and heavily restored: here they are seen from the monks' vegetable garden.

58 Within, the arcade, apse and ambulatory of the choir, with marble floor around the reconstructed altar.

59 St Benedict with the opening of his Rule, fresco of *c*.1150, Nonnberg, Salzburg, Austria.

60 St Gregory the Great (probably), fresco of *c*.1150, Nonnberg, Salzburg, Austria.

59

60

spread of the ancient books of Christian devotion and theology and classical learning were due to their long life, waking or sleeping, in monastic libraries, and to the reawakening of intellectual interest in old books at various epochs of the Middle Ages. Thus it is natural to look for a major development in the study of Benedict's Rule in the Carolingian renaissance.

The coronation of Charlemagne as emperor in Rome on Christmas Day, 800, marked the alliance of Roman tradition and Frankish monarchy, the assurance that the Roman Empire was still thought to be alive in the west. But it was in his new Rome north of the Alps, in Aachen, that Charlemagne organised the centre of an empire in which divinely ordained kingship, military power, central administration—such as it was in the ninth century—religious and monastic reform and intellectual revival had their nucleus. The emperor himself provided the force and power of the movement; in middle life, he felt himself thoroughly involved in everything which went forward, and sat on his lofty throne in the palatine chapel during mass directing the service. But the intellectual climate was made by men like Alcuin, by a group of scholars with a modest but definite reverence for the antique and a clear idea of how the treasures of ancient literature and the needs of contemporary schools were to be matched. Their central idea was to find and copy pure and exact texts of the Bible, the fathers, the classics and the liturgies and rules of the Church. To this process the modern world owes the survival of a number of ancient works of literature and learning, and the purity of text of still more. It is characteristic of the achievement of Alcuin and his colleagues that, although the oldest text of the Rule of St Benedict now surviving comes from seventh-century England, the best derives from the court of Charlemagne. This is the famous manuscript preserved for many centuries at St Gall, Sankt Gallen, the Codex Sangallensis.[5] It was once supposed to be a direct copy of the original manuscript, preserved in Rome after Benedict's death and the dispersal of his community. Its story is now thought less simple and satisfactory; yet it remains a faithful copy, made by Carolingian scholars, from a model very close to Benedict's own text, still close enough to mirror the degenerate spelling and syntax of sixth-century Latin much more faithfully than the copies to which we are used today.

Charlemagne's successor, Louis the Pious, decided that, if the monastic life was to flourish in his empire as he wished, a major effort of reorganisation must be set on foot. To this end he appointed the second St Benedict, Benedict of Aniane, arch-abbot of all the monasteries of Francia—or at least of those within reach, or of those capable of reform. The dissemination of the Rule of St Benedict and the appointment of Benedict of Aniane were grand gestures, whose practical result at the time was extremely limited. But they sowed the seeds from which the traditional monasticism of the tenth and eleventh centuries, with all its branches, was to grow.

62

63

61 Rome, Santi Quattro Coronati, the chapel of St Silvester, see plates 47-8.

62 Fleury. On the capital, right, from the choir, is the entry of Adam and Eve into the Garden of Eden, the fall and expulsion.

63 Fleury. The nave, twelfth/thirteenth centuries (consecrated 1218) is austere, Cistercian-like. It is seen here from the monks' choir, with the tomb of King Philip in its midst (died 1108, but the tomb is later).

Of ancient Aniane itself, Benedict's first home, nothing remains; but its near neighbour, Saint-Guilhem-le-Desert, is a remarkable monument to his generation of monks. For here in a wild cleft in the hills above Montpellier, a great noble of Charlemagne's day, William of Toulouse ('Guillaume d'Orange'), sought refuge. His hermitage became the centre of a fine monastery, which grew and flourished when William the saint drew pilgrims to his shrine and William the hero was inspiring epic songs, culminating in Wolfram's *Willehalm*.[6]

If we ask the question, when was the Benedictine Order formed, then the first, simple, strict answer is: never, or not yet. The history of Benedictine communities has been the story of a long struggle to preserve the independence which was traditionally regarded as an essential mark of Benedictine monachism. The abbey of the Rule is a world on its own, and Benedict's monks have commonly been inclined to prefer it that way. In the eleventh century groups of monasteries under a common head began to be formed, sometimes very large groups indeed, but still following the Rule of St Benedict; in the twelfth century articulated orders grew up with a constitution and a central organisation, some of them following the Rule. In the thirteenth century a powerful pope and a great

64 Fleury, Adam in the garden of Eden, detail of the capital.

65-7 Saint-Guilhem-le-Desert, France. In a remote place in the hills west of Montpellier, Charlemagne's vassal William founded in his retirement a hermitage that grew into a monastery; by the eleventh and twelfth centuries a small town had grown up round the abbey.

65 The town houses jostle the late eleventh-century apse (much restored).

council (the Fourth Lateran of 1215) put it on paper that the independent houses of Benedictine obedience should form themselves into provincial or national congregations; and on paper for the most part the doctrine stayed. In thirteenth-century England the first congregation was formed; but it was not until many centuries later that every Benedictine community had been dragged into some net or other, and not until the days of Pope Leo XIII in the late nineteenth century that a single abbot primate, a single head to the whole 'order', was set up; but the Benedictines are still not governed by the primate or gathered into a single, authoritative order; his primacy is one of honour, not of power.

A former generation of Benedictine historians viewed the early efforts at centralisation with a marked coolness, and this accounts for the comparatively bad press that Benedict of Aniane received, together with some of his most distinguished successors, including sometimes even Cluny itself. Yet even the great liturgical scholar Edmund Bishop, a devout upholder of the traditional Benedictine life, admitted that: 'After the great founder himself, Benedict of Nursia, no man has more widely affected Western monachism than did the second Benedict, he of Aniane'.[7] Stern and puritanical by temperament, authoritarian in intention, Benedict of Aniane found that the world in which he lived and the responsibility laid on his shoulders increasingly mitigated both his puritanism and his austerity. In 817 at a council at Aachen he was the central figure in the promulgation of a series of monastic customs which, joined to the Rule, was to form the basis for the traditional monasticism. Its most essential features were liturgical. God's work, the *opus Dei*, of the Rule, ceased to be

65

66

67

merely a part of a divided routine and became the *raison d'être* of the monastic life; and a liturgy of ever-increasing elaboration grew up to match its new vocation—new, or partly new, because in a measure this was the consummation of accretions to the Benedictine life begun in the Roman basilicas shortly after the death of Benedict of Nursia. But even more important than the growing liturgy was the consecration of the book itself. St Benedict's Rule ceased to be, what it had been for Bede, a revered model, one of many, and became the basic norm—to be studied and learned by heart as no other Rule or model was studied.

The tenth century

When Benedict of Aniane died in 821 his schemes collapsed; and the ninth century marked perhaps the lowest point in the history of monastic observance since the sixth. There are exceptions. Here and there about Europe great abbeys flourished; and this was the golden age of Reichenau, secure on its tiny island in the Bodensee, and St Gall (Sankt Gallen). From both these monasteries venerable confraternity books survive, revealing that already in the ninth century each had an alliance in prayer with a group of abbeys in south-western Germany and Switzerland.[8] These alliances were not institutional, like those of the later orders; yet they created unions in some ways very much like congregations of more recent times, and helped the knowledge of Carolingian monasticism to survive through the collapse of the Carolingian empire. The buildings of Reichenau remain perhaps the most striking monument today of this epoch in monastic history: the Mittelzell, the main abbey church, has a nucleus of the ninth century, and was greatly enlarged at the turn of the tenth and eleventh. What we admire today is a great Romanesque basilica; but in truth by the eleventh century its heyday was past. In the ninth century it had been a centre of life and learning, and furnished even St Gall with skilled painters. But centres such as these were exceptional; for the most part the ninth century was a period of decadence both in monastic observance and in monastic crafts.

It was between 909 and 940 that the foundations for the true monastic revival were laid, and laid over a wide area. From Cluny in Burgundy (909-10), north-east to Brogne (*c.* 920) and Gorze in Lorraine (*c.* 933), then west via Fleury, where St Benedict's relics rose again to preside over the temporal and spiritual revival of his flock, to Glastonbury (940): in this ample space the Rule of the first Benedict and the customs of the second found practical expression. The monastic life revived and flourished in several hundred monasteries in France, Germany, England, Italy and Spain. The scale and the variety of the modes of monastic life became far greater in the twelfth century, when monastic houses came to be counted in thousands. From the tenth to the late twelfth century the foundation and endowment and support of monasteries of every kind are the characteristic forms which the endeavour of the pious, lay or clerical, was to take. Numerous men of moderate wealth and conventional piety—and many supposed less than pious by their fellows—invested large sums, a substantial part of their wealth, in founding or en-

83-8
52-8, 62

66 Saint-Guilhem. The old houses come close to the tower porch at the west front.

67 Saint-Guilhem. Within the abbey, the blind 'Lombard' arcading on the church above the quiet shade of the cloister.

68-70 Reichenau, Germany

68 The island in the early seventeenth century, looking south across the Untersee, the western arm of the Lake of Constance, showing the group of churches, with the main monastic complex, the Mittelzell, centre foreground, inscribed 'Münster'. The full length of the church is shown to the north. The church is of many periods from the eighth to the twelfth centuries, and much restored; the main structure of the nave is of the late tenth century, the west work mid eleventh. This engraving is after an oil painting in the abbey church (for source see p. 8).

69 The west work, a substantial element in many great churches of this period, especially in Germany. It probably played an important part in the development of processions and liturgical elaboration.

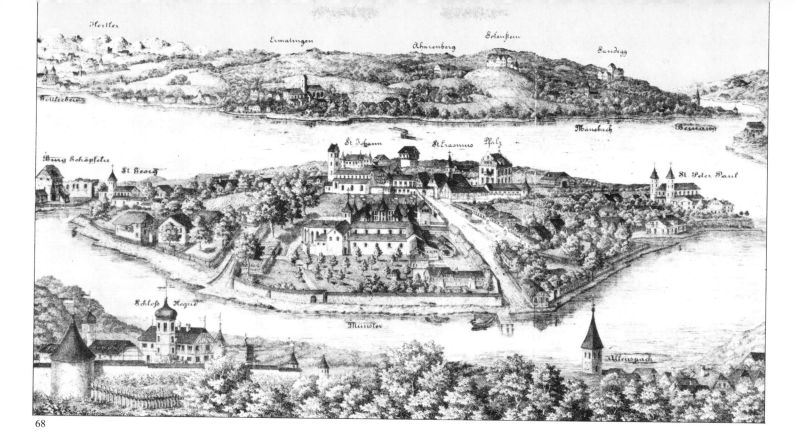

larging monasteries where monks or nuns could pray for their souls till the Day of Judgement. Here are facts of deep and lasting interest for the social, cultural and economic history of western Europe—also for the understanding of its politics, as we shall see—as well as facts of religious history.

Cluny and Gorze in the tenth and eleventh centuries

The houses which flourished in the eleventh century had mostly been founded or refounded in the tenth; all accepted the Rule of St Benedict of Nursia and the legislation of St Benedict of Aniane as the basis for their life; all accepted a much larger liturgy and much less manual work than the earlier Benedict had expected. Two main streams of influence flowed down from the tenth century into the eleventh and twelfth. First of all, that which stemmed from Cluny, whose prestige grew steadily as more houses accepted her customs, and as she continued to flourish under a succession of abbots of exceptional ability and saintliness, and also of exceptionally long life, for St Odilo (994-1049) and St Hugh (1049-1109) spanned the whole eleventh century between them. Numerous abbeys were reformed under the inspiration of Cluny. Commonly the patrons asked Odilo or Hugh for monks, books and advice; sometimes the monks themselves took the initiative in applying to Cluny; frequently the abbey remained for a time under the jurisdiction of one of Cluny's leading men, or of the abbot himself. In the end, down to the mid eleventh century, they became independent houses once again. But though these abbeys, reformed under Cluny's aegis later, owed no allegiance to the mother house, they continued to bear her stamp upon them. A visitor would find in the customs, liturgy, music, sometimes in the architecture and ornaments, signs that monks from Cluny had been there. From the mid eleventh century on, Cluny began to collect houses large and small which remained dependent on her, so that by the late twelfth century, spread over most of western Europe except Germany, there was a community of many hundreds of houses in the Cluniac allegiance. This meant that the abbot of Cluny was himself the patriarchal head of all these communities; the

69

monks professed obedience personally to him. The kind of constitutional or parliamentary structure established by other orders in the twelfth and thirteenth centuries was foreign to the simple hierarchy of Cluny.

Much of Cluny's influence was indirect, through disciples of her abbots and houses reformed by her which had preserved or recovered their independence. This can be seen most characteristically in Italy and Spain. In both lands Cluny had daughter houses. But in Italy its most powerful influence came through St William of Volpiano, abbot of Fruttuaria, who led a movement, deeply influenced by Cluny, which spread her customs and the communal ideal of the traditional monasticism in Lombardy, especially at Sant'Ambrogio at Milan, south to Farfa, and from Farfa to Rome itself; and also in Dijon,

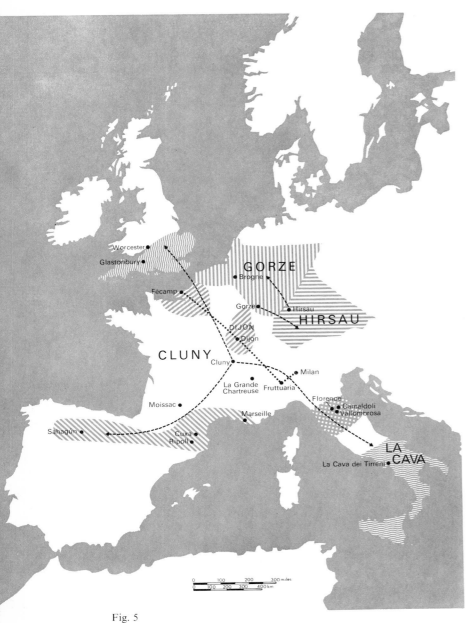

Fig. 5

where William was already abbot of the house of Saint-Bénigne, and from Dijon to Normandy, where he inspired and led the remarkable renaissance of monastic life with its centres in Fécamp and Jumièges, and which also influenced monasteries already under way, such as Mont Saint-Michel (see p. 211). In Italy, the abbots of Cluny had already established their customs in a number of houses, including San Paolo fuori le Mura at Rome, when St William started his work; and he greatly enlarged and extended the area over which Cluny's influence spread. Later in the eleventh century a number of Italian houses were refounded or revived under the direct sway of the abbot of Cluny; but the most widespread movements of Cluniac reform were technically independent of her authority. Monte Cassino itself, St Benedict's home, became a major centre of observance, monastic influence and craftsmanship under Abbot Desiderius, who was for a brief time at the end of his life Pope Victor III (1086-7). After the formation of the Norman dominion in south Italy and Sicily in the mid and late eleventh century, a new monastic centre was established at La Cava dei Tirreni, not far from Salerno—under Cluny's inspiration but never dependent on her. In the

329, 334-50

Fig.5 Map to illustrate the monastic movements of the tenth and eleventh centuries. Any attempt to plot the shifting pattern of influences, often very widely spread, must be impressionistic. Yet such a map is genuinely revealing, so long as the boundaries and arrows are not taken too literally, and so long as we make no attempt to put frontiers to the influence of Cluny, save where the sphere of influence of Gorze was felt (see pp.54-8).

70 Reichenau, the west work, exterior.

71-4 Rome, San Paolo Fuori le Mura. The basilica was built in the fourth century over the martyrium of St Paul; rebuilt after the fire in 1823. However, much remains of earlier mosaics, and the cloisters are intact.

71 The cloister with exquisite columns of cosmati, i.e. marble with mosaic inlay.

72 The apse with mosaic of Christ and the apostles, made under Pope Honorius III (1216-27), named at the peak of the arch, restored under Gregory XVI, 1836. A group of monks and clergy say office in the manner traditional in the Roman basilicas.

70

71

about 1050 the frontier of France and Germany, as it then ran, divided the sphere in which Cluny reigned from that of Gorze. The essential reason for this seems to have been political. The patrons of almost all these abbeys were kings and princes; it was not till the late eleventh and twelfth centuries that it became common for lesser men, barons,

that of the pope; to put it another way, she was founded in direct dependence on the pope, and was able in due course to draw out the logical consequence of her status. Successive kings of Germany had close personal relations with St Odilo and St Hugh, but the pattern of Cluniac independence was alien to them. Thus for their own monasteries they looked to

78

79

77 Camaldoli, Italy, the hermitages on the hill top. Buildings and chapel are mostly in seventeenth- and eighteenth-century style, but the setting and the plan have hardly altered.

78 Portable altar of Thidericus, abbot of St Godehard, Hildesheim, late twelfth century. *Thidericus abbas dedit . . .* the gift of Abbot Thidericus. From the British Museum, Department of Medieval and Later Antiquities.

79 Maria Laach, a characteristic example of a German Romanesque church with apses at both east and west and a forest of towers; mainly twelfth to thirteenth centuries, though much restored in the nineteenth and twentieth.

80 Maria Laach, sculpture in the Galilee; a head emerging from foliage, a motif common in the early thirteenth century.

80

knights and burghers, to found and play the patron to monasteries. In the tenth century the German kings, alias emperors, had kept a tight grip on their abbeys, whereas those outside their frontiers, especially those like Cluny which were remote from any centre of kingly or princely power in France, had developed a tradition of independence. Cluny herself had from the start a considerable measure of secular freedom, and in due course became wholly independent of every power save

Lorraine, then a part of their kingdom; and Gorze and its kin developed a system of external relations much more dependent on the king and the princes than Cluny's.

One of the central figures in German monasticism at the turn of the tenth and eleventh centuries was St Godehard, who ruled over Niederaltaich and Tegernsee abbeys, and by

81

the purity of his observance influenced many more. Late in life he settled in Niederaltaich, his biographer tells us, intending to end his days there. One night, after spending many hours in prayer and worship, he retired to his chamber just as dawn was breaking and laid down on his bench for a short rest. His sleep was disturbed by a dream, in which he saw a great olive tree in the midst of the cloister garth, and under it he was sitting and reading; presently there came messengers from the king-emperor, Henry II (1002-24), saying that their master had sent them to dig up the tree and carry it off for his use. Although they encountered roots of exceptional depth and other difficulties, the abbot awoke feeling sure that he would himself be presently uprooted. Sure enough, Henry insisted that he become bishop of Hildesheim, and as bishop he served both the monastic movement of his day, and the king. In combining these two roles, Godehard showed himself a true disciple of Gorze and the German monastic ethos of his day, and relations between the king and the monastic reformers were especially close under Henry II.

In the mid and late eleventh century the borders of France and Germany ceased to be a frontier between Cluny and Gorze; and one of the most powerful movements of the century had its centre in Hirsau in south Germany, and its founder in a disciple of St Hugh of Cluny. Yet the influence of William of Hirsau did not necessarily involve the waning of the older traditions which had flowed from Gorze, for in many parts of Germany allegiance to the king still meant adherence to the type of monasticism which had inspired St Godehard; and so when a loyal count founded Maria Laach in 1093, he looked to St Maximin at Trier, a house firmly set in the Gorze mould, for the monks and the monastic customs on which the house was to be founded.

The differences between Cluny and Gorze were mainly external. Their internal life represented still the customs of the ninth and tenth centuries, based on the Rule of St Benedict.

81 The setting: Maria Laach across the lake.

82 Maria Laach, the paradise or Galilee, early thirteenth century, c.1220-30.

82

4 Life, work and prayer

The daily round

What did monks do? How was their life spent? First of all, they dedicated a great share of their time to communal worship in the monastic church; in some communities, at some epochs, almost all the time that was left over from eating and sleeping. In all communities paying any kind of allegiance to St Benedict

83

84

and his Rule the day was punctuated by services. From soon after midnight till late in the evening the bell rang every hour or two to summon the monks to the office, to the recitation of psalms, hymns, prayers and readings from the Bible: in the middle of the night to Mattins,[1] in the small hours to Lauds, at dawn to Prime, about two hours later to Terce (the 'third hour'), about noon to Sext (the 'sixth'), early in the afternoon to None (the 'ninth'), early in the evening to Vespers, a little later to Compline. The times have been stated with deliberate vagueness. It is indeed possible to state the hours of the day when these events were supposed to have happened according to the Rule; but what these hours really meant, in the centuries before the clock (as we know it) was invented, is impossible to say; and a natural vagueness covers most medieval customaries. They had sundials and they had hour-glasses. To what extent they used them is an insoluble mystery. In practice, for most monks most of the time, the hour was announced by the bell; and we should be wrong to think in any terms more precise than the fairly regular toll of the bell punctuating a very regular day.

In winter, the monastic day may be roughly defined as running from 2 am to 6.30 pm.[2] By any standard, this meant an early start and a long day; though not unduly long. It meant an early start, but ended not long after dusk, at least in Mediterranean lands. The southern influence is still clearer in the summer timetable; for from Easter until mid-September the Rule allowed for a siesta in the early afternoon, and so a longer evening. Perhaps the strangest feature is the arrangement for meals. In winter and Lent one only was allowed, at about two in the afternoon in winter, in the evening (half-past five or six) in Lent; in the summer there were two, about noon and in the evening. Eggs, fish and cheese, beans, milk and honey provided the basic fare, with many variations in different times and places. Meat was forbidden by St Benedict, but it was widely held that he had not intended to include birds in his prohibition; and a number of special relaxations had already begun to creep in by the eleventh century. It was assumed that the very young monks and those who had serious difficulty in fasting would have breakfast or at least a drink between Terce and Sext; occasional extra dishes,

83 Cluny, France, the abbey in the eighteenth century from the north west, from an engraving by Née for J.-B. Lallemand, *Voyage Pittoresque*. The farther tower in the transept is the one that survives.

84 Cluny, the remnant of the third church (begun 1088): the main south transept and the somewhat later tower.

85

86

87

85 Cluny, the south transept within, showing the immense height of which St Bernard complained, and the arcading and fluted pilasters (top left) which inspired the architect of St-Lazare, Autun.

86 Cluny, capital, the Third Tone of Music. The tones are the fundamental plainsong melodies for singing the psalms, each in the corresponding Gregorian Mode. Cluny, Musée Ochier.

87 Interior of Cluny III, as reconstructed by K. J. Conant and T. C. Bannister.

'pittances', were added in most monasteries on Sundays and feast days and on a number of occasions which tended steadily to increase as the centuries passed. At the abbot's table, and in the infirmary—that is, where distinguished guests and the sick had to be fed—meat was commonly allowed.

In the refectory, then as now, an improving book was read from a pulpit or lectern. The monks were not allowed to talk—and silence was the rule throughout the day, save at certain times in special places, and apart from the public utterance of prayers and praises and instructions in church, chapter house, refectory and cloister. Thus a whole language of signs had to be devised to enable the brothers to communicate without breaking silence. A common sign for bread was a circle described by the thumbs and two fingers of both hands, for bread (we are told) was usually round; and for cherries a finger placed under one eye.

Apart from the brief time allotted for meals, the monk's day was divided between prayer, public and private, and work. 'Idleness is the soul's enemy,' wrote Benedict, 'and so at certain times the brothers ought to be engaged in manual work, and again at certain times in spiritual reading' (c. 48). It is

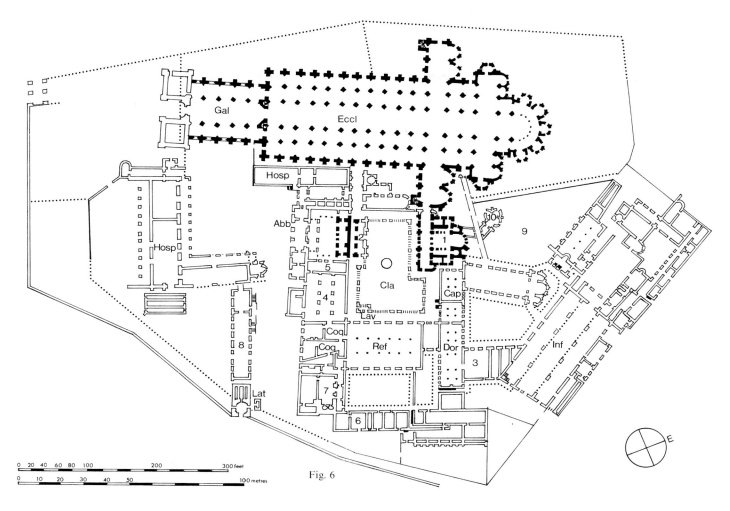

Fig. 6

Fig.6 Plan of Cluny in the twelfth century (after Professor K.J.Conant), showing the third church, Cluny III (begun 1088), and the remnant of Cluny II (tenth and eleventh centuries). 1.Choir of Cluny II. 2.Galilee of Cluny II. 3.Dormitory extension(?). 4.Storehouse. 5.Almonry. 6.Workshops. 7.Bakery. 8.Stables etc. 9.Cemetery. 10.Cemetery chapel.

88 Cluny, capital, the Sacrifice of Isaac. Cluny, Musée Ochier.

clear that he presupposed a routine in which communal worship, private prayer and reading, and manual work, were roughly balanced; and on the interpretation of this simple sentence innumerable passages in monastic history turn.

Let us consider first of all three possible approaches to work.[3] We may view it simply as the job to be done, like washing up or cooking: something essential for the life of any household, but not necessarily anything more. We may view it as a way of passing time, for the prevention of boredom or idleness. Or we may view it as a sacred thing, as the dedication of hand and brain to a lofty purpose. Now it is clear that if we start with the third view as our premise, then St Benedict's words must assume an enormous importance. But it is equally clear that it had never occurred to Benedict himself to interpret work in any such way. The passage itself describes work as the avoidance of idleness, and is evidently intended to provide some variety in the day to prevent the intense monotony that can follow from too homogeneous or monolithic a routine. But Benedict also goes on to define work as what is necessary, what has to be done; and it seems that he is essentially thinking of the chores of a community. He had no idea that the monks should be entirely self-supporting, should till the fields or

grow the wool or spin the yarn or weave the cloth from which their habits were made. He was concerned to see that the jobs that had to be done were accomplished, and in the process a useful element of variety enter the monastic day.

When one turns from the small and poor communities for which Benedict wrote to the large, elaborate and wealthy abbeys of the eleventh century, one can readily see why this chapter was interpreted in a manner very different from Benedict's intention. Granted a large team of monastic servants and a fairly large number of officials and specialists to do the various administrative and routine tasks of the community, there came to be little necessary work for the rank and file to perform. At the same time the development of more elaborate liturgy and of church music meant a much greater part of the day was spent in church.

Of how this worked the traditional monasticism of the eleventh century has left us many accounts, though none is perfect and all leave gaps; but far and away the best are the descriptions of the customs of Cluny. About 1075 a monk of Cluny called Ulrich visited the abbey of Hirsau in south Germany, and was eagerly cross-questioned by the abbot, William, on the customs of Cluny. On his return, Ulrich wrote the fullest surviving account of Cluny's customs; and they have for us a double interest, since they not only open wind-dows on every aspect of monastic life in the abbey, but also show very clearly how one monastery influenced another, how the customs of the traditional monasticism were passed down.

A great part of Ulrich's book is taken up with a description of the rituals and liturgy of Cluny. First he goes through the regular hours, from the moment the bell rang in the middle of the night for Mattins, when the monks rose, and dressed, and went down through the cloister to the church; he treats of how the office was sung, of how one of the brothers went round with a lantern to check that none was asleep in his stall; of the progress through the later hours, and the arrangements for mass, that is for the two masses attended by the whole community and the private masses said by each of the monks who was a priest. Then he turns to the Church's year, and observes the varieties of the feasts and fasts, from Holy Week round to Lent again. The ritual splendour is like a pendulum, swinging to the extreme of magnificence at the great festivals, to the extreme of simplicity in Lent. In Lent the ornaments, crucifixes, candelabra and reliquaries were hidden behind veils, and in place of the splendid golden frontal, the high

90

91

92

93

94

95

96

97

89 Head of Christ from a bronze crucifix, *c*.1070, originally from the abbey of Helmstedt, now in the Treasury of St Liudger, Essen-Werden, Germany.

Scenes from Monastic Life

90 Bede at Cuthbert's feet, f.1v.

91 Receiving postulants, f.16.

92-3 Fire fighting (see p. 9), ff.30, 31v.

94 Building with angelic help, f.39.

95 Monks digging, f.41.

96 A group of monks in conversation, f.53v.

97 Cure by a monk with Cuthbert's relics, f.84v.

All are from Bede's Life of St Cuthbert, British Museum Add. MS 39, 943.

83-8,
fig. 6

98

99

100

98-101 Essen-Werden, Germany

98-9 The abbey church of St Liudger, the central tower from without and within, showing the transition from Romanesque to Gothic in the thirteenth century—much later in this part of Germany than in the Île de France or England.

100 Ivory pyx of the fifth century and small reliquaries. The pyx was to hold the consecrated host on its visits to the sick and dying, or for the informal reservation sometimes practised in the early and central Middle Ages. The reliquaries are Islamic, from Sicily or South Italy, twelfth to thirteenth centuries. These ivory boxes, probably in origin bridal caskets or the like, were much in demand in northern Europe as reliquaries.

101 A panel from another box, eighth century, doubtless used as a reliquary.

altar had a cloth of white linen. On Easter Eve tapestries and carpets were hung round the church and all the finery restored to its place of honour; at Easter and Christmas nearly 500 candles were lit, and the altar was surrounded with candles and ornaments.

Ulrich freely admits that the services in the abbey church took up a great part of the day and night. The offices or hours consisted essentially of groups of psalms, with antiphons, hymns, prayers and readings or lessons interspersed. When a monk died during the winter, the whole psalter was recited the following night; if he died in summer, they were content to commemorate him with 100 psalms. Even allowing that their chanting was probably fairly crisp—medieval injunctions more often rebuke monastic choirs for going too fast than too slow—this was a marathon exercise. So were some of the readings: Ulrich tells us that he heard the whole of Isaiah read in six nights during one Advent. Thus there remained little time for manual work, and not even a great portion for private prayer and spiritual reading.

It is clear that the frontier between the *opus Dei*, God's work, public worship, and man's work, be it reading or labouring with the hands, had been redrawn; and the reasons for this throw a flood of light on the nature of medieval monastic life. The community at Cluny in the mid eleventh century was perhaps a hundred strong; when St Hugh died in 1109 the number had risen to three hundred. All books were handwritten on parchment at this period, and so extremely expensive, and by our standards extremely scarce. A thousand books made a large library in the Middle Ages, and if a hundred or two hundred monks wanted to read the same book, it could only be accomplished by public reading. Public reading was a much more essential part of their life than we can readily grasp; and this helps to make sense of the long lessons at Mattins and the solemn readings at mealtimes in the refectory. We have indeed a list of the books issued to sixty-four monks during Lent for private reading in the 1040s, and the list is a fascinating cross-section of the contents of the library and the interests of the monks. The Bible, St Augustine, Cassian and Gregory the Great reflect the basic literature of medieval monasticism; other fathers of the Church and the classics of the early Christian centuries, such as St Isidore of Seville, are well represented; the list also contains Lives of saints, a few works of history, including ecclesiastical history from Josephus to Bede, and one of purely secular history, Livy's *History of Rome*, rather rare in monastic libraries.[4]

Thus we can see that there was a practical element in the

103

104

105

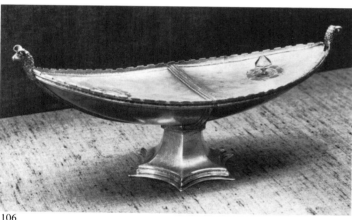

106

102-3 The Gloucester Candlestick (58.4cm high) made for Abbot Peter of Gloucester (1107-13), now in the Victoria and Albert Museum. Men and animals clamber in the foliage up to the inscription—*lucis onus virtutis opus doc(trina)* . . . the light's burden is virtue's work, is teaching aflame—and on to the candle above.

104 Ivory cross, *c.*1100, perhaps a pectoral cross to hold a relic, apparently from Canterbury, with the Lamb of God and the symbols of the evangelists. Victoria and Albert Museum (J. Beckwith, *Ivory Carvings in Early Medieval England*, London, 1972, no.45, p.128).

105-6 Censer, *top right* and incense boat, *above*, from Ramsey Abbey, fourteenth century, accidently discovered in Whittlesey Mere, now in the Victoria and Albert Museum.

arrangements at Cluny and that the Advent readings enabled the whole community to 'read' Isaiah simultaneously, which could not otherwise have been accomplished. But this only slightly lessens the ritual nature of the Cluniac routine. Ritual entered every aspect of the monastic life, and its effects are very visible in the buildings of the eleventh and twelfth centuries. Privacy was no part of the life of the period, whether for rich or poor. A peasant lived huddled with his family in a small cottage or hovel with a single room; a rich burgher or a knight spread himself a little more amply, but in two rooms

at the most; even a great castle might essentially consist of two main rooms and a chapel, without private apartments of any kind. Only a palace enjoyed a multiplicity of rooms of various sizes; and this was not because kings were more private than their subjects—this was hardly so still in the days of Louis XIV and Versailles—but because of the multiplicity of tasks which had to be performed. At first sight, a monastic complex seems more like a palace than any other kind of building of the age. But this was essentially because of the variety of folk and functions it had to provide for. In the Church, God, the saints, the monks and their lay visitors had each to have their compartments, linked in a unified whole, but yet separate and distinct. The centre of the domestic buildings was the cloister, in which much of the monastic work was accomplished. It was definitely a work room; but it was also the centre for much ritual. On great festivals the community processed right round the cloister. Every day they processed from church to the chapter house, their business centre. In the chapter house they listened every day to a chapter of the Rule—hence the name of the room; they solemnly considered their own and their colleagues' faults; they conducted business of a formal kind; on occasion they held discussions or listened to a discourse from the abbot or a senior monk on the spiritual life. At meal times they gathered at the wash-place, often a splendid and ornate affair, for ceremonial hand-washing, followed by a very elaborate grace in the refectory, and a meal as much punctuated by ceremony as by food. Liturgy and work had lapped over into each other's space, and the portion of the day allotted to necessary tasks had been severely curtailed.

The officials and the monastic economy
It became increasingly the practice to allot many tasks to specialists, and to release a number of monks from the full liturgical round to minister to other needs and wants. St Benedict had assumed a small body of officials under the abbot's close direction: a provost or prior to be the abbot's second-in-command, deans (literally, men set over ten monks

108

the occasional washing of the monks' habits. The razors for shaving were kept by one of the monks under the chamberlain's jurisdiction, locked in a box in the cloister near the door to the dormitory. At the appointed time he organised a group of monks in two rows in the cloister, one row to shave, the other to be shaven, and the task was performed to the accompaniment of a psalm. Normally the monks shaved weekly. 'As to our baths,' says Ulrich candidly, 'there is not much that we can say, for we only bath twice a year, before Christmas and before Easter'.[6]

The central figure in the administration of the abbey and its temporal welfare was evidently the cellarer, who had the largest team of assistants: a general assistant or sub-cellarer; a granarer who saw to the delivery of food supplies and to their storage, and organised the baking of the bread; a keeper of wine, who supervised the carting of wine from the abbey's extensive vineyards, its storage and use within the abbey; the gardener and the keeper of the fishponds; the refectorer organised the kitchen and the meals; and other officials managed the guest-house and the stable. The work of two other major officials is described by Ulrich: the almoner and the infirmarer. The almoner organised poor-relief in the neighbourhood of the abbey; and since a large part of its revenues consisted in tithes from the parishes under its jurisdiction, and tithes were intended for the relief of the poor as much as for the support of the clergy, in principle at least the almoner should have handled very substantial quantities of money, food and clothing.[7] How substantial they actually were is impossible now to say; and in times of dearth, and in later centuries, they tended for various reasons to be whittled down. In this too a ritual element entered in, and in most monastic customaries we hear as much of the almoner's duty to collect poor men for the liturgical feet-washing and serving by the monks on Maundy Thursday as we do of practical relief. But Ulrich has much to say of practical matters, and we may be sure that the almoner's office was onerous and important, that in such a society many men depended on charity, and that charity was abundant at Cluny in the days

each) to supervise groups of monks, a cellarer to attend to all their bodily wants, and door-keepers to guard the gates and the enclosure. By Ulrich's time these officials had grown more numerous and independent at Cluny. The abbot had often to be away visiting daughter houses, performing some mission for the pope, attending to the abbey's affairs; and in his absence two or more priors had to be ready to act; one as general administrator of the whole family of houses, a second 'claustral' prior to look after the domestic affairs of Cluny herself, and later (in all probability) a whole hierarchy of priors to whom the abbot could delegate his task. The deans at Cluny were external officials, administering groups of manors, seeing to the flow of food and money to the abbey's central funds, and also to the welfare, bodily and spiritual, of the abbey's tenants. Under the claustral prior there was a team of *circatores*, wandering spies as we are tempted to call them, whose business it was to tour the monastery and see that every monk was at his allotted task. The master who taught the young monks had one of the most crucial tasks in the cloister. The liturgy in the church was organised by the precentor, and in his charge came all the books, not only for the chant, but in the library—the book-cupboard as it was called, reminding us how modest a space a monastic library of this age filled, even in a great abbey like Cluny. The chamberlain and his assistants attended to the clothing, washing and shaving of the monks. The cloth was bought already woven and dyed,[5] and it was tailored in the chamberlain's department; he also supervised

107 Altar frontal or reliquary from Santo Domingo de Silos, twelfth century (see pl. 75).

108 Altar cloth, German, twelfth century, now in the Victoria and Albert Museum. St Bartholomew and St Paul.

109 Wine vats at Eberbach, Germany. The vats are modern but in an ancient cellar. The wine of the monks of Eberbach was famous in the late Middle Ages.

110

111

110 Ivory draughtsman, twelfth century, probably from St Albans, Victoria and Albert Museum (see J. Beckwith, p. 146, no. 117).

111 Tile from Chertsey Abbey, England: Tristan, thirteenth century, now in the Victoria and Albert Museum.

112-18 Vézelay, France. The most sumptuous of Cluniac abbeys. From the mid eleventh century it was the pilgrimage church of St Mary Magdalene; it was rebuilt *c.*1120-50 from the proceeds.

112 The mystic mill, Vézelay: the Apostle Paul turns the mill, 'urging us onward from the material to the immaterial', converting the words of the prophets into the message of the New Testament. This explanation is given by Abbot Suger, describing a similar scene in a lost window at St-Denis (E. Panofsky, *Abbot Suger*, pp.74-5).

of St Hugh. In the infirmary lived sick monks and some others who for various reasons were excused the full routine; and once a month or so all the monks had a blood-letting and a holiday, when they could enjoy the less arduous, more relaxed routine of the infirmary, where meat might be eaten and a briefer round of services attended.

Substantial as the bureaucracy appears when compared with the officials described in the Rule of St Benedict, the catalogue given by Ulrich is incomplete. He says little of the sacrist who was in charge of the church, its fabric and ornaments—suggesting that they were more modest than those later obtaining in large Benedictine and Cluniac communities. And it is clear that the officials at Cluny in Ulrich's day were not independent landlords, as many later became.

There is too a certain simplicity about the economic life of Cluny at this date which is interesting to observe. Its basic

needs were corn, especially wheat, beans, milk, butter, cheese and honey; wax for candles; cloth for habits; sheepskins and pigskins for parchment; timber and stone for buildings and furniture. In vine-growing country, such as the heart of the Mâconnais or, for Hirsau, in the Black Forest there were vineyards and grapes. From the large estates near the abbey came corn and wine in the enormous quantities needed to support a large community; from farther afield the produce came transformed already into money, with which the other needs could be purchased. Beans and vegetables such as were used in the eleventh century—onions and leeks, for instance, but not later discoveries such as cabbages or potatoes—were grown in the monastic garden and the home farms; milk in modest quantities was presumably to be had from the cows and goats of the neighbourhood, and also butter and cheese. Students of Cluny's estates have been struck by the absence of sheep, or large flocks of any kind.[8] This seems to be partly due to the absence of meat from the diet, and the practice, in Benedictine and Cluniac communities in the eleventh and twelfth centuries, of buying cloth ready-made; and this meant too that for the most part the animals whose skin provided the parchment had to be purchased, no doubt at considerable cost. Candles for the monastic church were probably made from pure beeswax in the Middle Ages, and honey was extensively used to sweeten the diet before the import of sugar began in the fifteenth century; thus bees and beehives were an important part of a monastic economy. In every large community the fishponds were vital, providing some relief from the salt fish which seems to have played a heavy role in the monastic diet—though it is probable that the fishponds would

have been rapidly depleted if salt fish from more distant waters had not been available: for, needless to say, fresh fish could only be transported very short distances.

The sacrist had the largest burden of all, the fabric of the church, the maintenance of its treasures and its equipment; and he had also the chief charge of one of the largest sources of income, offerings given to the church by visitors, pilgrims, friends and patrons. If we contemplate his work, and imagine the army of assistants he must have needed when the great church was being rebuilt, and the complexity of the relations between the sacrist and the many other leading monks and the master masons and the multitudes who cut and carried timber and stone and the other materials needed, fashioned and set it in the new building, we are almost tempted to think that the material structure had become so heavy as to obscure, for many monks, the worship and the prayer for which it all existed.

Cluny, the new monasticism and the twelfth-century renaissance
This would be a superficial view of the case, however, for the sense of devotion, the impact and the image of Cluny was something deeply felt by numerous visitors in the eleventh

and twelfth centuries. No doubt the enormous increase in population in Hugh's later years made it difficult to sustain such standards. Furthermore, Hugh's death in 1109 was followed shortly by a crisis in the abbey, since his successor, Abbot Pons, proved a failure. The disasters of Pons' abbacy coincided with a growing challenge from the new monastic movements of the early twelfth century, and his successor, Peter the Venerable (1122-56), was faced with war on two fronts—against disruption and decay within, and fierce criticism without. Criticism came above all from the new orders, and St Bernard of Clairvaux poured out his wrath against Cluny in his youthful intemperate *Apologia*.[9] Bernard accuses the Cluniacs of being too rich, of living too delicately, of adorning their churches with preposterous ornaments, and of not testing the vocation of their novices or giving them sufficient instruction before admitting them. This is no doubt a brief and unsophisticated statement of a large dispute, but it reveals at once certain essential features of Cluny as it had been under Hugh and remained under Peter. It was a traditional way of life, not greatly different in standard of living from the harsh uncomfortable world of the eleventh century. As living standards rose in the twelfth century, the difference between the ascetic Cistercians and the more luxurious secular aristocracy became much sharper, and the Cluniacs were tempted in some measure to follow the latter. The Cluniac life was a traditional mode, based on the Rule of St Benedict, no doubt; but based even more on custom, a tremendous ritual, which left little time over for most of its members for much adventure in the life of prayer or intellect.

But if we ask which had the better of the argument, Bernard or Peter?—the answer must be: both. Peter instituted a number of reforms intended to meet Bernard's scorching criticisms where they could not be rebutted; and Bernard was conquered by the abundant charity, and diplomatic skill, of Peter the Venerable, so that they became close, even intimate friends.

We should perhaps expect to find, in the early twelfth century, the variety and number of recruits coming to Cluny drying up. It was no longer avant-garde, no longer in the van of monastic movements; it represented the old world. Or so it seems to us. Yet the opposite is true. In the eleventh century Cluny had been famous for its splendour and devotion; under

Vézelay

113 Within the porch, the tympanum of Christ and the apostles, *c.*1140-50.

114 Through the door, one of the most beautiful of Romanesque naves, with capitals among the supreme works of Burgundian art, *c.*1120-35.

115 The west front, *c.*1140-50, with later additions, especially the south tower and west window, thirteenth century, and the tympanum showing Christ in Judgement over the west door, nineteenth century.

St Hugh it had grown in a spectacular fashion. Yet it had not, before the end of the century, been conspicuous as a centre of literature or art. Both these things it became for a time in Hugh's later years and under Peter the Venerable. Perhaps it should be remembered more as a patron than a centre of art; but the little that survives of Cluny herself, and the riches of Vézelay, brilliantly illustrate one aspect of the twelfth-century renaissance (see pp. 107, 112). Cluny in the 1070s was no great intellectual centre; it was the home of a way of life of immense prestige, and the books which came out of it were practical treatises on that life, like Ulrich's. In 1140-1 it became the last home of Peter Abelard; and although Abelard's theology had little to do with Cluny or the monastic life, it is significant both of Peter the Venerable's wide range of interests and of his charity that Abelard found there a safe haven after the disaster of his final condemnation.

Peter the Venerable was a theologian of considerable accomplishment. How he found time, in a busy life, between the endless routine at Cluny and his long journeys round the Cluniac world, in France, Italy and Spain especially, to write at all, seems to have puzzled him as much as it puzzles us. His was not an original mind, but wide-ranging; he was a theologian, who took pains to study Islam—he commissioned the first translation of the Koran into Latin—and contemporary heresy. His aim was to refute Moslems and heretics; but what is remarkable in that age is that he troubled to study them first, and that he showed something of the same charity towards them that won the friendship of both St Bernard and Peter Abelard.

The splendour of Peter's human insight comes out above all

83-8

114

115

in his letters. They are verbose and over-rich, reminiscent of St Bernard's picture of Cluny's diet, and so defy translation. But through the endless periods one can discern a mind of extraordinary sympathy and understanding. One of the most remarkable is a long letter, almost a treatise, addressed to Brother Gilbert, who was a hermit living in close association with Cluny or one of its daughters. Peter reveals at every point a sense both of the differences and of the common ground between the hermit life and the life of a large community. Essentially, he sees them both as expressions of the spiritual life set between earth and heaven. He outlines four elements in the life of the recluse—prayer, meditation, spiritual reading and work. The recluse cannot plant trees, or water his plants, or engage in any rural pursuit, because he is enclosed in his cell;

117

116

118

so he engages in the more useful task (*quod est utilius*) of copying books, thus cultivating the fruits of the spirit and the heavenly bread of the soul.[10]

The hermits who lived in association with Cluny lent variety to its life, and added, for some, a dimension to its character and appeal. For others the sharp difference between life in a hermitage and in a community represented a challenge, which inspired them to look for novel modes of the religious life. Where the hermit inspiration was deep and widespread, the first shoots of the new monasticism grew.

116 Bee keeping, taking the swarm, from a capital at Vézelay, twelfth century, in a design beautifully adapted from the model of a Corinthian capital with figures.

117-18 Capitals from Vézelay, early twelfth century; obscure mythological scene (117) and Daniel among the lions (118).

5 The hermits

The influence of Italy in the eleventh century

Life at Cluny was a continuous round of activity both ritual and communal: regular and dignified, yet without privacy and without leaving a large space for individual spirituality or private endeavour. In practice the variety of men who felt its inspiration was reflected in a greater variety of life than the customs suggest; in the hills around there were hermitages for those who felt the call to live in solitude.

No monastic community which took any note of the ancient literature of the religious life could fail to know that it had first sprung up in the desert, and that Cassian and Benedict had allowed a place in their schemes of life for a few to look for a more lonely and heroic approach to the divine presence. The anchorite ideal was never entirely forgotten; groups of hermits can be found in almost every part of western Europe where the monastic life flourished in the early Middle Ages—in Ireland, England, France, Germany, Switzerland; above all, in Italy.

The wastes of Egypt or north Africa were not accessible to them; but the word desert literally means any remote, uninhabited place, and they looked for, and found, the desert on the hill-tops, in the valleys, on small islands and other secluded places in western Europe.

The Italian contribution to the monastic movements of the central Middle Ages can easily be undervalued. Most of the houses which gave their names to religious orders were in France or (as the boundary then ran) western Germany. Assisi and St Francis have overshadowed all earlier Italian founders since St Benedict. Yet the traditional monasticism owed much of its influence to Italian monks in the eleventh century, notably to St William of Volpiano and the creators of La Cava; and it was from Italy that the anchorite revival stemmed.

St Romuald and St Peter Damian: Camaldoli and Vallombrosa

In the later Middle Ages there were recluses in every country, in every corner of western Christendom, in innumerable secluded valleys and in many places not at all secluded, for man must live and even a hermit needed to be sufficiently under the public eye to attract alms and food. But the farther one goes north, the weaker becomes the influence of the desert. The prehistory of the movement was in the tenth century, in the persons of a Greek and a Bohemian, Nilus and Adalbert.[1] They came to Rome in the third quarter of the tenth century and began the revival of its monasteries, and the formation of new ones in the neighbourhood. Adalbert died as bishop of

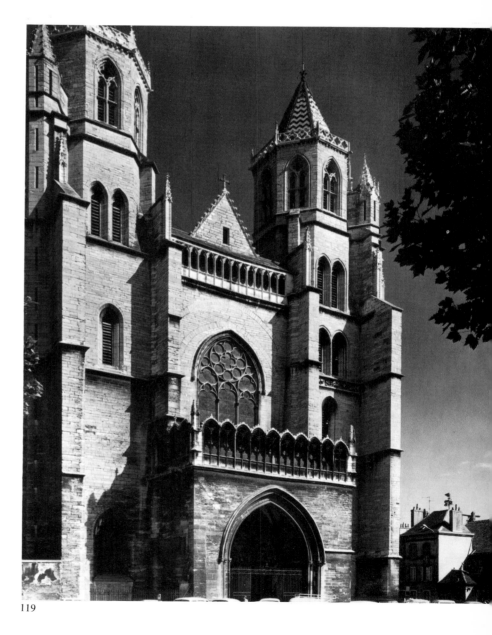

119

119, 121-22 Saint-Bénigne, Dijon, France. The abbey church of St William of Volpiano and Dijon, monastic reformer of the early eleventh century.

119 St-Bénigne was rebuilt in the twelfth century and again in the thirteenth to fourteenth.

120

121

122

120 At St Augustine's Canterbury, Abbot Wulfric, just before the Norman Conquest, planned a rotunda to link the main church and the eastern chapels in imitation of St William's at Dijon.

121 Of St William's church at St-Bénigne, only the crypt of the rotunda survives.

122 A twelfth-century fragment from St-Bénigne now in the Musée Archéologique, Dijon.

123-5 Jumièges, France. Another of St William's major abbeys, rebuilt in the mid eleventh century, the grandest surviving presentation of the image of Norman monasticism before 1066.

123 The nave looking west, through the tower arch.

124 The central tower from the north west.

125 The west front, similar to the west works in Germany.

In a secluded valley near Arezzo he founded a Benedictine monastery for beginners; and on the mountain top above a group of hermitages to which those long and carefully trained in the communal life could go, to recreate the life of the desert. The monastic life in general was seen by its finest proponents as a constant striving, 'you cannot stand still . . .: you go up, you go down; if you try to stay, you are ruined', as St Bernard was to say.[2] A similar inspiration can be seen in Romuald's younger contemporary St John Gualbert, who chose an even more dramatic site near Florence, and founded a remote, contemplative house among the leaves of Vallombrosa; strictly coenobitic, yet deeply influenced by the desert. Both became centres of small groups or orders of similar monas- 128

Prague and apostle to the Czechs in 997; Nilus, still a monk of comparative obscurity, near Rome in 1005. Their work was taken up by a more dramatic figure, the restless, heroic St Romuald, who began as a Cluniac monk and ended by founding Camaldoli. Camaldoli represented an attempt to interpret the final chapter of St Benedict's Rule quite literally.

77, 126-7

123

124

125

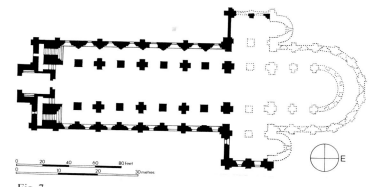

Fig. 7

Fig. 7 Plan of Jumièges abbey church, mid eleventh century; only
the nave and part of the transept survives, and the layout of the apse is
partly conjectural.

teries, and both survived, small but persistent, into the modern
world. Their monastic offspring included French houses and
orders, above all Grandmont and the Chartreuse, which were
strongly influenced by the disciples of Romuald and the call
of the Italian desert; but to gain first the flavour of the movement, let us stay in Italy a little longer, and consider the most
remarkable offshoot of the movement, St Peter Damian.   129-33

Peter Damian was a hermit and an intellectual. He had
enjoyed the best education that the Italian schools of the day
could offer; and in Italy, for all their vicissitudes, there were
never lacking from the tenth century schools in which a fairly
cultivated Latin and quite a wide knowledge of the deposit of
ancient learning could be acquired. We see in Peter Damian

126

127

126-7 Camaldoli, Italy, the hermitages, see pl.77.

128 Vallombrosa, Italy.

128

himself the beginnings of something more than this—he wrote a Latin of a quality, and showed an understanding of ancient books of an intensity, to make him one of the first notable figures of the twelfth-century renaissance, although his life lay wholly within the eleventh (c. 1007-72). His inspiration came partly from Romuald; equally, perhaps more, from a deep study of Cassian, of the Lives of the fathers, and of the ascetic literature of the patristic age. In his hatred of secular entanglements, and especially of marriage, in his great learning and eccentricity of temperament, and above all in his admiration for the monks of the east, he was almost a replica of St Jerome. Like Jerome's, his writings can be at once inspiring and absurd. On the whole, he disliked his fellow men, hated and despised their foibles and temptations, but just sufficiently

remembered that they were God's creatures and that Jesus had died to save them, to wish them all monks. He settled at a hermitage at Fonte Avellana, similar to Camaldoli and also inspired by Romuald; and there he lived the life of his ambition—a recluse, secluded in prayer, occasionally emerging with a fiery tract or sermon, for the most part hidden from the world.

But he was not permitted to stay in seclusion. When the new spirit of ecclesiastical reform captured Rome in the person of the German Pope Leo IX, Damian was one of the small group of great personalities—inspired, contradictory, quarrelsome monks for the most part—who changed the face of Christendom in the mid eleventh century. Damian found himself in due course cardinal bishop of Ostia, and a frequent visitor to places near and far from Rome as papal legate or ambassador. On one occasion he went to Milan with his 'holy Satan', the future Pope Gregory VII (see p. 93), and Damian, by force of character, polished eloquence and total indifference to what men might do to him, quelled a dangerous riot. Presently he returned to his hermitage, but not before he had helped to lay the foundations of one of the most remarkable movements within the papal reform, the attempt to make all clergy monks or quasi-monks, from which the orders of canons regular were to spring (see pp. 126-8).

Meanwhile, the stature of Damian's writings and the opportunities his office gave him to travel and to preach made him, what his predecessors had not been, an effective propagandist of the life of the hermitage. 'The solitary life is the school of heavenly doctrine, the training ground of heavenly skills. There everything that is taught is God. He is the path one treads, by which one comes to the knowledge of the highest truth. For a hermitage is a garden of heavenly delights; just as one might in a garden find the scents of different kinds of herbs, or the fragrance of luscious flowers, so in a hermitage the scent

129

130

of virtues fills the air with fragrance. There the roses of charity
burn rose-red, there the lilies of chastity shine in their snowy
vesture; there too the violas of humility enjoy their lowly
stature, and can be blown by no stormy winds. There the
perfect myrrh of mortification abounds, there the incense of
constant prayer ceaselessly rises. . . .'[3] And he likens the hermit's
cell to a shop in which transient goods are exchanged for
eternal; to a soldier's tent in God's camp; to the Holy Sepulchre, where sin died and the dead rose again.

The Carthusians

Peter Damian's writings were one of the means by which the
knowledge of the hermit ideal, and of monastic ideals in
general, spread through Italy and over the Alps into France
and the Low Countries. Local movements partly inspired by
Damian and other Italian leaders grew up in various parts of
northern Europe. In the forest of Colan in eastern France
Robert of Molesme presided over a group of monks and
hermits in the late 1070s and early 1080s; their ideas and ideals
were later to inspire him to found Cîteaux. About 1080 a
learned teacher from Rheims called Bruno came to join him.
In 1084 Bruno and two companions passed on to found their
own hermitage in a spot yet wilder and more remote; with the
aid of the bishop of Grenoble, they settled in a high wooded
valley and established the first hermitage on the site later
known as La Grande Chartreuse. Bruno presently moved on
to Rome, where he worked for the pope, and he died in 1101
in the south of Italy, in the act of founding another group of
hermits. But his hermitage at Chartreuse survived and prospered sufficiently to become the centre of a small but stable
order. The founder of the Carthusian Order as an organised,
regular pattern of life was Guigo I, who ruled the Chartreuse
from 1110 to 1136 as prior: the order had no abbots. He wrote
down the customs and laid firm the foundations of the

129-33 La Grande Chartreuse, France. Even in a Carthusian house, there
are some common buildings: cloister (129); refectory, fourteenth century,
furnished more recently (130); and the mortuary chapel (131).

131

institute, which have never since been fundamentally altered. In particular, they allowed for a much reduced liturgy, which gave ample time for private prayer, meditation, spiritual reading and work. The characteristic work of the early Carthusian was copying books, which helped to provide their priories with fine libraries. Meanwhile, from the start, though they lived in groups and communities, and had certain communal buildings, such as a chapel and a chapter house, most of their days were spent in their own individual cells; they formed groups of hermits, that is, living in permanent stone cells grouped round a large cloister. But it is not till the second half of the twelfth century that we are really well informed about their life.

One day in the middle of the twelfth century, about 1163, a young canon regular from the diocese of Grenoble, of noble origin and austere life, called Hugh of Avalon, came on a visit to La Grande Chartreuse. Hugh felt there an urgent call, an intense desire to join the community set 'almost in the clouds, . . . far removed from the turmoil of the world'. He approached one of the older monks, 'with groans and tears', asking for counsel. 'My son, how can you dare even to consider this? The men whom you see inhabiting these rocks are harder than the stones themselves, and have compassion neither on themselves nor on those who dwell with them. The very aspect of the place is frightening, but our way of life is even harder. The roughness of the hair shirt which you would wear would cut through skin and flesh to your very bones. The sensitiveness which I perceive in you would cause you to break down completely under the austerities of our way of life.' This discouragement, says his biographer, simply made Hugh hungrier for the banquet—for like St Lawrence viewing the instruments of torture with which he was martyred, he found the old man's horrid vision of Carthusian life draw him to it the more. It was indeed no easy course. His own superior, the prior of his house, put every kind of pressure on him not to go. The move from a less strict to a stricter religious community was a frequent event in that age, and must have caused many human difficulties and separations of this kind; but Hugh was shortly installed among the brothers at the Chartreuse, and stayed there in quiet contemplation and prayer and study of the scriptures and of the large library that the community had built up.[4]

'During this period Peter, the most venerable archbishop of Tarentaise, a Cistercian, used often to come to Chartreuse, and there alone in a cell among those of that holy community, dwelt for several months like an industrious bee making honey in his hive.[5] He might also be compared to the mild and gentle dove living in security and tranquillity with Noah in the ark, and fleeing from the tumult of the world as from the onrush of the waters of the flood sent to overwhelm almost the whole face of the earth. Passing his time in meditation and in converse on spiritual matters with these holy men, he believed that like Paul he had found himself in Paradise, and was often on the wings of contemplation borne up to the third heaven.

'The duty of waiting upon him was allotted to Hugh. Who was more fitted to be the companion of such a man? . . . To see the old man and the young one together you would imagine that Peter and John had once more returned and been reunited . . .

'There still exists on the side of the mountain, on the way from the cells of the monks to the lodgings of the lay brothers, a seat made as a resting place for the holy [arch]bishop, who became tired and hot through often passing up and down. [He] would seldom ride when there because the prior was forbidden to do so. The seat was of this type. There were two large firs growing side by side with a space between

them. Horizontal cuts were made in these into which a squared pole of yew wood of no great thickness was inserted. This was the only seat provided for the [arch]bishop.'

In later years, after he had become bishop of Lincoln (1186-1200), Hugh was able once at least to visit Chartreuse, and so his biographer had accompanied him there:

'We sometimes saw Hugh sitting on that seat, telling us affectionately this and certain other anecdotes about this former archbishop, now reigning in heaven, and wiping the perspiration from his venerable countenance, for the ascent was no small labour to him [Hugh was short and stout]. It was a pleasure also to us, who heard these stories from him, to sit on that lofty throne. It amazed us that as the trees grew the timber plank became so firmly fixed that the mark left by the incision could scarcely be detected. It also seemed wonderful that, although the trees had been growing vigorously upwards for fourteen years or more, the seat was never any higher, but remained near enough the ground for a small man to sit on it in comfort. It always seemed as fresh as if its original sap had not yet dried.'

The most remarkable character at the Chartreuse in Hugh's time (to judge from Hugh's Life) was Gerard, called by the biographer ex-count of Nevers, who had abandoned the world, but not his native wit or bluntness of speech. When asked whether he thought King Solomon was in heaven, he asserted firmly that he was—for Jesus called David his father, and David would undoubtedly have seen to it that his other son was properly treated. On another occasion he called on Louis VII of France (1137-80), a pious man and by no means a coward, but in great awe of Brother Gerard. The chess board with which the king had been relaxing was hastily removed when Gerard was announced, but not hastily enough; Gerard coolly observed that all his time should be spent trying to make amends for his failures as a king, not 'on these idle allurements'.[6]

Gerard reveals one remarkable consequence of the monastic life. Its comparative rigidity and uniformity have often been supposed to breed conformism, to diminish individual traits and eccentricities. This is not wholly untrue: communities can carry a single stamp, and the communal life has undoubtedly bred certain common characteristics. Yet the outsider who visits a lively community today is commonly struck by the opposite impression: that the common life has sharpened and strengthened the individuality of many of its adherents. This can be in even greater measure true of the more secluded breeds of monk; and brother Gerard and, in a different way, Hugh himself, reveal this very clearly.

The contrast of community and hermitage
The hermit ideal revived in a world in which its opposite, the communal mode of life, flourished as never before. The significance of this contrast is vividly revealed in such buildings as the dormitories at Eberbach in Germany or Sénanque in Provence. They are austere and simple and Cistercian; but they will serve as representatives of dormitories in any monasteries of moderate size. They are open, bare and unfurnished today. But all that we need to add to each in imagination is two lines of palliases filled with straw, and some rough

135-7

132 La Grande Chartreuse, the hidden remote enclosure, surrounded by woods and hills.

133 La Grand Chartreuse: within, the mortuary chapel and large cloister surrounded by cells.

132

133

S IVLI   AN

135

136

134 Santo Stefano, Bologna, Italy, the massacre of the Innocents, a Romanesque fresco, now in the Museo.

Monastic Dormitories. In contrast to the privacy and loneliness of the Carthusian cell, the communal dormitories of Eberbach (135-6) and Sénanque (137).

137

bedding. In later times such dormitories were fitted out with panelling and cubicles, and the monks of some houses abandoned them altogether for more domestic quarters; eventually the practice spread of providing monks with private cubicles in which to sleep. But privacy, or the use of small rooms, was the practice neither in the monastic life nor in the secular world in the eleventh and twelfth centuries.[7] A modern observer, accustomed to privacy, needs no further persuasion of the attraction of the hermit life than a picture of a common cloister, refectory and dormitory. A brief visit to the most celebrated of medieval hermitages—to the Chartreuse, to Camaldoli, the Carceri above Assisi, each set in a position of great natural beauty and quiet, surrounded by woods and streams and mountain tops—reveals some of the positive attractions of the hermit life. Not all the hermits lived in such places; surprisingly enough, the monks of the Chartreuse and Camaldoli set up houses in the middle of towns, such as Pisa and Bologna. But their natural habitat, and the country which inspired their founders, lay in the hills and woods. It was the solitude and peace which first attracted the hermits to these places. If they had thought of natural beauty as an alluring or distracting thing, no doubt they would have rejected it. In this guise it presumably appeared to Milton, when he counted the leaves of Vallombrosa:

Thick as autumnal leaves that strow the brooks
In Vallombrosa, where th' Etrurian shades
High overarch't imbowr—

and likened them to an army of devils. Yet if the founders of the Chartreuse, Camaldoli and Vallombrosa rejected the idea

7, 126-7,
306, 316

34
128

126-33

In France and Italy the pattern was different, because royal authority in France was slight, in Italy distant and intermittent. In France, to all intents and purposes, the Capetian kings were great nobles ruling over one principality among the many in their kingdoms. This was not quite the whole truth, and over bishops and monasteries the royal hand spread considerably farther in the eleventh and twelfth centuries than over lay barons. In any event, lay princes were more often to be found among the founders and patrons of monasteries than were kings; and at Cluny herself and among some of her disciples a new model of independence from local lay control had sprung up. The abbots of Cluny often had close personal relations with the surrounding princes—with emperors indeed—and with the bishops of Burgundy; but they

lived in border territory, in the Mâconnais, where it was still doubtful if any allegiance was owed to the king of France. They had been founded on Burgundian soil by a duke of Aquitaine.[2] Thus it was natural for their founder to set them free from secular ties to a rival dynasty; and in due course they

138-40 Santo Domingo de Silos, Spain. The strange and lively capitals in the cloister, late eleventh or early twelfth centuries, are of animals, grotesque and symbolic figures. They fall into two types, perhaps by different sculptors: in 138-9 the columns are apart; the relief is flat, and seems to imitate silks and ivories, and to show Moorish influence. Plate 140 shows capitals with the columns close together, and belongs to the second sculptural group.

138

won from the papacy, their temporal and spiritual overlord, exemption both from temporal and spiritual control, save that of Rome herself. They were exempt, that is, in principle, from the rule of kings and of bishops. But in practice a close relationship with many princes and bishops was needed to preserve the large estates and the numerous churches which Cluny came to rule; and over the houses reformed by her, or which in the eleventh and twelfth centuries became subordinate to her, a varying pattern of relationship with kings, princes and bishops came to be established. In Italy variety was in principle even greater, for the kings of Germany were kings of Italy too, but only rare visitors; local nobles and the reviving cities had in practice a larger part to play in their fortunes, even in the early eleventh century, than the king-emperors.

What was common to the monasteries of Germany and England, and in some measure to those of France and Italy too, was that the lay overlord regarded his monasteries in a very special sense as his own property; and what was common to them all was the sharp social division and difference of function between the monks who prayed and the peasants who worked and supplied them with food and the material basis of life.

There was a sense in which a monastic complex could never be a piece of property. A king or prince was not a priest or bishop, the functions of priests and monks in choir and cloister were tasks he could not himself fulfil, and could only imperfectly understand; in a real sense the monastic community was a spiritual power complementary to his, not subordinate to it. In a sense too the monastic estates, which supported peasantry, soldiers and the monks and their servants, were governed by a multitude of complex legal and social rules which divided the rights over them so that the whole social hierarchy was fed, and protected, and governed; and all were linked together as beneficiaries of the monks' prayers. And yet in another compartment of their minds kings and princes and lesser men regarded churches and abbeys and bishoprics as pieces of property just like the clothes they wore and the dogs they followed in the chase. If they were very secularly minded, like the Anglo-Norman William Rufus (1087-1100), they regarded them all as pieces of secular property, like manors; if they were spiritually minded, like Henry II of Germany, they were part of the whole system of kingly authority, over which the king ruled as Christ's vicar.[3] The phrase used in English formularies of Elizabeth I in the late sixteenth century, 'supreme governor of this realm . . . as well in all spiritual or ecclesiastical things or causes as temporal', very appropriately describes the attitude of Edgar or the Ottos or Henry II of Germany; save only that it in no wise implied—as it did for Elizabeth—any denial of the spiritual supremacy of the papacy. Henry II reckoned he could found and suppress monasteries, appoint and remove abbots, organise and reorganise, at will. They were in a quite direct sense the jewels in his crown, for they were his property, and the symbols of his divine authority.

It was a society in which freedom of choice was exceedingly limited. The sons of a baron or a knight were expected to learn the arts of war and the pleasures of the chase, the management of an estate and of a wife; but were not put to letters. The sons of the peasants were expected to work like their fathers and on their father's plots. But the estates of peasants and of lords could be extremely inflexible and insensitive to changes in population; in the eleventh and twelfth centuries growth in population was one of the main reasons for profound changes in society; already in this early period, it was becoming not uncommon for the well-to-do to place their younger sons in monasteries.

An essential element in the traditional monasticism was that it was for many a whole way of life, in which they joined as children and all, save the apostate or those who passed to a stricter or a higher role and became hermits or bishops, left by way of the cemetery. This is perhaps to us the most surprising feature of many monasteries of the early eleventh century, that a large number of their monks were not there of their own volition, at least in the first instance.

139

140

Recruitment in the eleventh and twelfth centuries

There is in the British Museum a manuscript written in Winchester in the time of King Cnut (1016-35) with a famous drawing of the king and queen presenting a splendid cross to the monks of the New Minster, the abbey which lay immediately beside the cathedral and was later moved to a more convenient site outside the city, called Hyde.[4] The manuscript contains a list of the community and of all its friends and benefactors, including not only kings and earls and citizens of Winchester, but the monks of the Old Minster, the cathedral community, and several other abbeys besides. We are here provided with a complete list of all the monks of the New Minster from its foundation in the 960s on—and it was kept up, not perhaps entirely faithfully, until the eve of the dissolution in the early sixteenth century. The most interesting part is that which reveals not only the names but something of the structure of the community in its first two centuries. It begins with the names of monks grown old or dead when the book was written c. 1031. These are mostly noted as having been priests or deacons. By the tenth century already, it seems, something approaching half a monastic community would be in

priests' orders, though it was not until the twelfth or thirteenth that it became the normal practice for all monks to aspire to priesthood and all priests to celebrate mass every day.[5] Some are merely *monachi*, monks, which may have no significance or may mean that they never aspired to any orders. The forty-eighth recruit is the first called *puer*, boy—the first to be noted as dedicated to the community as a child. From the moment when the record is contemporary, and when we may be tolerably sure that the names are being entered as the monks arrived, the *pueri* predominate. From some point in the 1030s we have a run of boys, with scarcely a mature recruit among them: between then and c. 1072 there are forty-one names, thirty-five of them *pueri*, two unspecified, two deacons and a priest, and one noted as 'convert and priest'. The convert in this setting was a man of mature years who came of his own volition. True, in strict law the *puer* could not take solemn vows till he was of man's estate; but by then, long since, his estate in life had been determined by his parents' choice. If he returned to the world there was no easy way to a livelihood open to him. The world accepted that a man's or a woman's vocation was neither more nor less than what their parents had determined. From 1072 on, the pattern begins to vary. Men who joined as lay and priestly converts alternate with the boys, and a class of 'young men', *iuvenes*, a term of various connotation, also appears. By 1150 the *conversi* much outnumber the *pueri*; but the last group which bear these designations, from the early to mid 1180s, still included three boys to five converts. These facts are the outward and visible sign of a period of rapid social change.

The Book of Life of the New Minster, Winchester, c.1031

141 Queen Emma—Ælfgyfu was her official English name—and King Cnut present the great cross to the abbey church, with God, the Blessed Virgin and St Peter blessing from above, and a group of monks worshipping below.

142-3 The opening of the list of monks. Each is identified as *abbod* (abbot), *sac'* (priest), *leuita* (deacon), *puer* (boy oblate), *c'* (converse or convert), *laicus c'* (lay convert). These pages span the years c.1031-c.1090. British Museum, Stowe MS 944, ff.6, 21v-22.

141

142

143

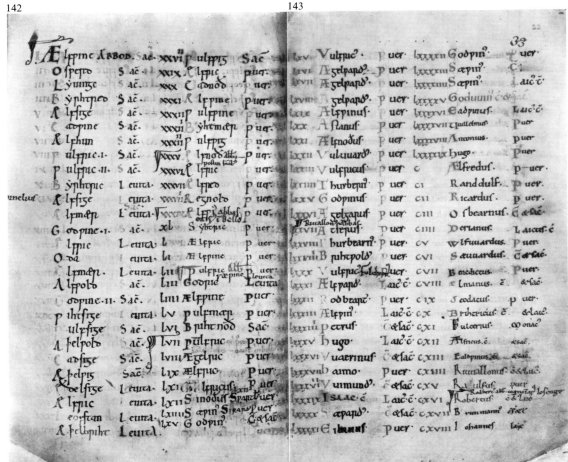

Social change, 1050-1150

In the late eleventh and early twelfth centuries the extreme pessimism of St Peter Damian or St Anselm as to the chances of any but monks escaping the pains of hell gradually subsided. 'The married are not condemned, but the continent are more easily saved' was the view expressed by Abelard in the early 1130s.[6] He was by then a eunuch and a monk, prescribing rules for the conduct of nuns; the view is, even so, notably less harsh than Anselm's. As heaven appeared more attainable, we might expect the monastic life to lose some of its attraction; nonetheless, it is a striking fact that as the numbers of layfolk expected to reach heaven increased, so the number of monasteries and their population increased with equal rapidity.

By 1050, so far as we can judge, the general rise in the population of western Europe which is so marked a characteristic of its social and economic history between the late tenth and the thirteenth centuries was well under way. In the twelfth and thirteenth centuries population rose steeply, to level off about 1300 and fall sharply again when plague struck in the 1340s. We cannot hope to know the fundamental causes for this rise. Even in much more recent times, the substantial increase in European population of the late eighteenth and early nineteenth centuries is still a mysterious phenomenon on which the experts feud; small chance of describing with any precision what lay behind the rise of the central Middle Ages. It seems clear that most western countries were somewhat more peaceful and that men were somewhat more inventive in the late eleventh and twelfth centuries than before. Increase in numbers by itself might only have led to widespread shortage and hunger; no doubt in some places, at some times, hunger was a very real threat, especially perhaps in the thirteenth century when the expansion had here and there outstripped the capacity of underdeveloped Europe to expand the land under cultivation or to adapt its techniques. What is striking, however, is that the growth of population coincided with a very marked increase in prosperity in many parts of Europe, and in a cultural and social movement which greatly added to the variety of art, literature, occupation, expectation and opportunity open to men, and even in a measure to women.

This was one of the notably creative periods in European history. The growth in population doubtless provided manpower for new occupations, and a challenge to those who grew food to grow substantially more; but it cannot in itself be called a cause of this prosperity—rather, it was a result, for the economic progress, however limited, was sufficient to feed far more mouths than hitherto. But in truth it is better quite simply to say, it was a part, and a crucial part, of the elements of change in a society which would still seem to us, if we viewed it with twentieth-century eyes, exceedingly static.

Change was most evident in two institutions especially characteristic of this period of the Middle Ages: its monasteries and its cities.[7] In Italy, the towns had never declined to anything like the extent that the cities of the north decayed after the barbarian invasions. In the eleventh and twelfth centuries the Italian cities staged a spectacular revival: they became

144-6, 149-50 Bologna, Santo Stefano

144-5 In the centre of the octagonal church, Santo Sepolcro, built in imitation of the Holy Sepulchre at Jerusalem, is the sepulchre, and within it the shrine of St Petronio with the Angel of the Empty Tomb, surmounted by altar and pulpit.

144

145

once again teeming and rich; as the grip of the emperors and the old aristocracy weakened in the late eleventh and twelfth centuries, the rich citizens argued with the bishops as to who should enter into their inheritance. In the late twelfth and thirteenth centuries innumerable cities were ruled by citizen oligarchies of local landowners and merchants—often the same people, or closely related. Even north of the Alps where few cities achieved either the wealth or the independence of places like Pisa, Lucca, Florence and Siena, the urban renaissance fundamentally altered the pattern of life—altered it by reintroducing the town as an element in the social scene, with permanent markets where corn could be sold to town dwellers and others who no longer grew their own food; and in this way the foundations were laid which created a large world of commerce affecting the whole community. Money came to play a leading part in the affairs of peasants as well as their lords, of merchants and artisans, clerks and monks.

202-6

The rise in population by itself does not explain the growth in monastic population, for that far outstripped the general increase. It is very hard to give precise figures; but they have been worked out for the English monasteries with some degree of precision. Between 1066 and 1154 (the accession of Henry II of England) the number of monasteries for men rose from just under fifty to about five hundred; these are figures that can be documented with fair exactitude.[8] Less certain, but probably not far wrong, is the calculation that the population of the English monasteries, the number of monks and nuns, rose seven or eight fold or perhaps even more over the same period of just under one hundred years.

England was relatively rich, and the Norman Conquest ushered in developments in some ways specially favourable to monastic endowment; yet we have no reason to suppose that conditions were greatly different elsewhere. In Spain the rapid extension of the area under Christian sway provided conditions as favourable as England, though the monastic population was always much smaller in this period. Germany was relatively less prosperous in the twelfth century than before, and in the western parts earlier endowment had been lavish: its expansion was probably less rapid than England's. In eastern Germany and those countries of central and eastern Europe which had become part of western Christendom, especially Poland, Hungary in fair measure, and Bohemia, the spread of monasticism was very slow indeed before the mid twelfth century; then it proceeded apace (see pp. 227-31). But Italy and France were the twin centres of the Church and of the cultural and spiritual movements of the eleventh and

146

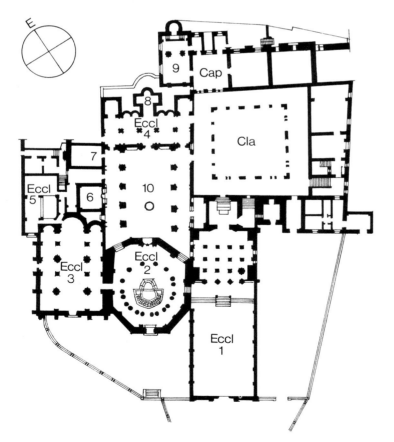

Fig. 9

146 Bologna, Santo Stefano, the courtyard of Pilate, 'Cortile di Pilato'.

Fig.9 Plan of the monastic complex of Santo Stefano, Bologna. Nine churches and chapels cluster together here, partly reflecting fashions of earlier centuries, partly the sentiment of the pious Bolognesi of the eleventh and twelfth centuries, when most of the churches received their present shape. The whole complex was known as 'Jerusalem' in the twelfth century. 1. Church of Christ the Crucified (Crocefisso). 2. Church of Santo Sepolcro (Holy Sepulchre, with the tomb of St Petronio). 3. Church of Sts Vitale (Vitalis) and Agricola. 4. Church of the Holy Trinity. 5. Church of the Blessed Virgin Mary. 6. Tuscan Chapel. 7. Chapel of St Giuliana. 8. Chapel of Holy Cross (La Croce). 9. Chapel of La Benda (a relic of the Virgin's head-scarf). 10. Courtyard of Pilate.

147 Verona, San Zeno Maggiore, west door, bronze reliefs, c.1138 (see pls.156-7).

twelfth centuries, and there, and especially in France, we have no reason to suppose the growth of monastic population slower than in England. Yet it is impossible to believe that the general rise in population between 1050 and the late twelfth century was anywhere in the region of sevenfold; even a doubling in one century puts some strain on our credulity.

Nor can the monastic rise have been won at the serious expense of any other sector of the community. It may be that even with the number of monks and clergy as it was in the 1150s the celibate element among the European peoples was not enough to check the growth of population in any significant degree. But in every walk of life—among the barons and knights, among the citizens and burgesses rich and poor, and among the peasants—the increase, with many local variations, and with all allowance for the large areas of our ignorance, went on steadily and, by the standards of an underdeveloped society, relatively fast.

In older monastic houses, so far as we can tell, the number of boy recruits remained fairly steady, or only slowly declined in the twelfth century; while the number of older recruits, of men who found their own vocations, rapidly increased. In the new religious orders of that period recruitment was mainly confined to adults. Thus although we may reckon that some of the increase in monastic population was due to fathers at their wit's end to provide for surplus children in a world where growing population could mean growing competition, it is among the grown up men and women of the age that we have mainly to look for the explanation.

No doubt it owed a great deal to social impulse and fashion; success multiplied success. In some parts of Europe the old fashion, represented by the German aristocratic ladies of the tenth and eleventh centuries (see pp. 167-8), for the highly born to monopolise some cloisters, spread in this age and became a permanent feature of the landscape for centuries to come. This remained especially the case in Germany, though there are a few cases in France, Spain and Italy as well. To the general explanation of monastic recruitment, aristocratic interest contributes nothing, for although monks and nuns continued to be recruited in the main (so far as we know—and so far as all our evidence suggests) from the well-to-do, it is precisely in the country where our evidence of growth is most secure, in England, that the aristocracy seem to have been most indifferent. Every age, even in England, saw a few men and women of the highest birth enter religion, such as Leofric (d. 1066), nephew of the earl of Mercia and abbot of half a dozen monasteries under the complaisant regime of Edward the Confessor, or Henry of Blois, favourite nephew of Henry I, brother of King Stephen, who was abbot of Glastonbury and bishop of Winchester from the late 1120s on. Yet as a class the English aristocracy conspicuously turned its back, almost throughout the later Middle Ages, on the clerical professions. They lavished money and land in the twelfth century, and occasionally showed generous patronage later; but their sons seldom became monks and their daughters almost equally seldom nuns.

If we cast our minds back to the age most nearly analogous in monastic history, the fourth century, we can recall that a similarly sensational and mysterious growth coincided with two features of the contemporary world—an intellectual and spiritual drive towards asceticism sponsored by men like Origen and his disciples in the generations immediately preceding the age of St Antony, and rising living standards, general prosperity and worldliness among the Christian community itself, as it became first socially respectable, then officially permitted, then the religion of the Roman Empire. The analogies in the eleventh and twelfth centuries cannot be exact; but they are at least helpful. Cluny and her friends and rivals had played a leading part in the wider movements of popular religious revival in the tenth and early eleventh centuries; then, in the mid eleventh, came reform at the heart of the Church's hierarchy, led by monks or quasi-monks, in the papacy itself. At the same time a rapid growth in the wealth of at least a sector of the population caused a kind of revulsion which has been common in economic history; and the great sayings—'Blessed are the poor . . . Blessed are the peacemakers'—reverberate through all the religious movements of this age. The richer men became, the more they might fear, for themselves or their neighbours, the torments of Dives or the eye of a needle. Yet revulsion was not the only feeling Christian men felt, then or since, for material prosperity. Increased wealth added greatly to the resources available for monastic foundations, and it became increasingly easy in a society in which silver and even, in the far south, gold, flowed more readily than it had done for many centuries, to add penny to penny for a building fund, or finance a new monastery from a syndicate of men of moderate means. Patronage ceased to be a monopoly, first of kings, then of nobles; it came within the reach of everyone who had an earthly surplus with which to pile up treasure in heaven.

The reform of the papacy and the advance of Mammon—strange allies in the monastic upheaval of the eleventh and twelfth centuries—affect our story in numerous different ways. The great popes from Leo IX (1048/9-54) to Gregory VII (1073-85) fervently believed that the clergy should lead ascetic lives, that as many as possible of them should be monks or at least live according to a rule. The separation of the clergy from the allurements of the secular world, from women and money above all, lay at the heart of their programme, and closely linked to these demands went an insistence on the authority of the Holy See as God's agent for the rule and reform of the Church. Leo came from a background steeped in the traditions of Gorze and its offshoots; Gregory—wherever he may have been monk[9]—counted St Hugh of Cluny among his few close friends; and his successor Urban II (1088-99) had been a monk of Cluny under St Hugh. These links were important; but more important still was the close union between the reforming popes and many leaders of monastic reform, their share in the ascetic fervour characteristic of the age. The papal reformers were practical men; but they were also dreamers, theologians, and, after a measure, lawyers, for their programme aimed to combine spiritual revival with the enforcement of major elements in ancient canon law, such as the law of clerical celibacy. Thus the revival in the study of theology and law was an essential companion to the papal reform, as it was of the monastic movements of the age.

The eleventh and twelfth centuries were exceptionally creative. The advance of Mammon greatly increased and diversified the resources available for monastic endowment, and the papal reformers encouraged investment in monastic communities, both by the fervour of their own belief in divine judgement on human, and especially on lay, sinners, and by

148 Verona, San Zeno Maggiore, the stone mason in bronze, late twelfth century.

149

monks joining in the activities of the rest of the clergy, serving parish churches, perhaps, even engaging in cure of souls. In the long run this was reckoned no part of a monk's work—the monk's place was the cloister.[10] But in this period the practice was accepted and widespread, so far as we can tell. However this may be, tithes and grants of churches, with the offerings which were laid by the faithful on their altars, frequently came into monastic hands. These offerings reflected the enormously increased use of money—of silver coins—throughout western Europe in the eleventh century. The resources which were mobilised could be astonishingly large. A great fire swept Saint-Benoît-sur-Loire twice in the eleventh century; twice the monks set to work to rebuild a large part of their church and other buildings to withstand the flames; and so far it has withstood them.[11]

52-8, 62-4

To us it seems an astonishing thing that such a religious community, however well endowed, could sustain the vast expense of rebuilding its church twice in a century—especially as the abbey lived on through the centuries which followed, and the church was scarcely altered after 1200. Even more surprising perhaps is the total aggregate of new abbeys and new churches in this period, which would strain the resources of a highly developed economy at the height of its prosperity, so one would suppose, and yet was the product of under-developed societies suffering ups and downs, good weather and bad. The concentration of resources on such buildings as these has

149-50 Bologna, Santo Stefano. The main cloister is on two storeys: the upper cloister is shown below, with spiral ornament imitated from a classical model and with a grotesque figure *left*, 149, curiously inappropriate in such a setting.

150

their efforts to gather spiritual endowments in religious hands. In the tenth and early eleventh centuries the bulk of monastic wealth had lain in land. But already from the days of Charlemagne on, and increasingly in this period, substantial resources were being collected for ostensibly spiritual purposes under the guise of tithes. Payment of tithes was now compulsory, anyway for landowners; and in principle a tenth of every man's income went to the charitable purposes organised by the Church—to relieve the poor and sick, and (by this date) to support the clergy. In practice landowners who owned churches, or who built churches in order to add to their property as well as provide for their own and their tenants' spiritual well-being, frequently gathered back into their own barns a substantial proportion of the tithes. To stop this abuse was one of the aims of the papal reformers; but like much else in the old system of proprietary churches the practice was deeply rooted in custom when they came to weed it out, and direct appeals proved of little effect. Furthermore, the charitable purposes which the Church wished to support were becoming increasingly diverse, and a large place in them was allotted to the monks, God's poor—even if the monasteries they served were often corporately rich. In origin it had been held that monks, as landowners, should pay tithe; and since they were neither impoverished nor engaged in the cure of souls, should not receive them. In the eleventh and early twelfth centuries this doctrine was reversed—not without protest or difficulty. The papacy came increasingly to see the only cure for secular control of spiritual things was to place control in the powerful hands of monastic leaders. Furthermore, for a time, the attempt to make all clergy monks or quasi-monks often also involved astonished many modern observers. Some have condemned them as wasteful—since they meant spending on stone, paint and reliquaries money which might have gone to feed the poor; others have been the more impressed by the dedication of funds and skills to a sacred cause. In an agricultural society, there may be very few who are wholly unemployed, but great numbers who have little to do outside the harvest season; and great building works, then as now, can provide much-needed employment. We do right to remember this, and lay some emphasis upon it; the point has been unduly neglected. Yet it was clearly not the first thought in men's minds when they planned these enterprises, not even the first material thought. The question must commonly have been asked: how can such an enterprise be paid for? Not only the number, but the size of these buildings is astonishing. Of the greatest of all, the third church at Cluny, only a fragment remains; yet this fragment still lords it over the little town.

Lay offerings

In the later years of St Odilo (994-1049) and the early years of St Hugh (1049-1109) the abbey's economy depended almost entirely on its estates.[12] From those near at hand came food and rent; from all came money renders of various kinds. A substantial community was amply, but not luxuriously provided for (see pp. 69-70). In the mid and late eleventh century numerous dependent houses were presented to the mother abbey, and so formed what we call the order of Cluny, and although each of these had to run its economic affairs in effective independence of the great abbey, they all sent tribute and offerings. Above all, there was a steady flow of presents to the abbey, offerings from visitors great and not so great, offerings and pensions from all over Europe. Cluny lies in the east of what we call France, although it had special privileges of exemption from secular control (see pp. 54, 57, fig. 5). The kings of León-Castile sent it especially rich offerings, and in the early twelfth century King Henry I of England competed with them. When the third church was finished (1088-1121)—and the nave had fallen and been rebuilt (c. 1125-30)—Abbot Peter the Venerable could say that the kings of Castile and England had contributed to it more than anyone else.[13] Henry had done this partly because (though commonly mean) he loved the grand gesture, partly because he was aware of terrible sins, partly because Cluny contained one of his favourite nephews, the son of his sister, Adela countess of Blois. The young Henry of Blois was presently removed to England, to become abbot of Glastonbury. He was soon promoted bishop of Winchester, but retained his abbey and so was provided with the income of a multi-millionaire. He never lost his affection for Cluny, and later in life his enormous wealth and financial ability helped to save the great abbey from penury and reduce its debt. By the 1140s and 1150s—indeed, even before this—the flow of gifts had dried up, the wealth of the abbey was reduced, the scale of building and the size of the community had saddled it with debts, and Abbot Peter the Venerable (see pp. 72-4) a man of great diplomatic charm, panache and wisdom, but not a great financier, struggled manfully but unsuccessfully against them until the return of the prince-bishop Henry of Blois set the abbey on the path to recovery. Economically, they were back in the eleventh century; they had to learn to live off their large estates; the days of the overflowing treasury had passed for ever. Innumerable houses of the eleventh and twelfth centuries enjoyed the rich offerings

especially characteristic of this age. Those who made offerings to these houses sometimes came as pilgrims to a shrine, sometimes as visitors to a church or monastic community; sometimes they did not come at all, but sent their messengers. In any event, the offerings presupposed that they could be received as honoured guests, if they wished. A pleasant fashion made it possible even for the great to lend a hand in building a church. The flow of offerings and the enormous richness of the result reflect the fact that there was an intimacy between the secular society of the day and the monastic order of a degree unique in the Middle Ages.

Of this the first St Dominic, Santo Domingo (c. 1000-1073) who refounded the great house at Silos, is an excellent example. He was a protégé of King Ferdinand I of León-Castile (1037-65), and also for a short time an advisor to his successor Alfonso VI (1072-1109). Domingo set the pattern of monastic observance and of relations between the monasteries and the king. In 1041 he was put in charge of the small, poor, struggling community at Silos; when he died it was flourishing and had a community of about forty—quite a substantial number for this date and for Spain, even if small compared with the greatest of twelfth-century communities. Its customs were Cluniac, and Domingo was one of those who inspired his kings to take the close interest in Cluny from which many of the monastic developments in Spain before the coming of the Cistercians were to spring. He himself frequently went on preaching tours; encouraged the development of a scriptorium and of various crafts at Silos—it is no accident that it remains a noble monument of Spanish craftsmanship, even though the author of the sculptures which survive is quite unknown. Domingo combined the life of a fervent monk with frequent visits to the royal court; and he showed his involvement in the world by so notable a concern for the treatment of slaves—numerous in Spain, as in all Mediterranean countries, throughout the Middle Ages—that he was remembered as the saintly patron of slaves and of those who freed them.

The art of Silos was to have some influence on painting and sculpture over a wider area; the saint himself inspired his royal masters to indulge in generous patronage to monastic houses far and near. It was Domingo's patrons, Ferdinand and Alfonso, who first provided St Hugh of Cluny with the royal benefactors needed to set the masons of the third church of Cluny to their task.

The ups and down of Cluny's economy faithfully mirror its relation to its estates and the people among whom it lived. It greatly affected their material and spiritual life. The enormous numbers of candles needed to light a great church encouraged the beekeepers of a wide area; the wine which flowed in its chalices and on its refectory tables played a part in fostering the vineyards of Burgundy (see p. 70). The huge monastic community and its large household of servants ate their way through the produce of many villages. The large estates of Cluny as of many abbeys in this age were organised to provide for the multifarious needs of the community—some manors to bring bread, others the cash or materials to provide candles, the vineyards wine, and so forth. In this activity some monks joined as 'deans' over groups of manors and administrators of part of the empire within and without the abbey walls; all this was characteristic of the age and of the traditional pattern of monastic life. But the tilling of the fields was for the most part the work of peasants, and organised by peasant reeves and lay bailiffs. The Cluniacs were not involved themselves

18-22,
138-40,
178

151

152

153

147-8, 151-7 Verona, San Zeno Maggiore

151 The image of Verona in the twelfth century; the west front with the lofty campanile, and on the left a fragment of the thirteenth-century monastic buildings.

152 The crypt showing grotesque heads and animals, and a twelfth-century fresco of the Crucifixion.

153 The main church, showing the storeys: crypt, choir, and the highly decorated walls of choir and apse.

154

155

in agriculture as were the members of the new orders by the end of the eleventh and increasingly in the twelfth century. In the reclamation of land and technological advance the new orders and the Cistercians in particular were, in the twelfth century, to play a crucial part. The Cluniacs remained old-fashioned, deeply affecting their tenants, but still themselves living as landlords.

Abbey and city: San Zeno, Verona

147-8, 151-7

Advancing wealth was chiefly expressed in this period by the rebuilding, extension and beautifying of cities. The cathedral and monastic churches often became the supreme status symbols of rich cities, as well as providing a spiritual counter to the growth of Mammon.

151

The western prospect of the abbey church of San Zeno Maggiore at Verona is in a sense the image of Verona, a great Italian city of the late eleventh and twelfth centuries; within, the church reflects the way the life of a city and a great monastic community mingled in this age. That this should be so in a building essentially of the early twelfth century, completed *c.* 1138, is hardly surprising; and the continued devotion of the people of Verona to their saint and his church is shown by the considerable embellishments which took place later in the century, and the rebuilt cloister, which was not finally finished till 1313. But essentially we are looking at what Verona thought fitting as an expression of piety and civic pride in the early twelfth century.

The first age of civic pride in most of Italy since the decline of ancient Rome was in the eleventh and twelfth centuries. At first the local bishop was commonly effective ruler of the city. His demotion was sometimes the result of violence, more often a gradual process, outwardly peaceful. Lay magnates first placed their own relations or friends in the see, then step by step removed them, as it were, to a more spiritual sphere. In the process much heat was sometimes generated, and no doubt a great deal of anti-clerical feeling; but it was also an age, in Italy as elsewhere, rich in generous feelings towards the saints and their shrines. Growing material wealth flowed

154-5 The sculpture of the west front, partly by the twelfth-century Italian sculptor Nicolo, *c.*1130-40. Below: Theodoric the Great, Dietrich von Bern (= Verona), by Nicolo; Theodoric chases the stag which according to legend led him to his death. Second storey: the creation of the animals and of Adam. Third storey: the creation of Eve, the fall; at the top the expulsion from Eden. 155, detail. Cf. pl.12.

to the adornment of cities, above all with beautiful churches. Even in a city like Florence dominated by later buildings, San Miniato sits on its little mount and smiles at the great churches of the *trecento* and *quattrocento* in the heart of the city. Elsewhere it is often Romanesque which is most in evidence; so it is in Pisa and Lucca and Bologna, in Modena and Parma and Piacenza; and so it is in Verona. The inside of San Zeno is heavily restored, but retains the essential features of the twelfth-century church. Our view is not impeded, nor our attention diverted, by such massive screens as divide up Canterbury Cathedral into a series of quite separate mansions.[14] San Zeno is one large room, set (as it might be) for an opera in form comparable to the final act of Aida: that is with a large auditorium all on one level, the nave; and an ample, though not very big, stage with crypt below and stately choir above. High aloft is a great crucifixion in fresco; more commonly, in Italian apses, one meets Christ in Majesty. This is, as it were, the part of the church which is God's alone, too lofty for man to walk there. Next below is the monks' choir and sanctuary, the home of the mortal community. Finally, in the crypt, but so arranged as to be fully visible from the nave—in a way one commonly meets in central and north Italy and southern Germany—the shrine of the saint, and an ample arcaded lower church in which pilgrims can gather or be led round in orderly procession to pay tribute to St Zeno in money and prayers.

202-6, 134, 144-6

In such an arrangement it was not at all easy for a layman, unless specially invited and conducted, to stray into the monks' choir. But the monks had no privacy; their offices and masses were conducted in full view of the layfolk in the nave, of the citizens, that is, of Verona, and of those who came to visit this fair city, set between the upper Adige—and so the

156

Brenner and Bavaria and Austria—and the plain of Lombardy.

Verona had been a strategic centre in Roman times; in the heyday of the medieval Empire, in the tenth, eleventh and twelfth centuries, it became one of the greatest strategic centres in Italy; and such it could be again, from time to time, down to the days of Napoleon. Of this the outward and visible sign is to be seen in the sculpture surrounding its western portal and in the bronze panels of the western doors. The panels represent two periods and styles of craftsmanship, whose date has been much disputed. The view thought most probable at the moment is that the first stage in the bronze panels belongs to the last stage in the main building programme, *c.* 1138—though an array of earlier dates has been propounded and is still defended; these and the later panels, and the stone sculpture

157

which surround them, make this west front a delightful storehouse of narrative art. The whole ensemble, though a strange jumble in some ways, sits amiably together, its reconciliation symbolised by the famous figure of the sculptor in stone represented in bronze. Yet the sources are very diverse. Here are many scenes from the Old Testament, and an outline of the life of Jesus. The style of the first bronze period is strongly reminiscent, crude though it is, of the splendid bronze panels at Hildesheim; there is little doubt that this is German work, and that German craftsmen, along with merchants and Bavarian knights, came over the Brenner and down the Adige to hammer the bronze into shape. The stonemasons have given us, as well as biblical subjects, the death of Theodoric the Great, Theodoric the Ostrogoth, who became, in Germanic legend, Dietrich von Bern, Dietrich of Verona and the legend of his last hunt, which ended in hell. Dietrich von Bern was taking his place in the poems which culminated in the *Niebelungenlied* in Germany at much the same time that he was taking shape in stone on the walls of San Zeno. Thus the west front broke into speech, in a tongue intelligible both to native Italian and visiting German.

148

154-5

We have explored a number of paths and by-paths leading to various explanations of the concentration of men and money into the monastic communities of the eleventh and twelfth centuries. If we put together what we have learned so far, we can say that for a host of reasons, from the fear of hell, through the search for peace, to the pursuit of the monastic virtues as an end both fervent and fashionable, recruitment soared. We have explored reasons social and spiritual; and it is not at all surprising, in view of the pace of the movement, that there were many bad monks as well as many good and indifferent, even some whole communities given over to bickering and brigandage. The traditional monasticism seems to have remained the monopoly of the well-to-do; the new movements, as we shall see, were sometimes more egalitarian. But within these limits, the power to recruit of the older monasteries was evidently spread very wide; they gathered in men of the most varied character and talent. It is this variety of talent which provides the monasticism of the late eleventh and early twelfth centuries with one of its most striking marks. In this period one finds an unusual concentration of men of great business gifts, of great gifts as thinkers and writers, and of notable craftsmen, within the walls of monasteries. There is no period in the Middle Ages when there was not diversity of talent and personality in the cloisters; but it is at this time specially marked. The variety and range of talent declined after the mid twelfth century; the rival opportunities open to men of an academic or peaceful turn of mind, the professional opportunities open to craftsmen, greatly increased in the world outside; the monastic movements lost their first bloom, ceased to be avant-garde. They continued to draw throngs of recruits right through the thirteenth century and in many places beyond; but they no longer recruited among men of original mind or special talent to anything like the same degree. This is one of the reasons for the relative decline of monastic influence in the Church in the late Middle Ages.

156-7 Verona, San Zeno. The early bronze reliefs, *c.*1138: 156, detail of the risen Christ; 157, detail of the door knocker (for later reliefs, see pl.148).

7 The monastic contribution to the twelfth-century renaissance

The movement of thought and culture which has come to be known as the twelfth-century renaissance began in the eleventh century at latest and was scarcely extinguished, even in part, in the thirteenth. It was the artistic, literary and cultural expression of the great epoch of change of the central Middle Ages. It began as an ecclesiastical movement, with the improvement of clerical education and clerical learning at its core, and the revival and reorganisation of ecclesiastical institutions as its first most obvious achievement. The creation of the universities on the one hand, and of the great churches of the Romanesque and Gothic periods, with their adornments and satellite crafts, were its most spectacular monuments; in this sense it always remained a movement clerically inspired. Yet as it grew it spread in all directions, came to include some very secular elements and some heresies, and inspired vernacular literatures of great variety, sophistication and worldliness.

Architecture and the crafts

The twelfth-century renaissance was a cosmopolitan movement, and we shall wander over the face of Europe in our pursuit of it; but its characteristic centres lay in France and Italy. In Italy and Provence the physical presence of the remains of the ancient world was a constant artistic influence, coupled with frequent contact with Byzantium and (to a slightly lesser extent) with Islam. To the historian of medieval art, Italy is often confusing, because some of these influences were always present, and could ambush the craftsmen of almost any age; none the less, Italy is crucial, since through it there flowed both the Roman and Byzantine influence which provided so many of the themes of eleventh- and twelfth-century art and architecture, and one of the routes of Islamic influence which inspired some elements of Gothic architecture, especially in the form of the Gothic arch. Provence at this time was part of the Italian cultural world, and if one wanders in Nîmes and observes the barrel vault and the fluted columns of the ancient Temple of Diana, or in nearby Saint-Gilles, where twelfth-century architects and sculptors contrived a building alive with classical entablatures and friezes, one may see something of the history of Romanesque architecture and sculpture in a small compass. Yet for clarity of vision, and a lucid chronology of the development of Romanesque, it is the rest of France to which we must chiefly look. The term itself has been given many meanings, and various sub-divisions, of time and country, have been proposed to confuse the layman. For our purpose, it is in its essence the architecture of the great churches of the eleventh and early twelfth centuries, the

158

158-62 Saint-Gilles, France

158 A famous pilgrimage church near the mouth of the Rhône, where travellers from the north embarked for Spain or Italy. The abbey was founded in the ninth century and rebuilt in the twelfth. Its modern fame depends on the west front, *c*.1160, where Romanesque arches rise over capitals, entablature and frieze copied from a Roman temple.

sculpture which came increasingly to adorn their portals and doors and the capitals of their arcades, the stained glass, the painting of their walls—and all the attendant arts and crafts which hung the walls with tapestries, laid occasional small carpets on their floors, laid against the altars splendid frontals, upon the altar finely wrought patens, chalices and pyxes of silver and gold and splendid service books, and on or behind the altars reliquaries of precious metals inlaid with stones or adorned with enamels. The most durable material in which they worked was stone, and their architecture is the most fully recorded of the arts; much sculpture has survived where the weather, or changes of fashion, or religious iconoclasts, have not defaced it. The illumination of books is also richly recorded in numerous surviving manuscripts. Almost all the tapestries and carpets of the age have gone; and of the other ornaments and wall paintings only a small part remains to show us the splendour of a great church in this age. But in some treasuries, especially in the Catholic areas of Germany, in parts of France and Spain, and in Italy, collections of early treasures survive; and many more are gathered in the world's museums. Such objects we illustrate from the varied collection in the treasury of the abbey church of St Liudger at Essen-Werden.

Thus the word Romanesque is most commonly applied to a style, and also to a scale of building—above all, to the fashion for building large churches with ambitious vaults. The style has

160

159 Saint-Gilles, west front, detail.

160 Saint-Gilles, from the west front, the flagellation of Christ: above, cornice with heads of animals; below, a lion and lioness; to the left, Corinthian capitals.

161 Saint-Gilles, from the west front: St John the Evangelist (*In principio erat verbum*, the opening of his gospel) stands beside St Peter, while St Luke's ox looks at them across the flowing classical ornament.

162 Saint-Gilles, the choir: fragments only survive, though nave and crypt, with St Giles's tomb, are still standing.

161

162

them principal centres of book production in the tenth century already. The Byzantine influence may be explained in a measure by the profusion of small movable objects coming into western Europe through the crusading world and Sicily, which could influence painting more readily than sculpture or building, and by interest in Byzantine ways of presenting the

and art, by secular masters; from about 1170 the monasteries rarely provided new thoughts or new inspirations—though in the thirteenth century the new religious, the friars, played a crucial role at least in the intellectual world and in the organisation of the Church. But from about 1170 arts and crafts once characteristically monastic had become the possession of

179   180   181

human body. Nonetheless, the difference from other crafts and from literature is striking. The most flourishing school of north-western France was the Norman, product of the conjunction of English and French which actually had preceded the Norman Conquest in this area; and one of the most flourishing in Burgundy was at Cîteaux of all places, founded by the English St Stephen Harding, the third abbot, and showing clear English influence.[3]

24-9, 221-2

Monks and Romanesque art
The first phase of the twelfth-century renaissance, by a simplification at once crude and drastic but not wholly false, might be dated from 1050 to 1140, and be defined as characteristically the monastic phase. The middle of the twelfth century saw the capture of the initiative, in learning, literature

179-80 Pages from a copy of Beatus's Commentary on the Apocalypse written at Silos in the early twelfth century, showing a corn and wine harvest, four animals (interpreted as symbols of the evangelists) and the twenty-four elders worshipping the throne (see pl.173). British Museum, Add. MS 11, 695, ff.168, 194v.

181 Saint-Savin, France, the crypt.

182 Saint-Savin, crypt, with the story of the saint (see pls.198-9).

183 Moissac, France, the cloister was reconstructed in the Gothic period, hence the Gothic arcade; but the piers and capitals are of c.1100 and the bas reliefs of apostles and abbots were preserved (see pls.169ff.).

184 Jumièges, France, the nave from the south, showing western and central towers.

182

183

184

professional craftsmen mostly secular. Monks never had a monopoly of any craft, nor of learning; but it may be said that the art and architecture commonly labelled Romanesque were characteristically monastic, Gothic art and architecture the mirror of the secular church. This is a bold saying, perhaps a desperate one. Many a great Romanesque cathedral—Mainz, Speyer, Worms, and dozens more in Italy, France and England, rise up to rebuke it. Nor will it stand confidently up against the mass of Gothic art and architecture in countless monasteries. Yet there is something to be said for it. From the first rude traces of Romanesque sculpture at Dijon, through the reliefs and the paintings at Santo Domingo de Silos, to the sculpture of Moissac, Cluny and Vézelay, Saint-Gilles and Saint-Trophime at Arles, the history of Romanesque can be traced in great monasteries; not without gaps, since if we may contemplate Cluny and Vézelay, in a book on monastic history we must leave aside the supreme triumph of Romanesque sculpture in the secular church of St Lazarus at Autun. Yet as a crude measure, the link of Romanesque with the monks survives; and if we inspect the countless examples cited in Emile Mâle's great book on French religious art in the twelfth century, a large majority down to and including Abbot Suger's later work at Saint-Denis, of about 1140, is monastic. His book on French religious art in the thirteenth century, which runs for his purpose from c. 1150 to the early fourteenth century, is almost exclusively based on Gothic, secular cathedrals.

18, 178, 179-80 169-77, 83-8, 112-18, 158-62

Monastic involvement

The word 'monastic' in this context is doubtless ambiguous, and for two reasons. First, it came in the late eleventh and twelfth centuries to cover a wide variety of new fashions and orders apart from the traditional Benedictine and Cluniac monasticism. The second ambiguity in the word monastic arises from the doctrine once held that medieval monasteries were built and adorned by the monks themselves. Many a romantic page in Montalembert's *Monks of the West* (1860-77) bears witness to that faith, and it took practical shape when the monks of Buckfast and Maria Laach of the late nineteenth and early twentieth centuries themselves set to work to restore and rebuild their abbeys. As applied to the masons and craftsmen of the Middle Ages it was dismantled by G. G. Coulton and his disciples fifty years ago. They showed that, so far as the evidence goes, the bulk of what we see is the work of professional masons and professional craftsmen. They made hay with the old, romantic view, and in the process, as so often happens when the pursuit of truth becomes trapped in controversy, they carted away more than they should. R. E. Swartwout's *The Monastic Craftsman* (1932) represents an intelligent exposition of the doctrine which had first been expounded at length in Coulton's *Art and the Reformation* (1st edition, 1928). Swartwout cited fairly some of the most telling evidence for monastic craftsmanship, and saw that one must take careful note of chronology. It has come to be increasingly realised, first, that the bulk of precise evidence comes from

23

186

185 Durham Cathedral, across the River Wear (see pls.163-6).

186 Saint-Trophime, Arles, west front with tympanum, c.1170, surrounded by a frieze supported by classical columns; a small and crude version of the façade of Saint-Gilles.

the thirteenth century or later, and second, that by then lay professionals were producing the majority even of finely written books, the most characteristically monastic of all the crafts before the twelfth century. The pendulum has swung back a fair distance—not perhaps yet quite far enough—but it is safe to say that in the eleventh and early twelfth centuries monastic involvement was common in many crafts, and played a crucial part in some; and in the same period monastic inspiration and patronage played its most vital role even where monks themselves were not engaged in artistic work. Equally, it is clear that there was no period when secular men did not play a large part in every craft. In the tenth century monastic revival in England St Dunstan and St Ethelwold were personally involved in the artistic work characteristic of their age; and of many of the eminent Norman monks of the eleventh century Orderic Vitalis notes that they had special skills, commonly in music and the chant. These are samples, but they can be multiplied sufficiently to show that in that non-specialist world, craftsmanship of various kinds was as normal inside as outside the cloister; that in communities dedicated, in some measure—even in the traditional monasticism of the tenth and eleventh centuries—to work, those whose talents

187

188

lay in that direction had nothing to hinder them, much to give them encouragement.

No doubt monastic involvement in heavy industry, that is to say in the building of enormous churches, was less common. The whole subject becomes more subtle and sophisticated in the early twelfth century. Multitudes of new monasteries needed buildings and furniture and (for the less austere) products of every kind of craft; and thus made unprecedented demands on the human resources even of that expansive age. They must have called on talent from within when it was available; though it could not always have met the need.

If we ask: was there a Cluniac style or a 'school of Hirsau' in the eleventh or twelfth century? Or a style developed by the Augustinian canons? The short answer must be, no. Great patrons with wide connections, like Cluny, could by the normal exercise of patronage influence trends and movements over a wide area. Yet it is interesting to observe that in the sphere of Cluny's influence, the sculpture of Moissac and Vézelay had more children than the architecture of the third church of Cluny; that in many parts of Europe, Cluny's churches and their decoration differ no whit from other local buildings;[4] that it is rare for us to be able to tell by looking at a building to what order it belonged, or, in the case of churches manned by canons, whether they were regular or secular. To this the Cistercians are the sole exception (see esp. p. 153 ff.).

83-8, 169-77, 112-18

When all is said and done, even before the mid twelfth century, it can never be taken for granted that a monastery could find a wide range of craftsmen within its own community. Sometimes a fine craftsman bred up a school of followers, especially in the days when communities were mainly recruited by children; sometimes these schools lasted for two or three generations. When a community or an abbot needed books or painting or building they turned to the best talent available; within, if it was to be found there, outside, if not. The new choir of Canterbury Cathedral, built to house the shrine of Thomas Becket in the years following the fire of 1174, is a monument to the zeal of the monastic community, and some of them were in a measure at least involved in collecting money, and in organising the masons' work. But the architect was chosen by competition, and once they had selected William of Sens, they accepted with him a professional design based on various contemporary French, early Gothic models. Canterbury is exceptionally well documented; in other respects it may well represent what had often happened before; it certainly represented what was to be the norm for the future.

Theophilus

Thus the first half of the twelfth century saw monastic involvement at its height; and it is not by chance that it has left us the two most sensational memorials of monastic craftsmanship. In early twelfth-century Germany the monk Theophilus, in

187 Saint-Trophime, Arles, tympanum with Christ, the symbols of the evangelists and the apostles.

188 Saint-Trophime, St John and St Peter, with the Three Kings before Herod.

189 Stained glass of the head of Christ, the oldest fragment of Romanesque stained glass in France, eleventh century, from the abbey of Wissemburg. Musée de l'Oeuvre Notre-Dame, Strasbourg.

18

his treatise *On the Various Arts*, laid out detailed instructions, very much in the manner of a renaissance manual, for illuminating books, making glass vessels and stained glass and creating ornaments in metal; on metalwork he is especially elaborate and thorough. It is highly technical, but shows us also something of the mind and spirit of the author.[5]

'Theophilus—. . . unworthy of the name and profession of monk—wishes to all, who are willing to avoid and spurn idleness and the shiftlessness of the mind by the useful occupation of their hands and the agreeable contemplation of new things, the recompense of a heavenly reward.

'In the account of the creation of the world, we read that man was created in the image and likeness of God and was animated by the Divine breath. . . . Wretchedly deceived by the guile of the Devil, through the sin of disobedience he lost the privilege of immortality, but, however, so far transmitted to later posterity the distinction of wisdom and intelligence, that whoever will contribute both care and concern is able to attain a capacity for all arts and skills, as if by hereditary right.'

He goes on to say, indeed, that a craftsman who refuses to ply his trade is liable to God's judgement like the man in the Gospel parable who failed to 'restore to his master his talent with added interest'.

Theophilus sees craftsmanship as a divine gift, and places his treatise in a theological setting. But it is also an extremely practical statement of all that he could tell from his own experience, or learn from others, on these crafts.

'If you will diligently examine it, you will find in it whatever kinds and blends of various colours Greece (Byzantium) possesses; whatever Russia knows of workmanship in enamels or variety of niello; whatever Arabia adorns with repoussé or cast work, or engravings in relief: whatever gold embellishments Italy applies to various vessels or to the carving of gems and ivories: whatever France esteems in her precious variety of windows: whatever skill Germany praises in subtle work in gold, silver, copper, iron, wood and stone.'

No doubt he exaggerated his knowledge of Russia and Arabia somewhat; but he was right to emphasise that his skill was genuine and cosmopolitan. He writes from within the cloister, but his vision was far from narrow. He neither assumed that his audience was monastic, nor suggested that it was not; and it is clear that the book was written for men who could read Latin without difficulty, both within and without the cloister, and that its early circulation was largely in monastic libraries. There is little doubt that he wrote in a west German monastery of the traditional mode, presumably one of the houses modelled on Gorze; and he has been identified with considerable probability as Roger, monk of Helmarshausen and noted craftsman in metal at the turn of the eleventh and twelfth centuries.

Work and books
Of the religious orders of the twelfth century, the most cosmopolitan—and the one which has left an architecture of striking uniformity—was the Cistercian. Their involvement sprang essentially from two facts—that their egalitarian method of recruitment opened their gates in a unique degree to craftsmen of a wide variety of skills, at least in the first generation or two of their existence; and second, that they insisted, as no monastic order had done to anything like the same degree, on the importance of work. All medieval doctrines of work derived from the book of Genesis, and it could only be seen

as the consequence of the Fall, which led Adam to dig and Eve to spin; and even after the Fall, Jesus himself observed that the lilies of the field owed their beauty in no measure either to digging or spinning. St Benedict had prescribed work for the good of the soul, and to ensure that necessary tasks were accomplished; the Cistercians took him to mean that all the work of the community should be performed by monks or lay brothers (see p. 139).

This was not a wholly new idea. In the traditional monasticism the hours set apart for work were often eroded to make time for more elaborate liturgy, and it has never been difficult to find excellent ways of passing time allotted to manual labour without unduly soiling the hands. It was official Cluniac doctrine that reading was equivalent to manual labour; none the less it is clear that even at Cluny much labour of various kinds was done. Several of the new orders at the turn of the eleventh and twelfth centuries followed the ancient and hallowed tradition and set their choir monks to work copying books. This was commonly regarded as monastic labour par excellence, and thus the new orders came rapidly to acquire libraries which could vie with even some of the oldest houses.

Books indeed were of great importance to all the new orders; and it is in their copying and reading that the most characteristic influence of the monasteries on the renaissance of the twelfth century can be discerned. It is because the books that were studied most frequently were found in monastic libraries, and the largest network of active schools lay in the cloister—and their pupils were mainly prentice monks—that the early stages of the intellectual revival were predominantly monastic in inspiration. There were always secular schools as well; and they came to flourish alongside the monastic. The old cathedral

190-1 Craftsmanship: 190, tenth-century ivory book cover, from the twelfth-century Siegburg Lectionary (for reading extracts of the Bible at Mattins), British Museum, Harleian MS 2889; 191, stall end of wood, late thirteenth century (*c*.1284) from the abbey of Pöhlde, Saxony, a monk carving, Landesgalerie, Hannover.

190   191

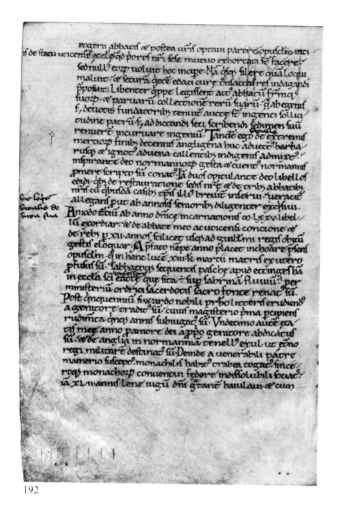

192

192 The handwriting of Orderic Vitalis. This passage gives his first description of his life: from the end of the 22nd line, 'at Atcham in the church of St Eata the Confessor which is situated on the River Severn [see pl.201] by the ministry of Orderic the priest, I was born again in the holy font'. Of the second account, quoted on p.122, his autograph does not survive. Paris, Bibliothèque Nationale, MS Latin 5506, ii, f.101v.

ferment of ideas which it produced, that the leading principles of most of the new orders were formed. It was an ancient idea that the active clerks in the world, those engaged in evangelism and popular preaching, and in pastoral work, were leading the lives of the apostles, that the apostolic life was essentially active, the monastic, the life of the desert or of the community was contemplative. Now many arguments arose as to whether the truly apostolic life was not the better; or whether the two lives could not and should not be mixed and mingled; or as to whether the monastic life was not after all truly apostolic. By a curious irony, these speculations led many monastic leaders of the age to believe that stable enclosure within the monastic precinct and a wandering life without, preaching and teaching, or setting up new communities, were both some-how simultaneously expressions of the truly apostolic life. Thus Robert of Molesme wandered from house to house and eventually founded Cîteaux; thus St Anselm's disciple, Honorius Augustodunensis, wherever he may have sprung from, wandered between Germany and England, gathering and spreading his master's and his own ideas among monks and secular teachers; and his ideas included some of the symbolic, biblical schemes most influential in the artistic iconography of the day.[6]

Biography and history
Throughout the twelfth and· thirteenth centuries history and biography were the two fields of literature in which monastic pre-eminence survived. Orderic Vitalis, Eadmer, and William of Malmesbury were characteristic monastic authors of this period: characteristic both in the range of their interests, centring on history and hagiography, and in their devotion to calligraphy: of all three we possess autograph copies, carefully and beautifully written, of some at least of their works. The interest in history was specially characteristic for a time of the Anglo-Norman monastic world; and the revival of an interest in the past and in English and Norman traditions was one of the inspirations that affected all three. In any case it was only in communities tenacious of their memory, with records and books giving some basis for historical study, that history could begin seriously to flourish. William of Malmesbury, the most acute historical student since Bede, inspired others no less acute to copy his methods in writing and inventing histories more secular than his. Bede had written the *Ecclesiastical History*, and Orderic's great ramble of a chronicle was also ecclesiastical, though it strayed into every path of interest to a Norman community: the settlement of the Normans in England, and the wanderings of the family of the founders of his monastery and their colleagues in the south of Italy and on Crusade. Eadmer wrote biography and history; his best works were his *Life of St Anselm*, and his *History of Recent Events*, which is a second life of Anselm in a different key—his part in public events. William was chiefly inspired by Bede; but he divided his major works into two: a history of the English bishops, and a history of the English kings, for he

libraries had always rivalled the monks' libraries, and came into their own again as the revival developed in the cathedral schools. In the first half of the twelfth century ideas which had grown up among monks were being developed far beyond their ken in secular schools.

Books and the apostolic life
The ascetics and reformers of the eleventh century read the classics on the spiritual life of earlier days: they were inspired by the literature of the desert, and above all by Cassian, to go out into the wilderness, to live as hermits, or to form new kinds of communities. They read the Rule of St Benedict, not in the context of the mass of custom in which it lived in the monasteries of traditional observance, but as if it had just been written, fresh and new. Cassian had found the origin of the monastic life in the New Testament, and every religious reformer, every Christian idealist, looked for his inspiration, or justification, in the Bible. At the heart of every monastic rule lay an echo or quotation of the words in the Acts of the Apostles which defined the life of the Apostles and early disciples—men and women 'united in heart and soul . . .' who had 'everything . . . in common' (see p. 13). Thus the monks began once again to study the life of the Apostles, to find their own root and inspiration in it. But the consequence of such study was to lead far beyond its original, devotional intent. For some monks observed differences between the life of the early disciples and themselves which they felt were not wholly to their advantage; and critics of the monks from outside advanced the opinion that quite a different mode of life was more truly apostolic. It was out of this controversy, and the

193

194

wrote for secular as well as monastic patrons, and it suited him to provide for their secular interests. His most distinguished imitator was Geoffrey of Monmouth, a secular clerk who wrote the most secular of twelfth-century chronicles, first for the same patron as William, then for whoever would read it; and the rich tapestry of good tales which he provided, and especially the elaborate account of King Arthur which he invented, ensured him the widest audience of any medieval chronicler. His account of Arthur also provided one of the crucial links between the learned, Latin world of the cloister, and the secular world of vernacular literature.

St Anselm, theology and humanism

St Anselm himself was an Italian (c. 1033-1109) who settled in Bec in Normandy and was already about sixty when he became archbishop of Canterbury. His philosophic insight and power to express his most abstruse thought in language both subtle and simple, made him the greatest theologian of his age. He did not command a large audience, but it was sufficient, in that peripatetic age, for some of his seminal ideas to spread; and thus he came to be the central figure in the devotional and theological revolution which placed the human Jesus and his Virgin Mother at the centre of the religious sentiment of the twelfth and thirteenth centuries. This sentiment united the world of devotion, of literature and art, with the world of learning; and adumbrations of the growing interest in the human Jesus, and the growing appreciation of human values which went with it, could be found in many parts of western Europe, perhaps especially in Italy. Anselm was austere and ascetic; but in the hands of those influenced by him his notion that God became man not to cheat the devil of his rights, but to establish a relation between God and man, became the basis of the Christian humanism of the twelfth century. No one would have been more surprised by the roads down which his concept led the academic and popular theologians of the century than Anselm himself. In the next generation the great secular teacher Abelard carried the line of thought on to the point of saying that Jesus came to give men a human example; and he coupled in his own thought and life a deep involvement and belief in human emotion which is a part of the story of his affair with Heloise. Later, in a moment of bitter penitence, Abelard became a monk, and he died eventually a monk of the community of Cluny. This illustrates how close the classroom and the cloister still were; it does not make Abelard himself a monastic theologian.

The cult of the Blessed Virgin was firmly established centuries before 1100. None the less, in the same meeting of Italian and English traditions in the circle of Anselm, it began to take on a new complexion. Not Anselm himself, but his

7, 31-8, 193-6, 200 Canterbury Cathedral

193-4 A rich ornate Romanesque tower of the twelfth century, in its setting on the south side of the cathedral; the south window of the main transept is Perpendicular.

195 The choir, late twelfth century, is an anthology of the ideas of early French Gothic, based on various churches, including Sens, home of the first architect, William of Sens; the east end of the Trinity Chapel was designed by his successor, William the Englishman, but still shows the inspiration of William of Sens.

196 *Overleaf* In contrast, a view up the tower, Bell Harry, begun 1493.

198

199

10-17
nephew and namesake, who was a monk at the Sagra di San Michele (or Chiusa) and later abbot of Bury St Edmunds, was the centre of a circle with a special interest in the Conception of the Blessed Virgin. Out of this circle, in which William of Malmesbury and Eadmer were much involved, came the doctrine and the cult; the first substantial collections of miracles of the Blessed Virgin, and the interest in her Coronation by her son in heaven, which was first represented, so far as the record goes, at Reading Abbey in the 1120s, then taken up at Saint-Denis, and so entered the mainstream of Gothic iconography.

The characteristic of the twelfth-century renaissance of greatest moment to us was its variety. Not everyone accepted the view that the human Jesus looked kindly on human feelings and failings; not everyone agreed that the exuberant techniques of painting, sculpture and jewelry were appropriate for the adorning of churches. In the early twelfth century some heretics were burning churches, some puritans arguing that they should be plain and unadorned, while Abbot Suger and the monk Theophilus saw God's glory revealed in the most sumptuous ornament and the most brilliant jewel. The stern asceticism characteristic of many monastic leaders went hand in hand with a view that the world was almost wholly evil, even though at first created by God and good. The narrowest of margins separated some eminent monastic thinkers, most notably the Italian Peter Damian, from the view that the world was evil even in its making—which was heretical, and the basis of the most successful of twelfth-century heresies, that of the Cathars. Yet it was within the walls of monasteries and among monastic leaders that the love of God's creation was at first most evidently fostered. If we ask what unites St Basil in the fourth century, the Irish hermits of the sixth and seventh, St Bruno in the eleventh, St Bernard and St Francis in the twelfth and thirteenth centuries, the first answer might be their love of natural beauty—though one might equally find it in their devotion to the ascetic life. Plants and fruit begin to creep over the pages of herbals about 1100, and frequently entrance us by the vivid observation shown in the craftsman's eye in minor sculpture a century later; love of nature is equally evident in the situation of the Grande

132, ·6, 316
Chartreuse, of countless Cistercian abbeys and of the Carceri above Assisi. All these places were the homes of ascetics, who renounced the world while rejoicing in it; yet we can hardly

197-9 Saint-Savin-sur-Gartempe, France. In the early tenth century the old abbey of Cerisiers was revived and dedicated to St Savin, an unidentified corpse, it seems, who was supposed to have been a Roman martyr and was provided with an appropriate legend. The abbey church was built in the eleventh century and contains one of the most complete sets of Romanesque frescoes (c. 1100). The intricate and elaborate scheme reveals monastic inspiration, though we cannot tell if monastic craftsmen helped to paint it.

197 *Preceding page* In the porch is an apocalyse: above, the scourge of the beasts (Revelation, 9, 1-10); below, the struggle of the woman (interpreted as the Church) and the dragon (Revelation, 11, 19—12, 18). The nave ceiling has the story of the Pentateuch, from Creation to Sinai.

198-9 In the crypt is the story of St Savin (see pls. 181, 182). Here he is arraigned before the Roman proconsul or governor, Ladicius (198, detail) and a second time before Ladicius (199), after being flayed and tortured with pincers.

200 Canterbury Cathedral, from the splendid twelfth-century glass, Lamech the patriarch, son of Methuselah. 200

wonder that in the same world of Bernard and Francis we meet in Latin and vernacular lyric and romance, copious evidence that the love of natural beauty, and delight in the world as God's and good, went hand in hand with an ever more consciously accepted hedonism, sometimes quite pagan in inspiration, sometimes devout. Clear traces of the doctrines of St Bernard have been found in Wolfram, the great German epic writer of the early thirteenth century, who was a thoroughly secular knight.

65-7   In the early twelfth century the fame of St William, the Carolingian count of Toulouse who had founded Saint-Guilhem-le-Desert, was spread far and wide, as Orderic Vitalis noted, in the Chanson de Geste on Guillaume d'Orange. Its main theme is the slaughter of Saracens; it is one of the

201

201 Atcham church, where Orderic Vitalis was baptised, 'by the mighty River Severn'. The Norman west door can be seen; the rest has been much altered, though the walls are basically eleventh century.

bloodiest of crusading epics. In the early thirteenth century, when the leaders of the Albigensian Crusade were slaughtering heretics round Toulouse, Wolfram issued his version of St William's legend, the *Willehalm*, whose theme, contrariwise, is a plea for tolerance. Wolfram had probably never seen a Moslem, nor even Orange or Saint-Guilhem. But human kindness was a deep part of his nature, and his doctrine of God's love for man shows how deeply he had drunk from the stream which flowed from the devotional and theological treatises of the twelfth century.

The sense of human values here portrayed comes most directly from St Bernard, but also makes Wolfram the heir of a wider tradition of twelfth-century humanism. In biography, autobiography and personal letters a few sensitive writers of the eleventh and twelfth centuries added greatly to the literary tradition of their age by revealing a capacity to express and expound human personality quite exceptional for the Middle Ages. Perhaps its most brilliant expression is in the letters of Heloise and Abelard (see p. 172); but more characteristic, and

nearer the heart of our subject, were the more modest endeavours of the biographer of St Anselm, the monk Eadmer, and the autobiographical efforts of the Norman chronicler Orderic. Eadmer was inspired to write in an original way by the extraordinary personality of Anselm, and especially by his conversation. In a famous passage he tells how Anselm, as abbot of Bec, tried to impress his idea of the monastic life on the boys of the cloister, in a manner less fierce than some of his fellow-abbots employed. 'What, I ask you, is to be done with them? They are incorrigible ruffians', grumbled one of his colleagues. 'We never give over beating them day and night, and they only get worse and worse' . . . 'You never give over beating them? And what are they like when they grow up?' 'Stupid brutes,' he said. To which Anselm replied, in effect, that this was no more suitable treatment for spiritual monks in the making than it would be for tender plants in the garden; and that even the goldsmith did not form his leaf of gold or silver by blows alone. 'He now presses it and strikes it gently with his tool, and now even more gently raises it with careful pressure and gives it shape. So, if you want your boys to be adorned with good habits, you too, besides the pressure of blows, must apply the encouragement and help of fatherly sympathy and gentleness.'[7]

The education of the cloister was for a whole way of life; here, in the monastic schools, much of what was most characteristic of the eleventh and twelfth centuries met; and the best of traditional monasticism is summed up in the devout and moving—yet quite unheroic—survey of his own life which concludes the life's work of Orderic Vitalis.

192

'On Easter eve I was baptised at Atcham, a village in England lying on the mighty River Severn. . . . When I was five I went to school at Shrewsbury, and dedicated my first lessons to you in the church of St Peter and St Paul. . . . It did not please you that I should lead my life there longer . . . in case I ran the danger of failing to follow your law owing to the human affection of my parents. And so, O God of glory, who ordered Abraham to leave his country, his father's house and kindred, you inspired my father Odeler to give me up and surrender me wholly to you. Weeping, he gave a weeping child to Rainald the monk, and sent me into exile for your love—nor ever after saw me. A small boy did not presume to contradict his father, but I obeyed him in all things, since he promised me that I should possess paradise with the innocent . . . ; and so I left my country, my parents, all my kindred and my friends. . . . At ten years old I crossed the Channel, and came, an exile, to Normandy, knowing no one, known to none. Like Joseph in Egypt, I heard a tongue I knew not. Yet by your grace I found among the strangers every kindness and friendship.'

He describes his reception by the abbot of Saint-Évroult; how the monks gave him the name Vitalis so that they would not have to use his barbarous English name; how he had lived there fifty-six years,

'. . . by your favour, loved and honoured by all the monks and all who lived here much more than I deserved. I have suffered heat and cold and the burden of the day . . . and I have awaited my penny wage with confidence. . . . Give me the will to persevere in your service, unfailing strength against Satan's crafty malice, until I may receive, by your gift, the inheritance of eternal salvation. And what I ask for myself, here and to come, I desire too, merciful God, for my friends and benefactors, and for all your faithful children according to your providence. Our own merits do not suffice to obtain things everlasting, for which the perfect ever ardently long. . . . May the glorious intercession of the holy Virgin mother Mary and all the saints help us in your sight. . . .'[8]

part 2
New orders

8 The Augustinian canons

The apostolic life

The inspiration for the new monasticism flowed through two channels, which met at the turn of the eleventh and twelfth centuries in what recent historians have called 'the monastic crisis'—*la crise du monachisme*. Yet perhaps it was not so much a crisis as the stirring of the waters, a whirlpool with ripples and eddies, with a noisy centre and still pools out of the flood's reach, such as one may find where two strong currents meet.

The first stream brought down from the early church and the old monasticism the Rule of St Benedict, the hermit ideal and the rules or regulations for a common life for canons. In the eleventh century all three enjoyed an enhanced prestige, partly because of the intellectual revival—our second stream— which led many to read these texts and interpret them afresh. The Rule of St Benedict was now firmly established as the basis of the traditional monasticism, which enjoyed the height of its prestige at Gorze, Cluny, Hirsau and many other notable centres. The hermit ideal enjoyed a renaissance, prepared in Italy at the turn of the tenth and eleventh centuries, blossoming both in Italy and in France in the second half of the eleventh century. Out of the papal reform came a movement to convert all clergy who were not monks into canons living under a rule; and the rule to which they were subjected was the Rule of St Augustine.

In the ferment of social, religious and intellectual life of the eleventh and twelfth centuries, it was natural that there should be argument and controversy about every aspect of the Christian life. No dispute is more characteristic of the age than the debate about the apostolic life, the *vita apostolica* (see pp. 114-15, 182-3). It had been the traditional view of all monks, and especially those under the Rule of St Benedict, that their life was apostolic. Yet it was an undeniable fact that one of the main functions of the apostles had been to preach and to evangelise; they were missionaries. So too had been many of the monks of early centuries, and there never perhaps was a time in the history of monasticism when the community and the world were in closer rapprochement than in the late eleventh and early twelfth centuries. This was the age when

large numbers of churches were given to monks, which they seem commonly to have been expected to serve; this was the age when they defended their enjoyment of tithes on the ground that the labourer was worthy of his hire.[1] This was the age when the citizens of Verona and Milan poured silver and gold into San Zeno and Sant'Ambrogio (see pp. 97-8, 219-23); and harmony, not the bitter conflict which was later to be common, was the norm between townsfolk and the monastic communities nearby. 147-8, 151-7, 353-4, 356

Yet there were many who thought that the monastic life was angelic not apostolic, rather one of prayer than activity; the monks' role that of Mary, not Martha. And it is precisely in this same period that the distinction between the active and contemplative became once more strongly urged. Ascetics and hierarchs agreed from time to time to forbid monks to serve parishes, and to foster alternative ways of providing for clerical service to the world. In their different ways St Peter Damian, hermit, monk and cardinal bishop (*c.* 1007-72), and St Anselm, a retiring monk and abbot who found himself one day, to his sorrow, archbishop of Canterbury (*c.* 1033-1109), served and fostered the growth of canons regular to rescue the secular clergy from their sins and the monks from the chores of Martha.

The canon living according to a rule was no novelty in the eleventh century: numerous communities paid service in some degree to the *Institutio Canonicorum* of 816 or 817, which is an anthology from earlier rules, especially those of Benedict and of Bishop Chrodegang of Metz, who had legislated for canons in the eighth century. In the mid eleventh century the papal reformers inspired a movement to draw clerics and canons into a type of institute whose base was the Rule of St Augustine.

The Rule of St Augustine

The document which has passed under this name since the eleventh century was not actually composed by St Augustine of Hippo in the early fifth century. He may have written down some principles of life for small communities of men and women; or the early rules may be the work of a slightly later age, perhaps of the sixth century. In due course both the male and female versions were enlarged, and it is a version of this enlarged rule for men which circulated in the eleventh century as the Rule of St Augustine and changed the face of the monastic world. It prospered for three reasons: for the prestige of Augustine's name; for its combination of practical sense and vagueness, which allowed a pile of useful customs to

202-6 Lucca, San Frediano. A fine city church served by a community of Augustinian canons. Stripes of reddish and white stone and arcading, characteristic of the region, make this a good example of the larger twelfth-century churches of Lucca and Pisa. The lofty campanile is also mainly twelfth century, restored in the nineteenth. 202 From the east.

be attached to it, and several quite different ways of life to be based on it; and because it came in due course to seem to its adherents that it was closer to the life of the Apostles than Benedict's Rule. Let us observe at once, then, its utility to the modern student: a monk was one who followed Benedict, a canon one who followed Augustine. There were orders of monks not strictly Benedictine, but even the Carthusians had great respect for Benedict; and there were orders vowed to the Rule of St Augustine who were not canons, notably the Dominican friars (see p. 190). But it is a decent working definition, none the less.

The early propagandists for Augustine's rule had no idea of setting it up as a rival to Benedict's. Many of them were devout monks who saw the Rule of Augustine as a thoroughly practical instrument for gathering into a regular, orderly, celibate and devout life all the many clerics who were not and never would become monks. But the inspiration for the spread of St Augustine's Rule came also from men who saw it as something more powerful than this; and as adherents grew in numbers, this point of view was likely to spread. It seemed to many who meditated on the apostolic life that Jesus had laid emphasis in his instructions to his disciples on poverty, simplicity and practical good works; and these three elements were emphasised, in varying proportions, by most monastic reformers of the late eleventh and early twelfth centuries. The Rule of St Augustine seemed to its own adherents to allow more space for these qualities; the followers of St Benedict strenuously denied it. No doubt Augustine left rather more scope for the development of good works, and this was observed as much by ardent Benedictines, like St Anselm—who clearly regarded the regular canons as a thoroughly useful second best in the religious life—as by reforming bishops not attached to a particular mode or order, anxious for practical help or for the means to reform their clergy.

If ever there was a time when monk and canon were distinct, it was in the canons' heyday in the early twelfth century. Augustine's Rule formed the basis of the way of life of canons regular, Austin or Augustinian and Premonstratensian, and also, later on, of the Dominican and Austin friars—and of other orders of more recent date. This gigantic feat of comprehension was due to the extreme vagueness and imprecision of Augustine's Rule. It is reminiscent of what Ronald Knox said of William Temple (after Dryden):

'A man so broad, to some he seem'd to be
Not one, but all mankind in effigy.'

Just at the point at which our definition appears to be most precise, it lets us down: the difference between the allegiance to Benedict and to Augustine is of great importance,[2] but it tells us little of the way of life of the canon. That depended on a whole body of customs added to the Rule. These were inspired by the papal reformers of the mid eleventh century, who were monks and devotees of the regular life.

The movement in Italy, France and Spain
To cure the irregularities of the secular clergy, Peter Damian and Hildebrand (Gregory VII; see pp. 77-9, 93) fostered a movement for the conversion of secular clerks into regular clerks, for putting the clergy under rules. Its first successes came in Italy, in Rome and Lucca and elsewhere. At Lucca, the link with the papal reformers was especially close in the

203

204

203 San Frediano, Lucca, from the west, with the original mosaic of Christ and the apostles (thirteenth century), considerably restored.

204-5 San Frediano, Lucca. The font, twelfth century (perhaps c. 1160) links city and community. Pharaoh rides to his destruction in the Red Sea, and Moses receives the Law. Pharaoh and his knights are in contemporary dress, much as the Emperor Frederick Barbarossa and his knights might have appeared when they invaded Italy in the 1160s and 1170s.

206

206 San Frediano, Lucca, within, showing a twelfth-century version of an earlier basilica.

time of Bishop Anselm, Pope Alexander II (1062-73); and in the second half of the eleventh and early twelfth centuries a whole group of churches were given communities of regular canons, including the cathedral. The centre of the movement, however, lay in the priory of San Frediano, whose growth and influence were encouraged by Alexander himself and by later popes. The present church, mostly of the twelfth century, is a remarkable monument to the relations of the world, the city and the canons of San Frediano; the large nave provided shelter for the Lucchesi and the sumptuous font, presumably, baptism for their infants. Meanwhile, the movement was spreading fast into France and Spain, and north into Germany and England.

The most notable community in southern France was at Saint-Ruf on the outskirts of Avignon. It was founded as early as c. 1039, and in the second half of the eleventh century became the mother house of a group of communities following the Rule of St Augustine and the customs of Saint-Ruf. The rays of its influence, and of the movement in general, spread very wide over Provence and the south of France and down into Spain. There in the early twelfth century began the conversion of the cathedrals of Toledo, Osma and one or two others to regular canons;[3] before the end of the century the canons of Osma were to include St Dominic of Caleruega in their number (see p. 190). In the 1140s the abbot of Saint-Ruf was an Englishman called Nicholas Brakespeare, who became Pope Adrian IV in 1154, and two years later wrote to the bishop of Toledo commending the canons of Saint-Ruf to him; and thus the influence of the canons from Saint-Ruf in the abbey of Santa Leocadia came to supplement those of the canons in Toledo Cathedral.

Germany, Austria and the British Isles

After France, its most notable centre lay in Bavaria and Austria, where its early development was inspired and controlled by St Altmann, bishop of Passau (1065-91), in close union with the reformed papacy. Over fifty houses were founded or reformed in this area, the most influential of them Reichersberg, established between 1080 and 1084 in Altmann's diocese, though not directly under his influence; for it was one of an increasing number directly under the archbishop of Salzburg. Here in the early and mid twelfth century lived one of the notable writers of twelfth century Germany, Gerhoh, author of many treatises on theology and the relations of church and state, of clerical and lay society.

Altmann himself suffered for his support of the pope against the emperor in the dispute between Henry IV and Gregory VII; and many of the houses were centres of papal influence. The canons indeed were in touch with almost every spiritual movement of the age: several houses grew from hermitages, or were linked with hermits; many were in towns and served parishes; several canons appeared as archdeacons in the diocese of Salzburg. The variety of their activities mirrored many fashions of the age, and their life and inspiration could be as varied as that of the monks.

The same was in due course true over much of western Christendom. Many of the earlier houses of canons were

207

208

209

210

207-11 Arles, Saint-Trophime. The canons' cloister is largely of the twelfth century, and the conventual buildings twelfth to thirteenth. The canons of the cathedral may have been regular about 1060, and were certainly regular in the second half of the twelfth century.

207 Capital, showing Joseph's dream, from the Nativity.

208, 210 The cloister. The fine capitals were carved elsewhere and brought here ready made, for some do not fit their present setting.

209 The memorial slab to Poncius Rebolli, priest, canon regular and master of the works (*operarius*) of St-Trophime, who died in 1183. He probably supervised the making of the western portal, though *operarius* does not mean he was a mason.

212

213

211 St-Trophime, Arles, capital in the cloister, entry into Jerusalem.

212-13 Jedburgh Abbey, Scotland

212 King David's Augustinian foundation, here seen across the cloister, with two Norman doors into the church, which was largely rebuilt at the end of the twelfth and in the early thirteenth centuries.

213 From the choir, second quarter of the twelfth century, looking west, past the twelfth to thirteenth century arcade to the Gothic rose window rising over a Norman arch.

founded by converting old churches or colleges of canons; these included a number of cathedrals, stretching from Cefalù in Sicily, via Spoleto and Arles,[4] on to Séez in Normandy and Carlisle on the northern frontier of England. All these lay in towns, as did the first great English houses, St Botolph's without the city gate at Colchester, and Holy Trinity within Aldgate in the City of London. Holy Trinity was founded by Queen Matilda, in 1107 or 1108; and she was the chief patron of the order in the British Isles in early days, inspiring in due course her brother, King David I of Scotland, a connoisseur of every religious order of the age (see p. 235), and her husband, Henry I (1100-35), whom she taught to be a benefactor to the religious, and especially to the Augustinians, whose houses rapidly increased in his reign; by 1135 there were about sixty-five in England, over a hundred by 1154, when their grandson Henry II became king.

Many of these foundations lay in towns; but in the British Isles, as in Germany, the Augustinian foundations reflected a wide range of inspiration. No house could have had a site

186-8

214

more remote than Llanthony in Monmouthshire, under the Black Mountains. One of its founders was a hermit, the other a former royal clerk, and when Matilda and Henry offered him rich endowments, he refused them, for he wished his house to be poor and hidden from the world. In due course its poverty, and Welsh raids, forced his successors to search for new pastures; and they founded a sister house in Gloucester, Llanthony Secunda, which became a notable town house and a centre of learning with a fine library. But Llanthony Prima still remains a monument of Augustinian seclusion.

Many early houses were endowed with churches and expected to serve them. Soon after Toledo was conquered from the Moslems in 1085, the cathedral was restored and the nucleus of a community formed under Cluniac inspiration and perhaps partly of Cluniac monks; soon, however, it acquired a chapter of canons regular, and from 1156 Adrian IV's initiative in founding the abbey of Santa Leocadia with canons from Saint-Ruf made Toledo a centre of Augustinian influence. In a similar way, shortly before 1100, the earl of Northampton gathered almost all the churches of that town to form the endowment of the Cluniac priory of St Andrew. When his neighbour the earl of Leicester undertook a similar merger

214-15, 224 Llanthony Priory, Wales. An Augustinian house in a remote place under the Black Mountains in Monmouthshire, home of a community noted for learning and asceticism. The buildings are mainly *c*.1180-1220.

214 The crossing from the south east.

215 Lancets and rose in the south transept.

of the parish churches of Leicester into a religious foundation in 1143, it was for the Augustinian canons.

All manner of considerations may affect a founder: efficacy of prayers, a contemplative ideal, friendship with a group of monks or canons. Many Augustinian houses were formed in close association with hospitals, to serve all the various needs of the poor, sick and aged. The earls were clearly influenced by a wish to see effective pastoral care in the growing towns; but they were also doubtless glad to find a comparatively cheap form of endowment. The conversion of a large church into an Augustinian abbey or priory and its endowment with churches simply concentrated resources which were of no use to a secular lord; and an Augustinian house could be founded on a modest scale. By such means, and by putting pressure on smaller men, Henry I came to be called the founder of numerous houses.[5] It is evident that the patrons and canons whom we have met in recent paragraphs were following a fashion, and knew what they were at. It is natural for us to suppose that this was always the case. Surely, we may think, the founders of the twelfth century understood these distinctions, however obscure they may be to us. For reasons which we shall discuss, it is doubtful if this was always (or perhaps commonly) true of founders of houses of nuns. For monks and canons, yes, one must concede that the founder knew what he was doing, up to a point. The proviso is important. Some founders were deeply involved and committed; but not all were so sure of the difference between one type of religion and another.

The founders of the tenth and early eleventh centuries were

215

kings, princes, great nobles or bishops. A lofty status and great wealth were needed—and influence over lesser men who were expected to contribute lavishly but not to call themselves founders. Nor was there any great range of choice: down to the mid eleventh century a Benedictine house, of monks or nuns, it had to be, founded, re-founded or (if the founder were mean or poor) made dependent on another house. But by 1100 already, and even more by 1150, the range of choice had become bewilderingly great. Nor was it confined to the rich. Poor men might found little cells, or band together to found a larger house.

Distinguishing between monks and canons: the canon of Liège
In the 1120s, or soon after, a treatise called the *Libellus de diversis ordinibus* ('On the different orders') was written by a regular canon in the diocese of Liège, where canons regular flourished in great profusion already at that date.[6] It is an attempt to distinguish between the various orders of monks and canons—not so much a guide-book for would-be postulants or patrons, as an olive branch, an attempt to quieten the storm of controversy among the various orders as to which was the most apostolical by suggesting that one and all had

their places in the sun, and their justification in the Testaments Old and New. It is cool, liberal and lucid; and no one who has read it can imagine that the difference between monk and canon was necessarily of great significance.

The author's intention was to show that all the species of monks and canons were within God's providence, and it never occurred to him that there was a profound or esoteric difference between Benedictine and Augustinian or Premonstratensian. To him, there were two types of religious communities, those that dwelt remote from man's habitations, and those that lived in towns, surrounded by the secular world. He has something too to say about hermits (whom he much admires, but treats quite briefly), and of the difference between monks and canons, and between canons regular and secular. The heart of his message is that those who dwell far from men are often more austere, more heroic in their prayers and their fasting; but that those who live in cities can combine contemplation with good works and practical influence. He simply takes it for granted that they engage in pastoral work and fructify the life of the city in quite a direct and practical way, and he makes little difference between monks and canons regular in this respect. If it had been widely read, which is unlikely, it might hardly have helped a doubtful founder to choose; but it would have brought comfort to any who had chosen, whatever his decision.

What is clear at once to the modern reader is that the good canon of Liège does not use the word 'order' in the normal modern sense. To him it is a mode, a norm of regular life, not an institution. Today a religious order has a rule, often supplemented by customs and regulations: a unitary system of authority; a single head. In this sense there were no orders in 1120. By 1150 or so the Cistercian and Premonstratensian Orders were in full swing; early in the thirteenth century they were joined by the first orders of friars. But large Benedictine houses were by definition independent at this date, and even Cluny's dependencies formed an order only in a loose sense; they were all subject to the single head, but beyond that had no constitution and no separate rule.

It is equally evident that the distinction between monks and canons which seemed so lucid to Peter Damian and Anselm was becoming rapidly less distinct. In due course canons ceased over large areas of Europe to serve churches and engage in pastoral work; they became more monastic.

Chaucer
Monks, canons and friars: all of us know the difference between these three types of men; or do we? May we not honestly confess, whether we are novices or veterans of the subject, that we have often been bemused by the distinctions? If so, we may take comfort from the thought that our medieval predecessors were equally confused.

Let us take Chaucer to witness. His monk is evidently a Benedictine, in some sense of the term, for he refers at the outset to the rule of St Maurus, Benedict's companion, and of St Benedict (Benet or Beneit) himself.

'The rule of Saint Maure or of Saint Beneit,
Because that it was old and some-del streit,
This ilke monk let olde thinges pace,
And held after the newe world the space.'[7]

He thought nothing—not a 'pulled hen'—of the saying that hunters were not holy men, and he conducted the cell of which

216

217

218

219

216-17 Hospitality: washing an angel's feet and offering food. British Museum, Add. MS 39, 943, ff.17v, 18.

218 Cuthbert instructing monks, f.35v.

219 Cuthbert preaching, f.22v.

he had charge as a hunting lodge. He thought equally little of the text that likened to a fish out of water a monk out of cloister—he thought it not worth an oyster. 'And I said; his opinion was good'—why sweat and toil, with a book, or with his hands,

'As Austin bid? How shall the world be served? Let Austin have his swink to him reserved.'

What is Austin doing here—St Augustine, lord of the Augustinian canons and of many other orders which did not follow St Benet (Benedict) or St Maurus? Many indignant critics have pointed out that he could not have been both monk and canon; and that, in a strict sense, Chaucer himself knew as well as anyone. He made the figures of the Prologue to the *Canterbury Tales* so exceedingly precise and lifelike that the temptation to identify them with living characters was irresistible. The game still continues, and some scholars have delighted to claim that this or that of the pilgrims was based on so-and-so. Yet a moment's reflection should surely reveal to us that the irony and satire of the Prologue collapses if they are taken simply as portraits. It is the union of individual and type, so that the reader is kept on a knife edge between saying—'of course this is only one individual' and saying 'of course, this is what monks were like'—that makes the Prologue still such delectable reading. By the simple trick of making it ambiguous whether the monk was indeed a monk or a canon regular Chaucer gives him a hint of universality. It is indeed possible that this had also the effect of helping to remind his readers of one of the great huntsmen of the day, William Clown, abbot of Leicester, an Augustinian.[8] But essentially he is surely enjoying an ambiguity which no modern student would dare to use: to confuse monk, canon and friar now is to commit a howler.

If we ask the question, what was the difference between a monk and a canon regular?—the final answer we should give, if we are honest with ourselves and with the evidence, is: 'I do not know'.

9 The Cistercians

Cîteaux, Clairvaux and St Bernard

Cîteaux was founded in 1097 or 1098 by one of the restless aspiring wanderers of the eleventh century. St Robert had been a leader among one of the amorphous groups of hermits of the late eleventh century from which several new orders sprang; in the forest of Colan, St Bruno, founder of the Carthusians, had studied under his direction. Then Robert moved off to found the abbey of Molesme in accordance with the ascetic principles developing in his mind. After some years Molesme seemed to him too well established and becoming set in its ways, and he moved on with a group of his monks to found yet another new monastery, which later was given the name *Cistercium*, Cîteaux. The monks of Molesme complained that he had gone without their leave; the benefactors of Molesme complained that they had lost the prayers they had provided for. Robert was forced to return, and the new community seemed to be struggling for life. It contained some notable talent and monks of strong conviction; but it is doubtful if it would ever have made much mark on the history of the religious orders but for the intervention of Bernard of Clairvaux.

220 Pastoral staff of *c*.1100, traditionally attributed to St Robert of Molesme, founder of Cîteaux. Musée de Dijon.

220

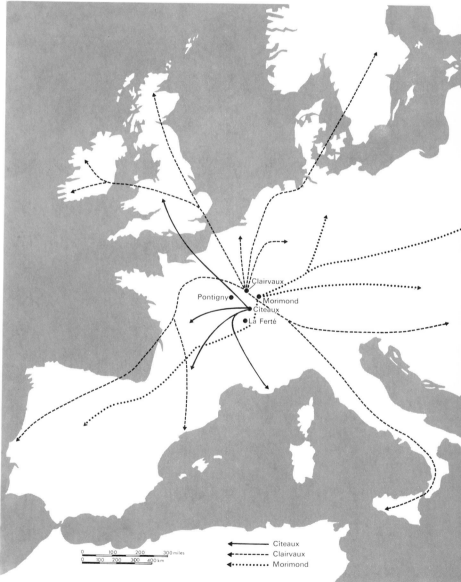

Fig. 10

Fig.10 Map showing the spread of the Cistercian Order. At the centre of the map lie Cîteaux and her four eldest daughters, La Ferté, Pontigny, Clairvaux and Morimond (founded 1115). It was from Cîteaux herself, from St Bernard's Clairvaux, and from Morimond that the greatest number of daughter houses sprang. The arrows give some idea of the direction of the order's growth.

221

222

St Bernard was born in the Burgundian village of Fontaine-lès-Dijon in or about 1090, one of the younger members of the large family of a landowner of moderate resources. Among Bernard's exceptional gifts was a power to influence men, not just by eloquence, nor just by force of character or moral strength, but by a combination of these qualities with a sense of urgency and spiritual adventure which proved almost irresistible. One greater than Bernard had observed that a prophet is not without honour save in his own home and among his own kin; and the most striking mark of Bernard's gift is that when he came to Cîteaux he brought almost all his brothers with him. Their arrival doubled the community, and transformed its prospects. He had one year as a novice, two years as a simple monk, then was sent out to be abbot of Cîteaux's third daughter, Clairvaux; and an abbot he remained till his death in 1153; an abbot, and more than an abbot, for in due course not only did his fellow-monks at Clairvaux and his colleagues in the Cistercian chapter enjoy his eloquence, but he was heard by bishops and cardinals and kings and popes. He felt called to settle the schism in the papacy in 1130, and had no hesitation in making his intention plain to the hard-headed and difficult monarchs of England and France; he allowed himself to be summoned to the preaching of the Second Crusade; he saw a disciple elected to the papacy in the person of Eugenius III (1145-53), and wrote an open letter to him—*De consideratione*—instructing him on how pope and curia should conduct themselves. No man insisted with more vehemence than he that a monk's place was in the cloister. If monks and canons ceased to do pastoral work in the second quarter of the twelfth century, if orthodox preachers disappeared behind the walls of monasteries, if every new religious order had something of Cîteaux stamped upon it, that was in a measure due to the extraordinary influence of Bernard. Yet he himself was never in his cloister for long at a time. He preached stability, but was in practice a wanderer.

221-2 Initials from Cîteaux, early twelfth century: S, gymnastic peasant with a flail; I, tree cutting, a monk in brown habit cuts at the root of a tree while a layman is still at work among the branches. Dijon, Bibliothèque Municipale, MS 173, ff.148, 41 (both reduced).

223 Rievaulx Abbey, Yorkshire, from the hillside. The abbey is set in the pleasant valley described by Walter Daniel (see p.157 and pls.259-62).

224 Llanthony Priory, Wales, the west front.

In his early years at Cîteaux, Bernard was a disciple of the English abbot, Stephen Harding, whose clear head and kindly nature formed a vital contrast to the tempestuous, ruthless Bernard, and perhaps taught Bernard that charity which he nearly always showed even to those whom he had at first severely trounced.[1] Stephen had been a monk of Sherborne in Dorset, and it seems that he set off in the 1090s in search of a house more austere; and yet he always retained an affectionate and grateful memory for his former home. One of the most attractive of the early Cistercian documents is the letter Stephen wrote to Sherborne between 1122 and 1134 expressing his humble gratitude and asking for the community's prayers:[2] it is an extraordinary contrast to the strident tones of Bernard's denunciation of Cluny, written at much the same time. Quite as striking, and as attractive, are the gay and humorous initials in the early Cistercian manuscripts painted under Stephen's eye.

24-9, 221-2

His chief monument is the *Carta Caritatis*, the Charter of Divine Love, the constitutional foundation of the order;[3] a succinct and simple statement of the basic arrangements of the Cistercian life. In recent years it has been shown that some provisions, especially those for the general chapter or parliament of the abbots of the order, are a later addition to it, that they reflect the order's growth and Bernard's heyday. But the basis remains a genuine product of the era of Stephen Harding. In different ways, and different measure, the charter, the initials and the letters of St Bernard reveal a vision of spiritual adventure; and in the order's buildings we find it, in some ways strongly and unexpectedly, translated into stone.

The Cistercian programme: choir monks and lay brothers

The Cistercians were dedicated first and foremost to the Rule of St Benedict, literally interpreted. They accepted from the traditional monasticism a monastic plan and a way of life essentially communal; they pruned the liturgy, but it remained a major part of their life. They accepted from the hermit tradition that prayer and spiritual reading should have a larger place in the daily round and the *raison d'être* of a community than could be squeezed out of the customs of Cluny; they inherited something of the ferocious asceticism of the Italian hermits. Above all, their early leaders were exceedingly well educated and had grasped the basic principle of the intellectual revival of their day—to study ancient texts as fresh and living books composed for their benefit. They took the Rule off the shelf and read it as if it had just been written; they tried to forget the accretion of customs which gathered

223
224

round it elsewhere, and to follow Benedict to the letter. They found too, in his epilogue, a call and a challenge to something beyond the routine of the common life. They read the Old Testament and the New, as Benedict had instructed them; and St Bernard frequently imitated an Old Testament prophet denouncing the world about him as literally as he imitated St Benedict; he also reckoned that he and his monks were walking in the path of the apostles, as did every monastic leader of the day. Above all, the Cistercian leaders found in the writings of Cassian and other early fathers the most advanced and sophisticated literature on prayer and on the individual's approach to God that then existed. Bernard has a major place in the history of mysticism, but hardly a very original place; he absorbed the doctrine of the fathers of the desert; infused it with a mystical theology derived from the Latin fathers, especially from St Augustine and Gregory the Great; and laid it out in his immaculate prose to inspire and edify his monks. What was new here was not the idea of contemplation or of the mystical life, but that they should be offered to large numbers of monks as an attainable ideal. In the full sense of the word the Cistercians produced few mystics;[4] but they produced a multitude which no man can number of monks who tried to live a life with spiritual aspiration at its centre. That is the first mark of their originality.

They followed St Benedict *ad litteram*; they were extremely austere; they pursued an ideal based on the personal pursuit of perfection. They aimed too at seclusion and self-sufficiency; they were the puritans of the Catholic Church in the twelfth century; and they developed a new kind of organisation aimed to keep a measure of uniformity undreamed hitherto in a spiritual empire so diffuse and scattered. The puritanism and the constitution were written into the order's early statutes, and directly reflected the personality of Bernard. But their supreme document is the order's surviving buildings, which reflect almost every aspect of the Cistercian adventure.

141-3   The buildings were designed to house two kinds of monks; choir monks and lay brothers. In the Book of Life of the New Minster at Winchester, one can see already, in a Benedictine house of the tenth and eleventh centuries, that a high proportion of monks ended as priests, almost all the rest as deacons; by the twelfth century advancement to the priesthood was becoming normal (see p. 88). At the same time the practice of daily celebration by every priest was also on the way—though far from general, and even further from being a rule. These changes had two notable consequences. First of all, ever more lavish provision of altars to accommodate these private masses was needed. The Cistercians from the first placed several chapels in their transepts, and, doubtless, altars elsewhere.[5] But the plain, blunt east end gave no space for more than the main altar.

The other consequence, likewise, was a general feature of the monastic movements of the eleventh century shown at its most complete and most highly organised in the Cistercian Order: the growth of a class of monks not suited for or aimed at the priestly calling, the lay brothers. One notable attraction of the Cistercian movement was that the doors were open to men from every walk of life. In theory this was already true of many communities and groups of houses in the eleventh century; the Cistercians, however, gave it an enormous

extension. Already before Cîteaux was founded the word *conversus*, the convert or converse, which had formerly meant any grown man turned monk, came to have also the special significance of a layman turned monk; a man who (in theory, if not always in practice) was illiterate, and would always remain so—age or temperament having rendered him impervious to book-learning and the cane. There has been much argument as to where and when the *conversi* first appeared; at the end of the day we cannot be sure, nor does it matter. The idea grew out of the religious climate of the eleventh century, out of the demand for wider opportunities and a richer variety of experience. In the group of houses reformed, with the aid of Cluniac customs, by the abbot and monks of Hirsau in south Germany in the late eleventh century, it was the practice to incorporate in a semi-monastic garb laymen living away from the abbey who administered its estates, a characteristic arrangement in the heyday of monastic offerings and involvement in the world. But more commonly the *conversi* everywhere were monks exempt from learning, who took a greater share of the manual work of the community in return for having a lesser share in the *opus Dei*.

Seclusion, self-sufficiency and manual work

It was the lay brothers who enabled the early Cistercian communities to be self-supporting, to be separate islands cut off from the world. The Cistercian dedication to the Rule of St Benedict naturally involved them in manual work. They expected, for instance, to grow their own corn and to produce their own clothes. The Benedictines had traditionally bought their own cloth ready woven and dyed black. The Cistercians reckoned to rear their sheep, and spin and weave the cloth for their habits from the undyed wool, which at first seems to have turned out brown or grey when they had finished it, but was later somewhat bleached to make them 'the white monks'. In point of fact St Benedict himself seems to have assumed that agriculture was mainly—though not exclusively—the work of lay peasantry, and that manual work normally meant the chores of the enclosure, washing up, sweeping and gardening, and a few simple crafts. The Cistercian lay brothers were farmers, shepherds, and masons; they were also millers, fullers, weavers and what-have-you. The rapid development in the twelfth century in the use of mills for purposes other than grinding corn owed much to them. The noise of the mill wheels echoes through the description of the rebuilding of Clairvaux in St Bernard's first Life. The author described how the monks and hired craftsmen worked together to rebuild the abbey of Clairvaux after it had been moved to a more ample site; how some of them 'divided the river, set it in new channels and lifted the leaping waters to the mill-wheels; fullers and bakers and tanners and smiths and other artificers prepared suitable machines for their tasks, that the river might flow fast and do good wherever it was needed in every building, flowing freely in underground conduits; the streams performed suitable tasks in every office and cleansed the abbey and at length returned to the main course and restored to the river what it had lost',[6]— no doubt with interest—but anyone who has closely inspected a Cistercian site where conduits and drains can still be traced knows how ample and how carefully planned the plumbing was; and the mill-wheels emphasise the technological skills involved. Nothing so elaborate had been seen since Roman times. The extreme simplicity and austerity of their life and their efficiency in all these crafts, and especially in rearing

24-9, 222, cf. 321

225 The Syon cope, early fourteenth century, a detail showing St Michael and the dragon. Victoria and Albert Museum.

226

227

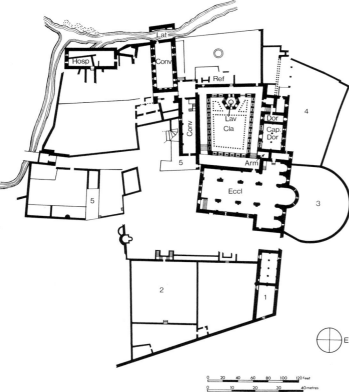

Fig. 11

Cistercian Houses of Provence 1: Le Thoronet

226-7 Church and apse are almost identical with Sénanque (pls.254-8), but the cloister is plainer and more rugged (see pls.229, 231).

228 The chapter house and the stone seats.

Fig.11 Plan of Le Thoronet, to show the medieval buildings, begun *c*.1146 when the abbey was moved from Tourtour, and mostly of the late twelfth and early thirteenth centuries. 1. Tithe barn. 2. Vineyard. 3. Cemetery. 4. Garden. 5. Later buildings.

sheep, enabled the Cistercians to amass wealth in early days, which helped their benefactors to pay for their tremendous building programmes, and tempted kings and princes to mulct them.[7] As the generations passed, recruitment became less varied and gradually fell off. After the Black Death in the mid fourteenth century the recruitment of lay brothers ceased, and the Cistercians finally melted into the monastic landscape.

Of the place of the lay brothers in early days Le Thoronet in Provence and Buildwas Abbey in Shropshire tell us as much as any documents; in particular they reveal the careful segregation of choir monks and lay brothers. Buildwas, like the houses in Provence, is an impressive monument to the determination of the Cistercians in early days to see that adequate, convenient and commodious buildings were provided. It was always a small house, and gives a good idea of what the order thought fitting for a community never expected to grow larger than a dozen to twenty choir monks and perhaps up to forty or fifty lay brothers. No benefactor providing for the needs of a community of less than a hundred

229

230

231

229, 231 Le Thoronet cloister; note the characteristic Provençal vault.

230 The lay brothers' quarters of *c*.1200 are exceptionally well preserved; they include the abbey grange, twelfth to thirteenth centuries, with later alterations, and the remains of a medieval oil mill and press.

2: Silvacane, France

232 The refectory.

233 Silvacane, the chapter house, with thick ribs, as at Sénanque, but a central pier more slender than at Sénanque, and Le Thoronet.

234 Silvacane, the calefactory, *c*.1200, with its window enlarged at a later date; note the plain capitals, typically Cistercian.

232

souls in the opulent societies of the twentieth century would conceive of building on this lavish scale today; and it is odd to reflect that this was thought appropriate for a group of men called to an extremely harsh, severe, ascetic, cold and silent way of life—cold in a physical sense, that is, in the Shropshire winter; for there must have been warmth of another kind to bring recruits flocking to these houses in their early days. However that may be, Buildwas is a large house for a small community, and as the community never grew larger than originally expected, its arrangements were never altered. The lie of the land at Buildwas affected and exaggerated one peculiar feature of the plan; the original separation, commonly lost by later expansion and rebuilding in the late twelfth century, of western range from cloister. At Buildwas this is

233

234

235

236

235-8 Buildwas, England. The best English example of a small Cistercian church of the mid twelfth century; small, but substantial, heavy in proportions, bleak in design.

235 The east end and crossing; the plain square end unaltered. Rough patches of stone on the nave piers show the shape of some of the screens (see pl.243).

236 The west front, without a door.

still clear. The lay brothers' quarters start at a lower level than the cloister and some feet away; they form a separate block, narrow, owing to the way the land lies, but unusually high, three storeys in all. Within the church there are striking roughnesses on the piers of the nave, which can only be due

to some arrangement for linking the piers to the screens and primitive furnishings of the church in early days.[8]

At Maulbronn there still survives, though heavily restored, the screen which separated the main choir from the choir of the lay brothers—that is, in the church of any other community, the nave. The choir and crossing were allotted to the choir monks for their masses and offices; then came a screen, at Buildwas approximately six feet high, at Maulbronn somewhat higher, separating off the nave, which was the lay brothers' choir. They attended mass and their simpler round of offices within the nave, in a box west of the screen, enclosed on both sides by wainscotting (at Buildwas) approximately five feet high. This separation continued outside the church. At Le Thoronet and Silvacane substantial remains can be seen of the

230

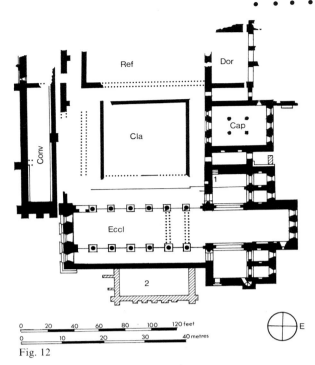

Fig. 12

237

238

239

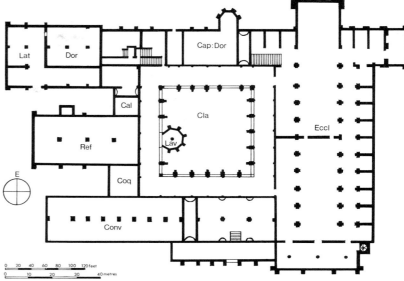

Fig. 13

Fig.13 Plan of Maulbronn.

241 The Romanesque west door.

240

237 Buildwas. The nave arcade, with the foundations of the later parochial chapel in the foreground.

238 The nave, within, looking west from the crossing.

Fig.12 Plan of Buildwas. It lies to the south of the River Severn, hence the church is on the south, the cloister on the north, as in many of the Cistercian sites illustrated in this book. 1.Night stair. 2.Chapel added *c.*1400, probably for lay parishioners. The rest of the buildings are twelfth to thirteenth century.

239-45, 248-9 Maulbronn, Germany

239 The approach to the abbey church: west porch or Galilee, early thirteenth century, restored.

240 The outer buildings of a great monastic complex, guest-house and other offices, in late medieval dress, much restored.

241

242

243

244

245

242 Maulbronn, the monks' choir, looking west, with fine late Gothic woodcarving.

243 Maulbronn, the twelfth-century nave, the lay brothers' view. The screen, though heavily restored, gives a fair impression of the scale and nature of a twelfth-century Cistercian screen (see pl.235).

244 Maulbronn, the staircase to the dormitory, fourteenth century.

245 Maulbronn, the cloister, Romanesque to the right, Gothic to the left with lavabo pavilion.

246 Altenberg, Germany, from the west (see pls.250-1).

247 *Overleaf, left* Pietro Lorenzetti, detail from Virgin and Child with St Francis and St John the Baptist, from the Lower Church, the Basilica of St Francis, Assisi.

248 *Overleaf, right* Maulbronn, the refectory, early thirteenth century.

247

249

250

lay brothers' buildings; and in particular, at Le Thoronet, the separate door by which they entered the church. At Buildwas the lie of the land dictated a building entirely separated from the cloister.

Puritanism and efficiency

Reflected in the Cistercian miniatures of *c*. 1100 is a gaiety such as one might expect in a young community clambering up the ladder to heaven. Artistic flair and a love of nature seem to have lived at Cîteaux before Bernard; and in an odd way he fostered them; odd, because he was an extreme puritan who succeeded in ignoring everything in the world that he regarded as inessential, including the physical setting provided by nature and by man. As a novice, we are told, he spent a year in a chamber at Cîteaux and had no idea at the end what sort of ceiling it had. In later years he rode for a day by the Lake of Geneva and claimed not to have known the lake was near. This could reflect a nature indifferent to physical things; but it is possible that the opposite was true. There is no doubt that he thought ornament of any kind in a church a distraction. He makes this abundantly clear in his attack on Cluny; and there is copious literary evidence that his puritanism was of an extreme kind, and one of his own contributions to the Cistercian customs. It may have been partly due to a temperament naturally sensitive to his environment, and there was one striking flaw in it. Bernard's Latin prose is among the most ornate and rhetorical of the century. It shows us that he was an artist.[9] But Cistercian architecture reveals with abundant clarity that the ruthless enforcement of puritan values all over Europe involved an obsession with this basic notion, that ornament and striking proportions distract. Abbot Suger, in a famous phrase, claimed to see the divine light reflected in jewels and glowing ornaments. To Bernard they distracted; and it is natural to see in the uniformity of the Cistercian idiom a reflection of this doctrine.

24-9,
221-2

There is nothing in Bernard's writings to suggest that he was himself an architect. The Cistercian documents occasionally tell us, when a new foundation was in the making, that this or that monk of Clairvaux, often a close companion, sometimes a brother of St Bernard, was responsible for establishing the order or customs of the Cistercians here or there; and this has sometimes been taken to mean that these eminent choir monks directed the planning of the buildings. Everything about Cistercian buildings of the mid and late twelfth century, however, suggests the professional hand of trained masons. At first sight, we seem to be faced with a paradox. The quality of the work is often extremely good, and they seem to have relied on first-rate masons. Local varieties of style show that the work was often executed by local craftsmen. The documents tell us from time to time that monks and local lay folk lent a hand, and there is no reason to doubt the truth of this; but key building work, the uniform plan and idiom were the

249 Maulbronn, the monks' lavabo.

246, 250-1 Altenberg, Germany. In the Dünsthal, east of Cologne, one of the finest Gothic churches in Germany, begun in 1255, completed in the fourteenth century. In contrast to Eberbach and Maulbronn, not far away, there is nothing specifically Cistercian about it.

250 From the east.

251 Interior, looking north east.

259-62 Rievaulx, England

259 Transepts and choir, with a corner of the cloister in the foreground.

260 The choir, looking west.

261 The choir arcade, triforium and clerestory, thirteenth century.

served. When they rest on their beds, each of them lies alone and girdled, in habit and tunic in winter and summer. They have no personal property; they do not even talk together; no one takes a step towards anything of his own will. Everything they do is at the motion of the prelate's nod and they are turned aside by a like direction. At table, in procession, at communion and in other liturgical observances, all of them, small and great, young and old, wise and ignorant are subject to one law. Personal standing is merged in the equality of each and all, there is no inequitable mark of exception. . . . The only test of worth is the recognition of the best. . . . Women, hawks and dogs, except those ready barkers used to drive away thieves from houses, do not enter the gates of their monastery. By their exceeding love they stifle among them the bane of impatience, and every growth of anger and the smoky emanations of pride.'[15]

259
260

261

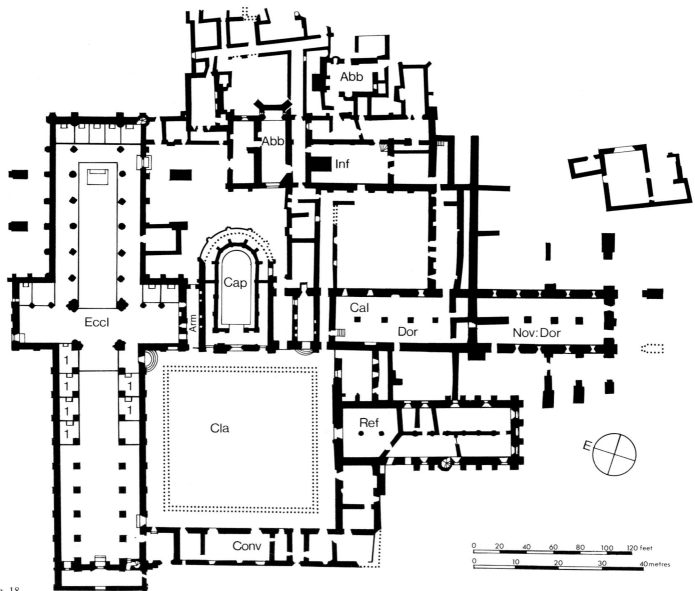

Fig. 18

Fig.18 Plan of Rievaulx. The buildings are still mainly twelfth century, the chief exceptions being the thirteenth-century refectory and choir, which is today the dominant feature of the church and is in fine mid thirteenth century English Gothic. In the fifteenth century there was much remodelling, especially of the infirmary, abbot's lodging and chapter house, which was shortened, though the shape given it by Ailred in the mid twelfth century can still be discerned. At the end of the dormitory farthest from the church the ground falls away: hence the flying buttresses whose foundations are shown in the plan. 1,1 etc. Chapels partitioned off (see p.254, chap.9, n.5).

The enthusiasm of this account of the early Cistercians can still communicate to us the message which inspired Ailred's biographer, Walter Daniel, as it had inspired Ailred himself. It helps us to understand how in one generation the small community at Cîteaux had come to spread all over the known world, and count many hundreds of houses and many thousands of monks in its allegiance.

The special emphasis on the beauty of the scene clearly answered something in Ailred's mind and in his friend's and can leave no doubt that for some Cistercians this beauty was accepted without puritanical qualms as part of the joy of life in a Cistercian solitude. The passage also shows that the life itself was hard, and as is here implied, uniform, disciplined and monotonous well beyond the Benedictine norm.

What is abnormal about Rievaulx is the spirit of Ailred, visible in some traces from his time of the scale of the place. The chapter house is large and spacious; it allows for much more communication, monastic conference—sermon and discussion—than most. It lacks the central pillars common in Cistercian chapter houses; in plan and scale it closely resembles that at Durham Cathedral priory, where Ailred's father had spent his last years. It suited the eloquence and expansive goodwill of Ailred; for in his later years Rievaulx held the largest community in England, perhaps, after St Bernard's own Clairvaux, in the order, with 140 choir monks and 500 lay brothers.[16] The exceptional numbers at Rievaulx were due to Ailred's deliberate act of charity in opening the gates. St Bernard, his master, had savaged the abbot of Cluny because the vocation of recruits there was inadequately tested and there was even at times no novitiate. That the Cistercians themselves put any close check on the quality of their recruits in this period of rapid expansion is hard to believe; it was evidently not so at Rievaulx.

262

263

262 Rievaulx. In the foreground, St Ailred's chapter house, stretching to the right; behind, the east end of the church, with the woods beyond. Within the chapter house can be seen the rows of stone seats for the choir monks.

263 In contrast, the normal Cistercian chapter house at Fountains.

'He turned the house of Rievaulx into a stronghold for the sustaining of the weak, the nourishment of the strong and whole. . . . Who was there, however despised and rejected, who did not find in it a place of rest? . . . And so those wanderers in the world to whom no house of religion gave entrance, came to Rievaulx, the mother of mercy, and found the gates open. . . . If one of them in later days had taken it upon himself to reprove in angry commotion some silly behaviour, Ailred would say, "Do not, brother, do not kill the soul for which Christ died, do not drive away our glory from this house. Remember that . . . it is the singular and supreme glory of the house of Rievaulx that above all else it teaches tolerance of the infirm and compassion with others in their necessities".'

And so we can understand how Ailred came to double

'. . . all things in it—monks, *conversi* [lay brothers], laymen [servants], farms, lands and every kind of equipment; indeed he trebled the intensity of the monastic life and its charity. On feast days you might

see the church crowded with the brethren like bees in a hive, unable to move forward because of the multitude, clustered together, rather, and compacted into one angelical body.'[17]

The adventure and its victims

The spiritual adventure of the Cistercians was inspired by Bernard in a very obvious and direct way. For all his wanderings he could not be personally known to the greater part of his confrères; no doubt to most of them Cîteaux or Clairvaux was known first and foremost as a way of life. Yet even strangers met Bernard in his writings. This was one secret of his immense influence. There were times in his life when his many illnesses and intense physical suffering made him physically repulsive to those who lived with him—he even had to live in a separate hut at Clairvaux for a time. But for the most part his presence was effective and compelling; it is said that when he preached the Second Crusade in Germany his audience were more moved by his own sermon in French than by the same sermon repeated by the interpreter in German. Yet he lives now, and always lived for most of his fellow-monks, in the written word. At every point in this story we have seen links between the austere Cistercians and the far from austere

264-5 London, the Temple Church

264 The round nave, consecrated in 1185, with piers of Purbeck marble, combining the Templars' devotion to the Holy Sepulchre with contemporary English fashion (much restored after bombing in the Second World War). On the floor, effigies of thirteenth-century warriors.

265 The head of a warrior, mid thirteenth century, presumably a secular patron of the Templars, and supposed to be William Marshal, the faithful royal servant and knight errant who became earl of Pembroke and regent of England, and is known to have been buried in the church (d.1219).

265

264

266

that they needed more space in a more salubrious quarter. By 1185 their removal to an ample riverside enclosure, which has been known ever since as the Temple, was accomplished; and the greater part of the present circular nave of their church had been built. The Latin patriarch of Jerusalem, visiting England in a desperate attempt to stir Henry II's conscience and recruit for the Third Crusade, was present at the consecration of their church and of the Hospitallers'. For the folk of London, the great round churches of Hospitallers and Templars provided an opportunity to worship in the gates of Jerusalem without leaving London. But they were also reminders, symbols of the earthly Jerusalem; to put the matter bluntly, they advertised the pilgrimage and the crusade.

Tomar, Portugal. A twelfth-century rotunda originally built for the Knights Templar, taken over later by the Ordèn de Cristo.

266 Interior, much influenced by Moslem art and with later paintings.

267 Exterior, with the late Gothic choir on the left.

Henry II himself had no intention of going on crusade—that could be left to his more romantic, gadabout son, Richard I—but he was compelled to be generous in his benefactions; and was thus duly impressed by the skill of the Templars in handling money and keeping it safe. The result was that he made the London Temple one of his principal treasure-houses: and it passes the wit of man to decide where in the Templar movement treasure on earth ended and treasure in heaven began.

In the end, their wealth was the Templars' undoing. The quarrels between the orders of knights undermined their prestige, especially when first Jerusalem fell (1187), then Acre (1291), in spite of (or as some thought because of) their efforts. Early in the fourteenth century Philip IV, the Fair (1285-1314), a king of France almost as greedy and egocentric as the English

267

Henry VIII two centuries later, urged on the pope their many crimes real and imaginary; and other kings cashed in. The result was the suppression of the order. Much of their property went to the Hospitallers, much to the royal patrons of the 'Process'. Today the Temple Church is a splendid chapel for the lawyers who live and work around it. But the tombs attributed to William Marshal, earl of Pembroke, the knight errant who rose to be regent of England (1216-19), and his clan—none of them Templars, but all of them closely involved with the order—remind us that the Temple once enshrined an ideal which could inspire men of heroic stature, and which played a part in English government.

The visitor to St James, Santiago de Compostela, who went from Tours to Conques and on to Compostela in north-western Spain, protected by the Knights of Santiago, passed by a series of splendid pilgrimage churches built on the model of Santiago largely from the gifts at the shrine of St Martin at Tours and Sainte Foy (St Faith) at Conques. But here and there about western Europe were churches, large and small, which were reminders of the greatest of all earthly pilgrimages. For the modest churches of the Templars at Tomar in Portugal, and at Laon in France, as well as the Temple Church in London, were directly imitated from the Church of the Holy Sepulchre in Jerusalem. Churches with circular, octagonal or hexagonal naves were built in different parts of Europe at different periods, especially in central and eastern Europe, where rotundas are or were relatively numerous.[2] Most of these were probably based, at one or two removes, on the palatine chapel of Charlemagne at Aachen. In the twelfth century a new fashion arose, based on the Church of the Holy Sepulchre, and disseminated mainly by the Templars; mainly, but not exclusively, for in England only half of the known examples from the twelfth century were Templar in origin. The Hospitallers built one in Clerkenwell, London, and one at least elsewhere; one or two were secular or attached to hospitals; and the earliest of all, the round church in Cambridge, was probably built for the ephemeral order of Augustinian Canons of the Holy Sepulchre.[3] Thus were the elements of several religious movements interwoven: crusading zeal, the love of pilgrimage, Cistercian austerity and the practical activities of canons regular and other founders of hospitals. The Temple church in London is at once the monument of a local fashion and one of the most cosmopolitan buildings in Western Europe.

264-5

266-7
268

268

Laon, the Templar church

268 A miniature octagonal church of the twelfth century, with open porch to the west, a small chancel to the east.

11 On abbesses and prioresses

To the eleventh century

'A woman must be a learner, listening quietly and with due submission. I do not permit a woman to be a teacher, nor must woman domineer over man; she should be quiet.' Thus thought the elders of the early Church, as represented by the First Epistle to Timothy (2, 11-12). None the less, they allowed elderly widows to take special vows to lead an austere and ascetic life; to the young ones—with surprising abandon—they recommended that they marry as often as they wish. The group of elderly respectable widows became in time, especially in the circle of ladies harassed, harrowed and inspired by St Jerome (see p. 21) in the late fourth century, one of the primary institutions of early monasticism. St Augustine probably wrote a rule for such ladies, and St Cesarius of Arles in the sixth century, provided the community in his own city with another.[1] Yet in the long run, patrons or founders of monasteries in the early Middle Ages tended to neglect the nuns, so that by the mid eleventh century there were four monasteries for men in England to every one for women, and in France the disproportion was probably even greater.[2]

There were exceptions. In seventh- and eighth-century England, for example, a succession of princesses of strong character and powerful aversion to marriage provided a principal impulse in the monastic life. Such were Hilda, great-niece of King Edwin of Northumbria, who presided over the famous abbey of women and men at Whitby in the mid and late seventh century, and Werburga, daughter of King Wulfhere of Mercia and presiding abbess over a group of Mercian convents a century later, which were in their turn ruled by abbesses younger or less eminent in birth and sanctity than Werburga herself. At much the same date as Hilda, an Anglo-Saxon slave in France called Balthild had risen by character and charm to be first a queen and then an abbess. These instances reflect a society in England, and in a measure too in the Frankish kingdoms, in which women could hold their own, and achieve a status rare in the central Middle Ages; and also a society in which it was fashionable for aristocratic ladies to take to the religious life. In the tenth and eleventh centuries we have to look to Germany for an interest in convents and nuns at all comparable. The various monastic documents issued in 816-17[3] included a rule for canonesses; and houses of both nuns and canonesses flourished in Germany in the centuries which followed. The Saxon dynasty looked with favour on these houses, and so did its daughters; Matilda, daughter of Otto the Great, was abbess of Quedlinburg, where her father died (973) and is buried. In the next generation, Otto II's

269

269-71 Nonnberg, Salzburg. A great abbey since *c.*700 when it was founded for St Erentrudis by St Rupert. The first Romanesque church was consecrated in 1009, enlarged later in the eleventh century and adorned with frescoes which survive *c.*1150 (pls.59-60). The vaults of the crypt and the main church were rebuilt in the second half of the fifteenth century, and the whole building restored in the nineteenth to twentieth centuries.

269 St Erentrudis's tomb in the crypt.

daughter Adelaide was abbess of Quedlinburg, Gernrode, Vreden and Gandersheim; nor did the line end with her.[4] Among this group, Matilda's cousin and namesake, Matilda abbess of Essen (from before 974 to 1011) has left us the most remarkable memorials of any abbess of the age. She was descended from both the German and the English royal lines. She was a grand-daughter of the Emperor Otto the Great, who sent her to Essen with a dowry consisting of one of her own estates, and of his English wife, Edith, sister of King Athelstan. She was sufficiently interested in her English ancestors to write to a distant cousin in England demanding some account of them; the reply took the form of a Latin translation of the Anglo-Saxon Chronicle made by the same relative, the Ealdorman Æthelweard. She was also the patroness of fine craftsmen, and the collection of crosses, the tiny crown and other rich ornaments, which still adorn the treasury of Essen Cathedral (as it now is) are the most perfect collection of the age to survive. Matilda was one of a line of aristocratic princesses who presided over Essen in its golden age; and who won protection and patronage from local nobles and from the emperors, as well as admiration from the local bishops, so that the convent prospered spiritually as well as temporally. As we should expect, high patronage flowed to the aid of these great ladies, and in Germany nuns were by no means as neglected as in France and England.

Even in Germany far greater funds and estates were at the disposal of the men. Yet in France and England neither patrons nor princesses altogether ignored the convents of nuns. The Princess Christina, sister of Edgar the Atheling and of St Margaret of Scotland, and so a member of the Old English royal line, presided over a school for young English princesses at Romsey and perhaps also at Wilton, and attempted to keep them safe from the lust of the Normans. One Norman princess meanwhile was dedicated at birth to the abbey at Caen which her mother, Queen Matilda, had founded, and grew up to find herself abbess; her sister Adela became in due course dowager countess of Blois and a nun at the Cluniac priory of Marcigny.

Marcigny was a very significant phenomenon of its age.[5] The abbots of Cluny of the eleventh century, like most of the great monastic organisers of the eleventh and twelfth centuries, were averse to nuns, who distracted monks from their proper tasks and laid difficulties and temptations at their gates. Such men set their faces sternly against the double monastery, though a few survived and a few more were founded. But the holy and importunate widow could not be held indefinitely at bay, especially if she were rich and strong of will. Such a lady sometimes set up house in a male community and became a mother to the community as did Eve Crispin at Bec in St Anselm's time. Marcigny was established by St Hugh, abbot of Cluny, in 1055, to provide a home for his mother and sister and a group of like-minded persons. His biographer notes his success in converting women from the world—'not an easy task', he observes—but the nuns of Marcigny were noted for a way of life more austere than was general among their menfolk. None the less, St Hugh insisted that it remain firmly under his own rule, although the Blessed Virgin was elected perpetual abbess.

The comparatively small part played by women in the religious movements of the eleventh and twelfth centuries is puzzling, and the explanation is not fully revealed to us. Clearly, it owed something both to the prejudices of monastic reformers and to the patrons who provided funds for new buildings and endowments for monasteries. Endowments were provided as never before or since; but chiefly by male patrons for men. No doubt this reflects a society in which the reins of power were in men's hands; in some sense, as we shall see, this was the heyday of male dominance in medieval social history. Furthermore, if you lavish a substantial part of a large patrimony on investment in heavenly treasure, you must be sure that the treasure is of the best metal. None doubted that women could lead holy lives, but they could not sing mass, and there were a number of reasons, sensible and absurd, for supposing their prayers less efficacious than those of men. In Germany the monasteries played a crucial part in imperial administration and their lands were the recruiting grounds of armies.

270

271

270 Nonnberg, Salzburg. twelfth-century fresco, a saint.

271 Nonnberg, Salzburg, the nuns' grill in their enclosed chapel.

272-4, 276 Fontevrault, France. Most of the abbey was rebuilt on the grandest scale in the sixteenth to eighteenth centuries. From the twelfth there survives the church, with a lofty apse (272), and a nave covered by a series of cupolas—much restored (273).

Needless to say, the monks themselves were not expected to fight; but it could readily be assumed that it was normally more satisfactory to have male communities and male religious working with the lay 'advocates' and recruiting officers. At the social level, furthermore, a man who was well enough off to imagine his children entering religion would certainly not be expecting to pay very substantial dowries for his daughters. The lavish endowment of a great house like that of Queen Matilda at Caen might be occasionally possible for a queen of exceptional wealth; and her foundation was a part of the penance imposed by the church in its strictness for a marriage of doubtful legality. Most of the new houses of nuns of this age and the next struggled into existence on a very modest scale; often they were small and poor, little more than depositories for daughters with moderate dowries. Sometimes even the poor houses grew to considerable wealth if they were near great cities and the dowries and legacies fell thick upon them.[6] Sometimes they were the lineal descendants of great houses of the past, and had a stately existence like Essen. They were commonly served by chaplains from one order or another; and it sometimes happens that the documents fail to specify to what order the nuns themselves belonged.[7] The explanation may be that they obeyed the rules provided by their chaplains, or followed the rites that they performed; and that these themselves varied from time to time when chaplains of one order were replaced by a group from another.

272

The chaplains were an essential feature of any house of nuns, since the sisters could not be in holy orders; and in most houses there were a number of male officials and servants, beside the multitude of maidservants that attended any flock of well-to-to ladies. Even very poor houses must have had some menservants, to act as porters and guardians of the house, and there was usually a male steward to represent the nuns in business affairs and litigation. In court and counting house women were reckoned at a disadvantage, although there were doubtless plenty of women of shrewd business sense and ability in the Middle Ages as in every age.

The twelfth and thirteenth centuries
In most parts of Europe, the nucleus of the convents consisted of ancient houses like Essen, some of which continued to flourish and prosper, especially if they preserved their noble connections. In the twelfth and thirteenth centuries they were joined by a much more numerous band of smaller houses. But every age saw one or more really notable exceptions.

No stranger exception could be found than that which appeared about the year 1100, in the Forest of Craon on the borders of Anjou and Touraine. Shakespeare in imagination peopled the Forest of Arden and Windsor Forest—or the Athenian Forest of *A Midsummer Night's Dream*—full of folk. When one reads of all the people who lived in the Forest of Craon at that time one gets a similar impression. From the monks and hermits who settled there sprang no less than three quite different religious orders.

Robert of Arbrissel was born about 1047 in the diocese of Rennes. After a career as a student, archdeacon and schoolmaster, he found his true vocation, and became a hermit and wandering preacher. This seems to us at first sight an odd combination; but we have met it already in Peter Damian and some of his Italian colleagues, and we shall meet it shortly in St Francis. Robert was evidently a preacher of enormous impact. He helped Pope Urban II to preach the First Crusade, and he

273

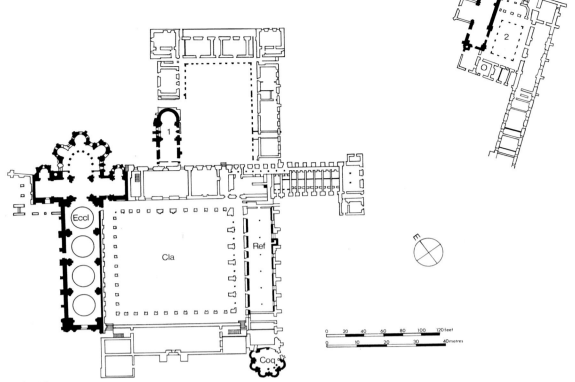

Fig. 19

274

Fig.19 Plan of Fontevrault, with the twelfth-century buildings—church, kitchen, etc.—outlined in black; the rest are of the sixteenth and later centuries. 1. Chapel of St Benedict. 2. Priory of St Lazarus (S Lazare).

274 Domestic survivals of the twelfth century are the abbess's kitchen with its forest of chimneys and great central cone, and the walls of some of the conventual buildings and other fragments. Similar kitchens survive at Glastonbury and Durham (275), but neither is so grand, nor so heavily restored, as this. Much of the roof may give a misleading impression of the original design.

275 Durham, the kitchen, late fourteenth century.

went on preaching tours till shortly before his death in 1117. But the major effort of his life went into organising the groups of penitents who gathered round him from which sprang orders both of monks and nuns. Over one of these he presided himself for a time. Over another he set Vitalis de Mortain, another preacher turned hermit; and in one of the various groups was a preacher of almost equal eminence, Bernardus Grossus. Vitalis founded the abbey of Savigny in Normandy, Bernard that of Tiron in Le Perche; both were to grow into ascetic male communities very similar to Cîteaux in her early days; and Savigny, with her progeny, which included numerous English houses—Buildwas among them—was to merge with the Cistercian Order in 1147.

Robert of Arbrissel was dedicated, like so many of the reformers of the day, to the apostolic life, to the direct imitation of the apostles. In the Gospels he read how Our Lord from the cross had given St John to the Blessed Virgin as to a mother; and he took this to mean that John and the other apostles were set (in some sense) under her authority. In 1096-9 he established a church and a community dedicated to the Blessed Virgin; and as her earthly representative he chose a lady of great piety and noble birth, Petronilla, widow of the baron of Chemillé. As time passed, the new monastery, which presently came to be called Fontevrault, became more highly organised, more feminine, more wealthy, and above all, more aristocratic. So strange is the reversal of the values of the world which placed earnest male ascetics under female control, that

276

276 Fontevrault. Within the church are the tombs of Henry II and
Richard I of England (d.1189 and 1199), made to Queen Eleanor's orders
shortly before her death in 1204; between them is her own tomb of c.1220.
The fourth is of much the same date as hers, and so can hardly be (as
commonly asserted) of Isabel of Angoulême, widow of King John,
who died 1246.

elaborate theories have been propounded linking it to the
origin of courtly love, or of the Provençal lyric;[8] and it is
indeed a fact that the first of the troubadours, William IX,
count of Poitou and duke of Aquitaine, was very friendly with
Robert, and that his grand-daughter Eleanor, widow of
Henry II of England and a celebrated figure in the courts of
love, is buried there. Perhaps it is best simply to say that the
devotion to the Blessed Virgin, so signally represented in
Robert, and courtly love both reflected, in very different ways,
fashionable reversals of the order of the world; and also that
contemporaries saw as clearly as we do the analogy and the
contradiction between them.

At Fontevrault the fine church, with its northern apse and
its southern cupolas, still survives; and in its transept, though
heavily restored, is a row of royal tombs. Here are Queen
Eleanor, her husband Henry II, her son, Richard I, and a
wooden effigy wrongly identified as Isabel of Angoulême,
widow of King John. For the first two tombs are the work of
Eleanor, who brought here, after his death in 1189, the husband
with whom she had so bitterly quarrelled; and ten years later
laid her son beside him, raising tombs to both of them shortly
before her own death in 1204.[9]

In the world of chivalry most literature was composed by
men—though often in women's honour—and so we have comparatively little direct contact with the nuns of the Middle
Ages. It is possible that the inferior education offered to women
at this date reduced the number of vocations. It was assumed
that monks could read Latin, and nuns too, it seems, in the
tenth century; but instructions for nuns in the twelfth and
later centuries were commonly in the vernacular, like the
famous *Ancren Riwle* for English anchoresses; and the French
inscriptions which appear in the illustrations to some of the

most magnificent of twelfth-century psalters, such as those of
Winchester and Shaftesbury—both of which were at Shaftesbury Abbey in the late Middle Ages—seem to be due to the
needs (real or supposed) of nuns for whom they were composed. To this there are striking exceptions.

The surviving letters of Heloise to Abelard were written when
she was abbess of the Paraclet, a house on the way to becoming
the centre of a small order similar to Fontevrault. They are
famous for their intensely moving account of her relations
with her former lover and husband; but the greater part of
them is taken up with the life of the nuns of the Paraclet.
From their pages we can conjure a vision of a remarkable
personality, Abelard's humble servant, yet as forthright, and
masterful in her own way, as he, and fully able to hold her
own in intellectual debate with the greatest master of logic
of the age.[10] After she had spent her passion in describing to
Abelard how her love for him was as intense as ever, she
submitted to his will as her lord and master, and, as many
a submissive wife has done, set him to work. She asked for
some account of the origin of the religious life for women,
and she demanded a rule. At this date, he was a very unsuccessful abbot, while she was already a widely respected
abbess. She can hardly have been unaware that she knew
more about the monastic life than he did. Partly for this
reason, no doubt, she took the precaution of telling him what
to say in his rule: especially, that he was to make up for the
deficiencies of St Benedict, who had written for men and took
no account of women's special needs in clothing and so forth,
nor of their physical weakness: 'who lays such burdens on an
ass as he deems fitted for an elephant?', she asks. She sought
for a retired life, free from the inconvenience of having to
entertain men, who were dangerous company, and gossipy
women of the world, who were worse. Her demands were
austere and practical, though occasionally eccentric. St
Benedict, she explains, though a holy man and spiritual
adviser, was occasionally silly: thus he refused to allow meat
although everyone knows that fish is often more luxurious
and expensive than meat, and allowed wine, which is dangerous
stuff—'Wine and women make the wise to fall away', she
quotes from Ecclesiasticus 19, 2—even if women can hold
their wine better than men. In later years, it seems, she became
more conventional and rejected meat; meanwhile her letters
reveal a brilliant mind critically at work on the role of nuns
and their traditional manner of life.

Heloise was in every way an exceptional figure; and we
shall not be surprised to find more evidence of an intellectual
tradition among nuns in Germany. There a notable creative
writer appeared in Hildegarde, abbess of Bingen, poetess,
philosopher and mystic; and at Odilienberg or Saint-Odilien
in Alsace (then also in Germany) was composed the famous
illustrated encyclopedia of Abbess Herrad, the *Garden of
Delights*.

There is copious evidence, furthermore, of a strong demand
for greater opportunities for women in the religious life in
the twelfth and thirteenth centuries. Early in the twelfth,
Norbert of Xanten found himself head of a mixed order
centred in Prémontré (see pp. 181 ff.) which was alleged in the
middle of the century to include ten thousand women.
Significantly, the canons who won control of the order soon
put a stop to the recruitment of women, so that the female
element presently withered away. Meanwhile, in the 1130s and
1140s, the English St Gilbert of Sempringham succeeded in

founding a double order, similar in conception to Norbert's, and similarly influenced by the Cistercians, with the blessing of the hierarchy and of St Bernard of Clairvaux; no doubt Bernard felt relieved that these importunate women should be managed in someone's else's order. Yet his path was not altogether smooth; for in spite of repeated and plain refusals by the Cistercian general chapter to countenance nuns within the order, convents of Cistercian nuns began to spring up all over western Europe in the twelfth and thirteenth centuries, and even, in Spain, to rival the men in influence, and in Germany, greatly to outnumber the convents of men. Here again is a puzzling but significant movement. The ladies of the twelfth and thirteenth centuries rebelled against their lack of opportunity. While the age of the twelfth-century renaissance saw the enrichment, in all manner of ways, of the choices and professions open to men, respectable women had to accept marriage to whomsoever their overlord or father chose, or hope for one of the scarce places in a convent. They expressed rebellion in ways carnal as well as spiritual; but their pursuit of a Cistercian vocation is one of the most characteristic of the age. None the less, it remains puzzling. The abbesses of Las Huelgas near Burgos, for instance, were ladies after the fashion of the abbesses of Essen and Fontevrault. Queen Eleanor's daughter, Queen Eleanor of Castile, was one of their founders, and she lies there amid a galaxy of royal tombs. The abbesses insisted that they were Cistercian, and they insisted that they would not obey the general chapter at Cîteaux in which no woman sat.

The difficulties and frustrations—and ultimate success—of an intelligent girl who wished to find her own vocation as a nun, are uniquely presented to us in the Life of Christina of Markyate, a contemporary of Héloise of the first half of the twelfth century. She was the daughter of a well-to-do burgher of Huntingdon, who felt the vocation to become a recluse. Such ladies and groups of ladies formed the spiritual nucleus of many of the new houses of the age, just as the citizens' dowries provided their temporal base. Christina won through to be foundress of Markyate Priory; and she inspired not only her remarkable biography, but the St Albans Psalter, one of the notable works of art of the age. Her parents were decent and worthy people, but they thought it quite out of the question that Christina should choose for herself: her vocation could only, in their eyes, be a childish fancy. The story of her struggle against her parents, of how she spent her wedding night converting her husband to her point of view, and of how, even so, she still had to face stiff opposition and the attempts of one of her spiritual advisers to seduce her, show quite starkly the difficulties encountered by young women who

277-84 Las Huelgas, near Burgos. The Fontevrault of Spain: here in 1187 Eleanor, daughter of Eleanor of Aquitaine and Henry II of England, and her husband King Alfonso VIII, founded a convent of Cistercian nuns, to be also a royal mausoleum.

277 Most of the church was built *c.*1220-30 and later; the porch and tower are also of the thirteenth century.

278 In the nave, which was used as the nuns' choir, the mausoleum of the founders and their family. In the centre, the founders' tombs, with the arms of Castile and England. Screen and tapestries are sixteenth century.

279 *Overleaf, left* The later Gothic Crucifix is a characteristic expression of Spanish religious sentiment.

280 *Overleaf, right* Thirteenth-century sarcophagus in the porch.

277

278

281 Las Huelgas, tomb, probably of Prince Fernando (d. 1275). It was hidden by a hanging when Napoleon's troops sacked the church.

282 Las Huelgas. Here an Islamic door sits in a thirteenth-century Christian arch.

283 Las Huelgas. In twelfth- and thirteenth-century Spain, Christian and Moslem still lived side by side; religious persecution only became severe in the fifteenth century. In the chapel of the Assumption a soul is carried to heaven above arches of distinctively Islamic form, of *c.*1200.

284. Las Huelgas. A beautiful thirteenth-century ceiling of Mudejar work, showing peacocks surrounded by Arabic inscriptions.

282

wished to choose their own way of life. One of the deepest of medieval prejudices was the view that women were incapable of conducting their own affairs, and must be protected from the dangers and temptations of the world—or else they would themselves rapidly become part of those dangers and temptations. Even so original and imaginative a religious founder as Francis of Assisi accepted this view; not perhaps with complete consistency, for he allowed Jacoba of Settesoli to bring him marzipan as he lay dying though women were not permitted in Franciscan convents. But 'Brother' Jacoba was

283

284

allowed to be an exception; the normal rule applied even to St Clare herself, and so the Franciscan nuns were enclosed as strictly as any religious, in contrast to the male Franciscans whose function was to wander (see p. 192).

Yet the powerful urge to the religious life evident among the ladies who flocked to St Norbert, and among the nuns who

sought to be Cistercian was not without influence. In the thirteenth century great numbers of new houses were founded, mostly Cistercian, especially in Germany and the Low Countries. Here they found a patron and helper in the abbot of Villers, the chief Cistercian house in what is now Belgium, who directed and encouraged the Cistercian nuns as they no doubt hoped and wished to be helped elsewhere too. The establishment of convents was only one segment in the religious movement for women of the age, which also witnessed the formation of the informal groups of Beguines, ladies dedicated to a religious life but without any elaborate rule of permanent vows, who flourished first in Liège and Flanders, then in Cologne and the Rhineland, and ultimately throughout the north of Europe in the thirteenth and four-

285

286

287

288

285-8 Villers-la-Ville, Belgium. A Cistercian house founded in 1146, which flourished in the time of Abbot William, patron of the Cistercian nuns, in the mid thirteenth century. To this period belong the refectory (285); the church (286) looking north east; the transept (287); and the kitchen (288). They are early Gothic, but still Cistercian in inspiration and sentiment.

teenth centuries. Thus for the women, the thirteenth century saw the largest number of new foundations, and worthy successors to Heloise and Hildegarde in St Elizabeth of Schönau and the Blessed Agnes of Bohemia. Yet the movement never had the same impact in France and England as in Germany and the Low Countries; and in Spain, although a few houses, like Las Huelgas, were large and influential, they were much less numerous. Elsewhere, the glimpses we can

289

290

289-90 The life of nuns, from a French manuscript of *c*.1300.

289 God the Trinity, with angels and saints—the Blessed Virgin, St Peter and the symbols of the evangelists—gives his blessing to the nuns' way of life. Below on the left, two novices are instructed, under divine blessing.

290 The superior and the nuns attend high mass celebrated by their chaplains, and (below) walk in procession singing hymns. British Museum, Add. MS 39, 843, ff.1v, 6v.

obtain of the life of nuns in the late Middle Ages suggest domestic comfort or discomfort rather than any deep penetration of a religious movement among women. Yet religion was not entirely cold in the fourteenth century—the age of St Bridget of Sweden, founder of the Bridgettines, and St Catherine of Siena, recluse and hammer of the popes—and it was to enjoy a mighty revival in the sixteenth, in the days of St Teresa.

Epilogue

In conclusion, to set beside Fontevrault and Essen, we have chosen a small house which may be inspected in domestic comfort; a house of no great size, yet not poor; a house not founded until the thirteenth century, whose buildings range in date all over the late Middle Ages; a good setting, that is, for one of the most famous of medieval nuns, Chaucer's prioress. Of the history of Lacock we know little. It was founded by Ela, countess of Salisbury, in 1232. She seems to have wished it to be Cistercian, but in the event it became a community of Augustinian canonesses. It was moderately well endowed; it suffered no great scandals. It escaped the poverty into which some houses fell in the late Middle Ages through the drying up of dowries or by sheer mismanagement. The cloister was largely rebuilt in the fifteenth century, which reveals that there was still a flow of funds, and that the nuns still lived and worked in the main monastic buildings. In 1535-6 there were still fifteen nuns—there had perhaps been twice that number in the thirteenth century—four chaplains, and nearly forty servants. At the Dissolution in 1539 the buildings were in such

291

291-4 **Lacock, England.** This home for a community of Augustinian nuns or canonesses was founded in 1232, and converted into a country house by Sir William Sharington, a courtier of Henry VIII's time, after the dissolution; and thus it was in part preserved. The church was demolished, but more useful parts of the building were kept, including the sacristy of *c*.1232-8, with two chapels in it: note the piscina by the door once leading to the church (291).

296

297

298

in the long run his order of canons regular differed little from monks. Norbert himself, meanwhile, was able—rather briefly, since he died in 1134—to deploy his exceptional gift as a missionary and inspiration of missionaries in the area of eastern Germany and beyond where German settlers and Slavs met and mingled. His presence ensured that Premonstratensian canons and Cistercian monks played a leading part in German settlement in the east.

The apostolic life in the twelfth and thirteenth centuries
It could be said that the most powerful evidence of St Bernard's impact on the twelfth-century scene was a negative one. The most curious fact about the orders of the twelfth century is how very monastic they were: all save the knights settled down

299

296 Ratzeburg Cathedral.

297 The interior, looking east.

298 The cloister.

299 The south porch of *c.*1215, with interesting glazed bricks.

eventually within their cloisters. This is all the stranger because many of their founders were men of missionary urge. Thus Robert of Arbrissel remained a popular preacher to the end of his days, even when under the rule of the Blessed Virgin and the Abbess Petronilla. Indeed we may suppose that his promise to obey her had about as much effect as St Francis's

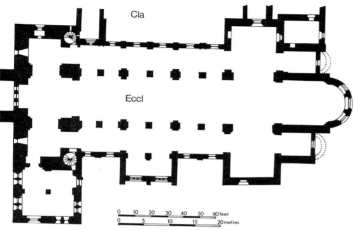

Fig. 21

300

Fig.21 Plan of Ratzeburg Cathedral; the original shape of the small apses is known from excavation.

300 Ratzeburg Cathedral, inscribed tombstone of Bishop Volrad von Doren, d.1355, formerly a canon.

301-2 Dryburgh, Scotland. A Premonstratensian abbey standing in a corner of the River Tweed.

301 Looking across the transept to the night stairs leading up to the canons' dormitory.

promise to obey the beasts of the field. But the point is that it was made.

It was natural enough that beside a cauldron in which so many new flavours of religion were cooking, there should be controversies both gentlemanly and bitter between the devotees of rival tastes. There were secular clerks who denounced all monkcraft, monks who replied in kind;[1] all manner of men interpreted and reinterpreted the apostolic life from which it was all supposed to come. For a long time, the free range of opinion on how the apostolic life should be imitated was checked by the prestige of the monastic vows.

301

A place was found for laymen living in the world—and in the long run for groups of married penitents—within the spectrum of the religious life; but in the early twelfth century movements of this kind usually ended in some kind of orthodox monasticism—or else in heresy.[2]

After Bernard, the most inspiring figure in this world in the early twelfth century was Norbert of Xanten; and when he gathered penitents and clergy around him and set them to follow a way of life which was ascetic and apostolic, he himself clearly continued to feel a strong call to be a missionary. Yet the order which he founded soon became almost indistinguishable from the Cistercian. He was a personal friend of Bernard, and deeply influenced by him; one cannot but think that the disciples of Norbert who converted his inspira-

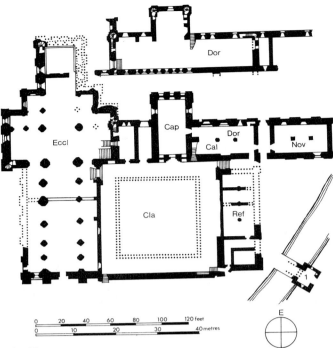

Fig. 22

Fig.22 Plan of Dryburgh, showing the medieval buildings. Most of those which survive are twelfth to thirteenth centuries. The west end of the church and the gatehouse (1) are fifteenth.

302 Dryburgh. A fine Norman door leads from the cloister to the church, whose transepts and choir are late twelfth and early thirteenth centuries. The nave is of *c.*1400.

302

tion into institutional form were even more influenced by the Cistercians. It seems exceedingly paradoxical that Norbert, of all these founders the most devoted to practical ends, should have founded an order which became enclosed, austere and remote. Some of the German houses still show their relation to the extensive new settlements in Germany east of the Elbe characteristic of the *Drang nach Osten* of the twelfth and the thirteenth centuries. The remoteness of a house like Blanchland, hiding in a little valley amid desolate moors just to the south of the border of Scotland, or the beauty of Dryburgh, a little to its north, perched in an angle of a great river, surrounded by splendid trees and water, tell us still that Norbert and Bernard were friends.

Yet in its own context all this is quite intelligible. Bernard preached stability, put down practical good works, built large walls round his enclosures, and himself wandered about outside, answered almost every call to practical action which came. Norbert felt the austere authority of the Cistercian life, and wished to follow it; the inspiration of the world in which he lived led him to Cîteaux and Clairvaux. He felt too, as an intellectual deeply read in the ancient and modern literature on the Christian life, that the rule of St Augustine was more apostolic, more biblical, than St Benedict's. Meditation on the life of the apostles led him to Augustine, to practical good works, to the mission field.

In spite of the prestige of Bernard and his ideal, the view that the apostolic life should still involve practical aid to ordinary Christian folk, and missionary work within and without Christendom, retained its strength throughout the twelfth century. From time to time little groups of penitents or wanderers gathered into a community; poverty and good works were their aim, or else they wished to live mainly withdrawn from the world. There was much diversity. Many of them developed into communities of monks and canons; one— the followers of the English St Gilbert of Sempringham, like Norbert, an admirer of St Bernard this side idolatry[3]—formed an order of nuns and canons, living in double houses though carefully segregated. As time went on, and the world became richer, reaction against growing interest in material goods led to a sharper emphasis on poverty. The merchant of Lyons, Waldo, who reacted against his own desire for wealth and formed a community of poor preachers in the late 1170s, was at first accepted by the pope on condition of swearing, among other things, that he did not believe all the rich to be in hell. Presently he passed beyond the pope's ken, and became the founder of the Waldensian Church; and many of these groups became 'heretics' in the mid and late twelfth century. The consequence was that orthodox hierarchs—especially the group of stern Cistercian bishops whom the popes placed in and around Narbonne to reform the church and stave off heresy—regarded all such poor wanderers as potential heretics.

Thus was Christendom making ready for St Francis; or rather, one is bound to say, staving off the time when he should come. The prestige of the cloister, and the fear of heresy, were both very powerful at the turn of the twelfth and thirteenth centuries. They go a fair way to explain why the friars started no earlier than they did—though some of these earlier groups were not heretical and were almost indistinguishable from the friars in their way of life.

303-20, 326 Assisi, Italy, and St Francis

303 The friars' cemetery, with arcading of the late fifteenth century.

304 *Overleaf* Assisi from the west, with the Sacro Convento and the basilica in the foreground. The Basilica looks like a fortress to protect the saint and his city.

303

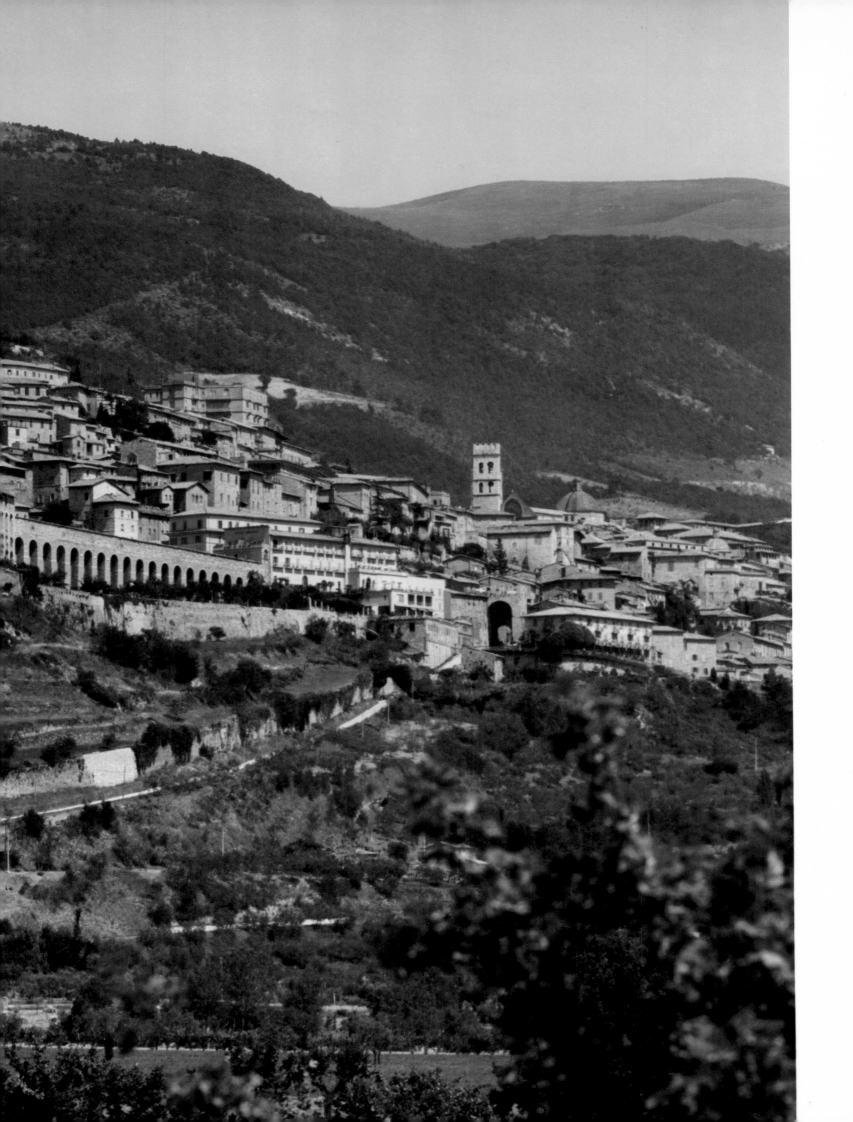

307

307 Assisi, the Basilica of St Francis by night. It commemorates the death of Francis on the night of 3-4 October 1226; it was mostly built by Brother Elias, 1228-39.

world in which they grew up, and yet showed all the more clearly for that certain striking marks of originality.

Francis and Dominic were very unlike one another. Dominic, the Spaniard, grew up an earnest, conventional Augustinian canon with a strong urge to preach, and an even stronger urge to obey his superiors. This led him to years of work in the most discouraging mission field of the day, among the Cathar heretics in the south of France. He formed a group of fellow-workers in Toulouse; he took steps to have it recognised as an order. But in 1215 Pope Innocent III had presided over the Fourth Lateran Council, and had been compelled to allow the fathers of the council to pass a decree forbidding new orders—or rather, as the clause was interpreted by the curial officials, new Rules. Ironically, this deflected Dominic hardly at all: he took the Rule of St Augustine, to which he was already professed, as his base, and its alluring vagueness once more served a religious movement well. But a much more powerful influence completely altered the whole frame of his intentions. He suddenly abandoned Toulouse, turned his back on the heretics, spread his order (all sixteen of them) throughout Christendom, and began to organise a missionary, peripatetic movement; in short, he made them friars. I have little doubt that the bouleversement was in a measure due to meeting St Francis.[4]

308 Assisi, the Upper Church by day. The western end of the city was reconstructed to provide for a great monastery and Basilica.

Assisi, Italy, San Damiano. Francis's first task after his conversion was to restore the poorest churches of the neighbourhood. San Damiano was one of the first homes of Francis and his companions, and was later handed over to St Clare.

309 The cloister.

310 The west front.

311 The oratory.

The apostolic life had always grown from fresh meditation on the Gospels; and it is no chance therefore that it should be the direct imprint on his mind and imagination of a passage from St Matthew heard one morning in the Gospel at mass that directed Francis's thought and life. 'As you go proclaim the message: "The kingdom of Heaven is upon you." . . . Give without charge. Provide no gold, silver or copper to fill your purse, no pack for the road . . . ; the worker earns his keep.' He felt called, as by God's direct inspiration—'the Lord Himself revealed to me' how to live and form an order of men living and working in the world. Francis was naturally fastidious, he had a dislike of beggars, a horror of lepers. He taught himself to conquer this, but their lot remained one of the central facts of his view of life. Why had the apostles been sent

312

313

314

312, 314 Assisi, the Sacro Convento, the Gothic gallery, part of the additions made by Cardinal Albornoz, who ruled the papal states for the Avignon popes in the mid fourteenth century.

313 Assisi, the large cloister of the Sacro Convento, built by Pope Sixtus IV in the fifteenth century.

315 Assisi, the rose window of the Upper Church.

out poorly dressed and even more poorly provided? On this question learned men were to write many treatises in the thirteenth and fourteenth centuries. To Francis it seemed obviously to answer a fact of experience: to help the poor to find Christ's path in their grim existence one must be as poor as they; only so could one hope to show them by example that poverty was a holy thing, even an exciting thing. He was a teacher of genius, yet always reckoned example far in advance of precept: he recruited all manner of different kinds of folk, and expected only a small minority to be able formally to preach; example was the basis of his way of life, and when called on to preach to the college of cardinals he danced a jig to show them how God's love should be conveyed. In the long run, indeed, he embraced every walk of life in his 'religion'— celibate friars formed the First Order, nuns strictly enclosed his Second—for even Francis could not countenance wandering women as a religious order—and married folk living according to a simple rule of life the Third Order, the Tertiaries.

The life of the friars itself showed an equally catholic appreciation of the traditions Francis had inherited. We can see this in the churches in Assisi in which he still lives: in the tiny chapel in the Portiuncula, so long as we can shut our eyes to the later church which surrounds it, in San Damiano without the walls, in the Carceri, high on the hillside above the town, and in his own shrine, the magnificent Basilica which stands at the city's edge. St Dominic's monument is in Bologna, but in quite a different sense. It stands in the city to which the ageing *déraciné* founder came to renew his own and his order's youth by recruiting among the university students. Bologna and Paris were his headquarters. Francis

306, 3
304

had originally spread his activity more widely than Dominic, and he accepted no frontiers. He himself travelled to Egypt to visit the sultan, and throughout Italy, visiting Rome on several occasions. But from time to time he came back to Assisi, which was always the centre of his life; and they brought him to Assisi to die.

The Carceri is an enchanted place, where the Peter Damian of the fifteenth century, San Bernardino, founder of the Observant Franciscans, restored the ancient home of Francis and his closest companions. Their cells may still be seen and visited, each with a traditional attribution to one of the well-known names—Francis, Leo, Rufino and Masseo. 'Those who wish to lead the religious life in hermitages', said the saint in one of his writings, 'let them go in threes and fours at most. Let two of them be the mothers and have two sons or one at least each; let the former lead the life of Martha, the latter of Mary'.[5] This is most characteristic: first in expression, for everything Francis wrote was succinct, simple and yet subtle; second for its doctrine, since this most gregarious of religious founders loved and cultivated the hermit life as well. The spirit of the Italian anchorite movement lives at the Carceri, and one of Francis's strongest temptations was to stay there for good. He often felt the call to be Mary himself, and sit at Christ's feet, and never underestimated the value of this call in others. When considering what this or that

316 Assisi, the Carceri (see pl.306).

317 Assisi, the soaring French Gothic of the Upper Church.

318 The west end of the Lower Church, added mid to late thirteenth century.

319 Assisi, the vault of the Lower Church with the Allegory of Chastity, school of Giotto. The frescoes in the basilica were painted in the late thirteenth and early/mid fourteenth centuries by Cimabue, Pietro and Ambrogio Lorenzetti and others; the extent to which Giotto was himself involved is much disputed (see pl.326).

316

317

318

319

friar should do, he always faced the problem as a human and personal one; not as an administrator planning a scheme of work, but as a director considering with sympathy and subtlety what was best for an individual soul. Looking back, it must seem to us now that he sometimes preached and practised a sublime anarchy; and he showed his attitude to the administrator's lot by writing to one much bothered by the importunities of some of the friars: 'and show your love for them by *not* wishing them better Christians'![6] Yet Francis the spiritual adviser and hermit also felt a very powerful call to preach, and to prepare his friars to work in the towns of Umbria and the world.

309-11 And so we go down with him to the convent not far from the city gates; to San Damiano, where he lived in the early days of his conversion. It then became for a time the home of the nuns, of St Clare and her early companions, but it still gives a living idea of the way of life of the early friars once the order began to grow. But what shall we say of the Basilica? Here is a splendid building, made famous by the frescoes which encrust its walls. Many a devotee, from early days down to the present, has denounced its magnificence: a rich monument to the apostle of poverty is either a sublime paradox or a scandal.

305, 307
5, 317-20

'One day while St Francis was lying ill at the bishop's palace at Assisi, one of the friars who was pious and saintly said to him joking and teasing: "For how much will you sell all your sackcloth to the Lord? Many rich brocades and silken cloths will be put on to cover this little body of yours which is now dressed in sackcloth". For St Francis had at that time a leather bandage because of his illness, which was covered with sackcloth, and a habit of sackcloth. St Francis replied, not himself, but the Holy Spirit through him, with great fervour of spirit and gladness: "You say true, for so it will be".'[7]

But Francis's vision was of paradise, not of the Basilica of San Francesco.

When he was dying, the citizens of Assisi sent soldiers to guard him and bring him home; for they knew that when he died his body would become a collection of relics of infinite value, and that all the cities of the neighbourhood would try to seize him. So after his death they hid his body in the rock, in the lowest level of a tremendous church in three storeys; and they set about it a large convent, so that the final effect is of a fortress looking defiantly out towards Perugia, the greatest of Assisi's rivals, in whose prisons Francis himself had once spent some unhappy months. He would have preferred to be buried without fuss at the Portiuncula, yet the grandeur of his shrine is not wholly inappropriate. For all his love of simplicity and humility, Francis recognised that he was the centre of a personality cult, and welcomed the fact.

If Dominic turned his missionary canons into friars in imitation of Francis he showed by almost all his other dispositions a shrewd appraisal of the difficulties which the Franciscans must encounter. He wished his order to be a

321

320 Assisi, Cimabue's St Francis from the Lower Church. Francis had a special devotion to the human Jesus: he made popular the Christmas crib, and towards the end of his life received the impress of Jesus's wounds, the stigmata. Here Cimabue imagines Francis, with the stigmata, in the presence of the Virgin and Child.

321 Fra Angelico, Coronation of the Virgin, Florence, San Marco.
The Saints are thought to be St Thomas Aquinas, St Benedict, St Dominic, St Francis, St Peter Martyr and St Mark, and they make a fashion parade of the religious habits of the fifteenth century: three Dominicans, one Benedictine, one Franciscan—St Mark's costume is perhaps that of a hermit.

320

collection of trained and disciplined preachers, drawn from a select class—the aspiring university students, chosen not for their learning, but because to be a student in the incipient universities of the day, one had to combine sound education and a love of adventure. In place of the loose-knit structure of the Franciscan Order—always in ferment, always in crisis— he began, and his successor Brother Jordan of Saxony completed, the erection of an orderly structure of committees. Francis made his own inspiration and example the standard, the stabilising point of his order: Dominic hid his own personality, and is indeed as a man, compared to Francis, still comparatively obscure. In its place he set a framework for development and discussion from which an order which did not depend on the divine spark in a single breast could grow. It was extraordinarily successful, and compels our admiration, even if we feel at best a doubtful gratitude to the apostle of committee government. Thus two contrasting personalities combined to bring to birth the apostolic order from which the twelfth-century founders had so often turned away; and in this story the personality of Dominic is as crucial as that of Francis, for each contributed to the other's success, and when the founders were gone the two orders were free to grow more like one another, even if in the process they sometimes drew away from the intention of both their founders.

Near the outset of our quest we observed the humility of St Benedict, who clothed his ideas of the monastic life very largely in another's words. In a similar way the basis of the Dominican way of life was taken by St Dominic from two previous rules. His order was founded on the Rule of St Augustine. The regulations which Dominic drafted for the daily round within the convents of his order were adapted from those of Prémontré, which themselves owed much to Cîteaux. Thus the ascetic, monastic traditions of the twelfth century still lived and reigned; but a clear limit was set to their kingdom. For the Dominican constitutions were at all points adapted to suit the practical needs of an Order of Preachers.

In two ways the friars were in evident contrast to monks and canons as they were in the early thirteenth century: it was their specific task to wander, to preach or to set an example in the secular world; and they were beggars, seen to live wholly on such alms as they could collect. Monks and canons could take round the begging bowl, and many a building was partly financed by a begging tour undertaken by a group of religious and the relics of the saint whose church was about to be rebuilt. But the friars lived wholly by begging: they had no property.[8] They were and are the Mendicant Orders. The abuses to which this could lead have been made notorious by Chaucer's portrait of a friar in his Prologue, perhaps the most cruel of all his gallery. The satire presupposes that it was well known that such abuses could exist; it is always a mistake to judge any order solely by its ideals and its saints. But if all friars were like the princely beggar of Chaucer's imagination the joke would fail and the satire become a bore. It is equally false to judge a religious movement by its notorious failures. Few men have enriched the world more evidently than Francis and Dominic.

Yet that is not quite the last word; for our present concern is especially with their relations with the monastic orders. The friars provided a calling for those who wished to wander and preach as well as to lead a regular life; they were for a century or more leaders in the avant-garde religious movement of the age. They stole the initiative which the Cistercians had enjoyed in the twelfth century. The monastic orders were never quite the same in the later Middle Ages. They survived; they kept a way of life in being; here and there appeared local revivals of exceptional fervour. In the sixteenth and seventeenth centuries, and again in the nineteenth, more general renewals changed the nature of the religious orders as the friars had done in the thirteenth. But the orders of monks and canons have never since held the place in Christendom they enjoyed in the heyday of St Bernard and the Cistercian movement in the middle of the twelfth century.

part 3
Gathering the threads

13 Three visits

I Fountains

We have traced the history of the religious life from the New Testament to the thirteenth century. As we draw the threads together, the first and most challenging question which faces us is: can we fit our narrative together with the visible remains of medieval monasteries? Can we draw 'oil from the hardest stone' and make these buildings reveal their story? If not, the attempt to weave together text and pictures has failed. This is a real challenge, and it would be wrong to answer it lightly; and the answer lies in the reader's mind and imagination. Yet something may yet be suggested by taking a variety of samples rich both in history and in remains, which can show us in depth the sort of answers we can hope for. It is for this that we set off to explore three of the most evocative monastic sites in Europe.

Fountains Abbey in Yorkshire sits at the end of a fair lawn, framed by the wooded banks of a narrow vale, set off by a chattering stream: the greatest of eighteenth-century follies or, to see it another way, a thoroughly functional monument of twelfth-century Europe. Here is a strange alliance between the most practical aspect of the twelfth-century renaissance and the most romantic aspect of the Gothic spirit of the eighteenth century; a piquant contrast, which stirs the mind and the imagination, and urges us to ask many questions about its history.[1]

At first sight, the comparison between the two ages which conspired to give us Fountains Abbey as we know it seems nothing more than an intriguing contradiction. The Cistercian monks who built the abbey in the twelfth century chose the site because it was comparatively remote from towns and villages, and they wanted to be alone; they chose the valley because it provided the two things they most needed: a convenient flat space on which a great complex of buildings could be constructed, and plentiful running water to fill their wash-basins, to flush their drains and turn their mill-wheels. They built a large abbey, solid, commodious and practical;

322-5, 330-2 Fountains

322 The abbey church: the heavy plain nave arcade, with pointed arches and round-headed windows.

323 'Fountains Abbey, from the Lake' by J. or J.C. Buckler, c.1818-20. showing the setting created for the abbey by the younger Aislabie (owner from 1768 to 1781) and his successors, British Museum, Add. MS 36, 394, f.42.

323

322

325

324 Fountains, the Chapel of the Nine Altars, a lofty addition of the first half of the thirteenth century.

325 Fountains, looking from the nave to the east window.

but neither comfortable nor ornamental—save for the mid thirteenth-century Chapel of the Nine Altars at the east end of the church and the fine sixteenth-century tower. The rest of the buildings are mainly of the twelfth and early thirteenth centuries, a striking monument to the efficiency of the Cistercian architects of the order's early generations.

In contrast, it is the well kept lawns and the trees which give the scene its romantic charm, and these are of the eighteenth century; so far as we know, the valley was only modestly wooded in the Middle Ages; and the park to which it is appended was pasture and grazing land. The eighteenth-century landlords beautified the European landscape and added something of permanent value to our civilization. In the late twentieth century, when so much of what they created is in danger of destruction, we are learning to value their creative appreciation that produced this beauty of landscape of a special kind—owing as much to man's improvements as to nature's raw deposit. There was another side to their work, however, for they sometimes treated the human inhabitants of their landscape as cavalierly as its natural lineaments. Many a contemporary and many a modern historian has commented on the activities of eighteenth-century improving landlords, who enclosed fields and laid out parks, something as follows:

'They proceed to raze villages and churches, turn out parishioners . . . level everything before the ploughshare, so that if you looked on a place that you knew previously you could say, "and grass now grows where Troy town stood".'

But these actual words come from the pen of a twelfth-century satirist writing about the Cistercians; and although the tone is that of satire, not cool appraisal, the basic facts have been shown to be true. ' . . . It is prescribed to them that they are to dwell in desert places, and desert places they do assuredly either find or make. . . .'[2] Walter Map wrote, it must be admitted, with the freedom of the satirist who does not really expect his satire to be read—nor was it read till the nineteenth century—and some of his cruder charges cannot be checked. However it is now clear that the Cistercians not only insisted that their founders give them sites and fields untrammelled

VEIPEDEMROSVSCALCATDOLENTE

VLTIMADSEVIDETVENTENTE

VIIOCTAVODIEORDINATVREPS

VISVEALTAREDORMIENSTVRONIAMETE

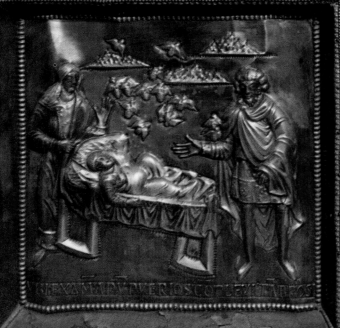

EXAMIDVTVERIOSCOTELLEARBOS

DEAROSSEMILLAPETITAGLICVR

house, giving the monks direct access to the church.

A part of the buildings had to be rebuilt after a raid by the abbey's enemies in 1147, and the bulk of what one sees today dates from the period 1150-1250. So solid and substantial was the building effort of that period that most of it never needed to be redone; nor may it have been easy to afford major changes in the fabric in later times. Fountains had numerous granges and extensive properties, especially sheep runs, yet it was never comparable in resources to the ancient royal foundations, like Glastonbury and St Albans. For two centuries at least its community was substantially larger than theirs, while its revenues remained considerably lower; and after the great building period it may not have found offerings and alms for the fabric so readily available. Thus only two substantial changes took place later: the reconstruction, on a far larger scale than before, of the abbot's house and infirmary, mostly in the fourteenth century; and the building of the handsome bell tower, in defiance of earlier Cistercian custom, by Abbot Huby in the early sixteenth century. Many changes were made in the abbey's furnishings in the later Middle Ages, but these have disappeared, leaving the abbey ruins essentially a monument to the Cistercian model as it had been in the twelfth and early thirteenth centuries.

It has often been disputed in recent years whether the Cistercian model was something essentially new; how original the order was; how great was the break with traditional monasticism? This is a question Fountains can help us to answer: documents and ruins are in perfect accord. The documents have been subjected recently to ruthless criticism, and the romantic story of the flight from St Mary's Abbey, York, the painful winter sojourn under the rough shelter of a great elm tree, is now threatened with demolition.[6] But no one doubts that the story begins in York, in an abbey built deliberately to combine the finest monastic inspiration of the late eleventh century in northern England with the other most notable type of community of the age, the rising town. Essentially, St Mary's York represented traditional monastic ideals into which some new ideas had infiltrated.

After a generation a group among the monks were unsettled by the passage through their midst of English disciples of St Bernard on their way to found the first of the major Cistercian houses in the north, the abbey of Rievaulx, in 1131-2. Next year they presented reforming proposals to their ageing abbot, Geoffrey; and it seems that it was his incapacity to handle the human problem involved in a divided community which precipitated the real crisis. The archbishop of York, Thurstan of Bayeux, came to make some inquiries, and the result was a riot, from which the archbishop narrowly escaped without a beating, carrying off the reformers with him. Presently a few melted back to St Mary's, and for some months the rest lived on the archbishop's hospitality and wondered what to do. Eventually they decided to join the Cistercian Order. They were settled at Fountains, on the archbishop's

330

331

estates; and Bernard sent one of his monks, Geoffrey of Clairvaux, to complete the transformation into a Cistercian abbey. From this group came some of the most distinguished Cistercian leaders of the middle of the century. In some respects their careers and actions reveal that they thought their world very different from the traditional world of St Mary's, York; but they had hesitated for some months, perhaps for a year or two, before joining the Cistercians, demonstrating (as has recently been observed)[7] that they were not in the first instance aware that the Cistercian challenge could not be fully met within the precincts of an older house.

Similarly in the buildings: there are plenty of elements which Fountains, along with virtually all Cistercian houses of the

329 Mont Saint-Michel: St Michael's view from the choir roof, looking north east, across the Merveille to the estuary of the Sée and the Norman coastline.

Fountains 330 The monastic buildings: the west front, showing the long line of the lay brothers' quarters running from the church, and, across the lawn, the guest-house. 331 The lay brothers' quarters within: the largest Cistercian range surviving in England.

day, shared with traditional abbeys. The basic model—the large and stately church; the cloister garth and walks forming the centre for the monks' domestic life; the common rooms for day and night, chapter house, refectory, parlours, dormitory—all are essentially in the same situation in Benedictine and Cistercian houses, or in those of other orders. Some peculiar features all Cistercian houses show: an unusual measure of uniformity, and a large wing devoted to housing the lay brothers. But it is in the style and fashion of the building that the contrast shows most clearly, and must indeed have been far clearer in the twelfth century than now, for they always avoided rich sculpture, sumptuous paintings, stained glass, shrines, grandiose vistas. Plain glass made them far lighter than most churches, plain or whitewashed walls made them far duller; even the proportions were deliberately lumpish. Thus the buildings, like the documents, enforce what at first sight seems mere confusion: the Cistercians were at once very much like and utterly unlike the other monastic communities. Yet this is as true to human nature and human experience as it is tiresome to tidy minds, and it is reflected in the personal tastes and friendships of many eminent monks. Among the leaders and the rank and file of monasteries old and new were many who engaged in controversy; but even more who made close and lasting friendships. The man who made possible the founding of Fountains, Archbishop Thurstan, thus became a notable patron of the Cistercians; he died a Cluniac, at Pontefract Priory. He was also, it may be noted, sprung from old corruption in the shape of being the offspring of a married canon of St Paul's; from a similar dynasty in the north came the greatest of the English Cistercians, St Ailred of Rievaulx, and Ailred's friends included the eminent Cluniac Gilbert Foliot, bishop of Hereford and London (1148-87), who counted other Cistercians among his closest friends, and one of whose nearest relatives died clothed in a Cistercian habit.

An academic cannot fail to notice the analogy with some modern universities and colleges. From within, the differences may appear profound, and be the subject of much keen observation. To the outsider the same institutions may seem utterly indistinguishable; and if he has penetrated into them, bewildering as well, for the mark of some modern academic communities is a strange combination of a spirit humane and liberal and cosmopolitan, with a spirit sometimes almost equally narrow, parochial and intolerant. It was the same with the medieval religious orders, and it is this which gives them a special fascination, if we have the patience to sit amid the ruins and look closely at the stones; and to read both the stones and the books.

II Mont Saint-Michel

The famous house of Mont Saint-Michel, of 'St Michael in peril of the sea', commands our attention first of all because it successfully withstood the assaults of men and of the elements for many centuries. Its foundation[8] in 708 represented the first peak in the cult of the militant archangel; it only ceased to be an abbey at the French Revolution.[9]

The cult of St Michael showed its first bloom in the seventh and eighth centuries, then flowered as never before or since in the eleventh and twelfth. Its chief centre in western Christendom has always been Monte Gargano in Italy, but many a hill top was adorned in the Middle Ages with a chapel or a shrine dedicated to the archangel. In 708, according to an

332

333

332 Fountains. A large drain runs beneath the monks' latrines; beyond, the refectory and lay brothers' quarters also make use of the conduits, and drains run from and to the river.

333 Fountains Hall, the early seventeenth-century house built by Sir Stephen Proctor, with stone quarried from the monastic ruins.

early legend probably with an authentic base, St Aubert, bishop of Avranches, translated relics—whatever they may have been—from Monte Gargano to the spectacular small hillock of rock which juts into the sea where Brittany and Normandy meet. Doubtless it was in early days the spirit of Breton or Celtic monasticism which reigned on the mount, and we may suppose it the home of a small group of hermits, at most, living in a cell or group of cells round the chapel on the peak, surrounded by the sea and the sea-birds like their brethren on and off the west coast of Ireland. But in the ninth and tenth centuries the diocese of Avranches became part of the new Viking, Norman principality, first pagan, then re-converted under new influences. Pilgrims continued to flow to the mount, and the Vikings brought trade; thus in the tenth century there grew up a small town with its centre in the little church whose nave survives now within the crypt—the oldest part of the present monastic buildings (see pp. 258-9). In 966 Duke Richard I converted this church into an abbey, bringing monks from Saint-Wandrille. Of its early history we know little until, at the beginning of the eleventh century, it joined the main stream of Norman monasticism, was put under the custody of St William of Volpiano, and became one of the notable centres of the flourishing monastic world of eleventh-century Normandy (see pp. 51-2). The transepts and their crypts, and a part of the nave, show clearly that it flourished in the early eleventh century—are indeed among the earliest monuments of eleventh-century Norman monasticism to survive. In the temporal sphere the abbey undoubtedly flourished; like the seafaring community which nestled at its feet, it took to the sea,[10] received rich endowments in Jersey, and, after the Norman Conquest, in England. These included, most appropriately, the Cornish St Michael's Mount, the nearest equivalent in Celtic Britain to the Mount itself.

Abbot and monks must often have been in peril of the sea, but their own needs combined with the fame of their church as a pilgrim centre to keep them perched on their narrow platform of rock. The site of the abbey of Le Mont Saint-Michel is a dramatic illustration of the triumph of religion

329, 334-50 Le Mont Saint-Michel, France

334 The abbey from the south: to the right, the east, the little town at its feet and the causeway.

335 From the north east.

334

335

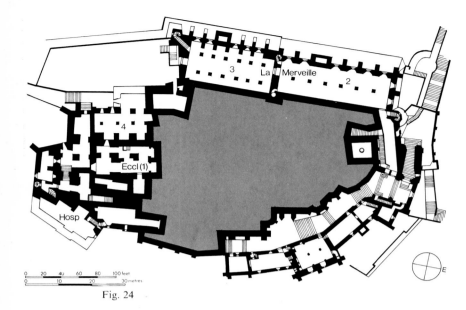

Fig. 24

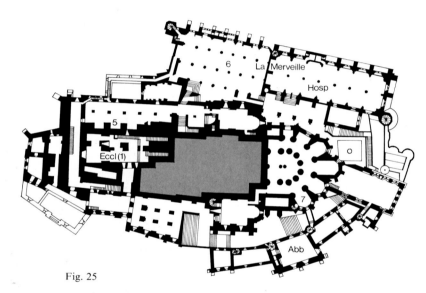

Fig. 25

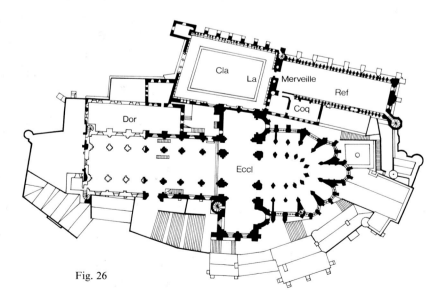

Fig. 26

Figs.24-6 Plans of Mont Saint-Michel, at low, middle and high levels,
as in c.1500. 1. The ancient church, 'Notre Dame sous terre'. 2. Almonry.
3. Cellar. 4. Old Almonry, Salle de l'Aquilon. 5. Monks' parlour or
promenoir. 6. Calefactory, later Salle des Chevaliers.

over common sense. One can scarcely imagine a more awkward
situation for the two expressions of medieval communal
living—town and monastery.

The town still bears witness to the close links between
monastic life and secular society, even in so isolated a place.
The way these links worked is more precisely revealed in the
monastery itself. As the great church occupied the whole of
the top of the little hill, the monastic buildings had to perch
precariously on its cliff-like sides. Thus a series of two- or
three-storey buildings set one on top of another contain the
elements of the monastic complex normally spread out over
a level plain; and the way order came out of the disorder of
the scene is fascinating to observe. To the north lies the sea,   334-5
separated from the monastery by a small wood and steep
slope. Here between the sea and the solid bulk of the church
on the summit of the hill lay the monastic buildings, as secluded
as the site allowed from the human throng, from all distractions
save the sound of the gulls and the waves. To the south, between the church and the town, lay the abbot's lodgings, the
buildings of the lord of Mont Saint-Michel, where the head
of the community met important visitors and the leading townsfolk. The main staircase still leads up from the town between
the abbot and his church, crossed by a charming fifteenth-
century bridge. Here in the late twelfth century the historian
abbot, Robert of Torigny, recorded in his chronicle the history
of Normandy, and incidentally of his abbey, and added to
the abbey's cartulary a register of the charters of his own
abbacy.[11]

The monks' quarters north of the church lie in two complexes, the smaller of the eleventh and twelfth centuries, the
larger, 'La Merveille', of the thirteenth. La Merveille includes   342-50
some of the most beautiful monastic buildings in Europe,
but the first thing we must say about it is that it hides and
disguises the original layout of the cloister of earlier times.
The smaller group consists of the old almonry, where the poor
were fed and humbler guests received in the Salle de l'Aquilon,   339
the monks' parlour (with the old kitchen and refectory) and
the monks' dormitory (or as some think their chapter house)
on the two floors above. Thus from the original entrance one
proceeds from the most to the least public rooms in the house.

Behind the old almonry lies the remnant of the tenth-
century church, now a crypt dedicated to the Blessed Virgin,
Notre-Dame-sous-terre, with the surviving portions of the
Romanesque church of the eleventh and twelfth centuries
around and above it—for most of the church is of this period,
save for the choir and western end, both of which collapsed
at various later dates.

The patron of Robert of Torigny was Henry II, king of
England, duke of Normandy, count of Anjou and duke of
Aquitaine. In 1204-5 Henry's youngest son, King John, was
driven from Normandy and Anjou by King Philip II, Philip
Augustus, of France. In the course of this conquest, an attempt
was made to defend the Mount, a natural fortress of great
strength, and Philip's vassal, Guy de Thouars, burnt the
town and some of the monastic buildings in his efforts to
reduce it to surrender. The efforts were successful; but King
Philip, determined to reconcile the Mount and its lord and
chief inhabitants to the new regime, gave his patronage to a
splendid rebuilding. From this stems the Merveille, which in

336 Mont Saint-Michel, flying buttresses supporting the choir vault

337

338

its present form is almost a complete monastic complex in itself. At its base is a large store-room, such as any abbey needed—for a large medieval household reckoned to keep imperishable goods for long periods, since transport was (by our standards) exceedingly expensive; and the monks of the Mount were never unmindful of the possibility of a siege, especially in the early thirteenth century. Also on the ground floor lies the new almonry, the hall for receiving the poorer guests and for dispensing the abbey's charity. The community were the lords spiritual as well as temporal of their town and seafaring kingdom; and the functions of the welfare state, in so far as they were performed at all, were squarely laid on the Church in the Middle Ages. The building, like the treatises on canon law which enshrined the rules of the welfare Church,

340

339

Mont Saint-Michel: the Church

337 The Chapel of St Martin, the eleventh-century crypt of the south transept.

338 The fifteenth-century choir, looking up.

341 The nave, mainly eleventh century, the north arcade rebuilt in the early twelfth century.

The Domestic Buildings

339 The entry to the older, southern block: the Salle de l'Aquilon, or almonry.

340 The western end of the monks' *promenoir*, gallery or parlour.

342

is a dramatic reminder of the monks' duties; how they performed them it cannot in its nature tell us.

La Merveille symbolically represents the hierarchy of medieval society. The second storey contains (like the first) two large chambers. In one, the ordinary guests of the abbey were entertained, fed and put to sleep—the guests not poor enough for the almonry, nor grand enough for the abbot's table. The second chamber was originally the calefactory, the monks' warming room and winter parlour. It is now called La Salle des Chevaliers, after an order of knights founded in the late Middle Ages and based for a time at Mont Saint-Michel; and the present name of the Salle des Chevaliers may serve to remind us of the feudal element in the hierarchy of the Mount and military nature of the cult of St Michael. In the thirteenth century an abbot, in Normandy as in England, was a feudal baron as well as the head of a monastic community, and for his own and his duke's defence he had to be able to mobilise a platoon of knights; these would have gathered, however, not in the Salle des Chevaliers, but in the abbot's hall. On the third storey of the Merveille, the monks ate and worked, in refectory and cloister; and above the cloister looms the great pile in which the monks and their visitors worshipped, the home of St Michael himself, where God was his guest at

342

343-4

346-50

Mont Saint-Michel: the Merveille

342   The guest's hall.

343   The calefactory, later the Salle des Chevaliers.

344   The fireplaces in the calefactory.

343

344

345

Mont Saint-Michel

345 The wheel to lift stores and provisions up an inclined stone ramp.

346 The refectory with the pulpit on the right.

346

347-50

the altars when mass was celebrated, and yet also, in his nature, present everywhere, and all the time; the all-pervading summit of the living hierarchy of mortals and immortals.

The cloister is one of the most delightful products of the Gothic architecture of Normandy. No doubt it carries reminders of the cradle of Gothic not far away in the Île de France from which King Philip sprang. But its style indicates still more the paradox of Norman Gothic: that in the years when the French king became, not merely the distant suzerain, but the immediate overlord of Normandy, the Gothic masons of the duchy developed a style of their own with closer links to England than to France. Something of its quality may be seen in Rouen Cathedral; it is at its best and most lucid at Coutances, since the destruction of Avranches Cathedral the nearest of the

347

348

347 The cloister, showing how the double arcade gives a shifting vista of arch shapes and a miniature vault. The profusion of Purbeck marble shafts is reminiscent of Salisbury Cathedral and other English work of this period.

348 Mont Saint-Michel, cloister, from the western walk: in the centre, Christ crucified; to the right, Christ enthroned.

Norman cathedrals to the Mount. The shape of the arches, the deep mouldings within them: both are strongly reminiscent of Coutances.[12] There are many reminiscences of Salisbury Cathedral too. But the foliage of the cloister at the Mount has a richness and a fantasy all its own. It also illustrates the religious sentiment of its age in quite a direct way. Should Jesus be viewed as a suffering human or as a king? King and judge He still was, and as such appears in one of the scenes on the western walk in the cloister. But human too; and another depicts a suffering Christ upon the Cross. The great apostle of the human Jesus in the early thirteenth century was Francis of Assisi, and near the crucified is a representation of St Francis, now almost worn away, dated to the year 1228, informing us that he was canonised in that year. This gives us

a vital clue to the date of the whole building, and shows that traditional monasticism could still flourish when the new monasticism of the twelfth century had passed its prime and the apostolic life of the friars had risen to challenge it. It is interesting too to reflect that it should be in France that we find the earliest known picture of the saint called the Frank, the Frenchman, Francesco, though by birth, life and death he was a man of Umbria.

Throughout La Merveille one may study the development of Norman Gothic; but in the church itself one is back with traditional monasticism in its heyday. In the crypt of the choir and in the nave we have a solid, rather plain, monument of the eleventh century. In the ruins of Jumièges, the most notable survivor of that first group of large solid Romanesque monastic churches in north-western France, we see the moment in the eleventh century when the fashion for enormous churches first broke through to the sea. Soon after, the largest of all the building explosions of the age took place in Norman England and in Normandy together. Jumièges and Bernay and the Mount were followed by the abbeys at Caen, Winchester, St Albans, a multitude of others, and finally by Durham. Durham is mainly of the early twelfth century, when the west end and the west front of the Mount were rebuilt. To the modern observer it makes little difference whether the churches were originally secular cathedrals, monastic cathedrals[13] or abbeys—that is to say, whether their choirs were expected to provide homes for communities of secular canons or monks. Both needed space for a full round of offices, and stalls for a large community. In the abbey or monastic cathedral the community was more regularly present in force, there were more priests to be provided with altars every morning (anyway in the twelfth and thirteenth centuries), and there remained certain liturgical differences between monastic and secular uses. But architecturally the differences were never very conspicuous. These enormous churches represented fashion, generosity, religious sentiment— the efforts of the Norman layfolk, and bishops and clergy, to win the approval of Christ the judge. They were also built large so that they could house within them lay pilgrims and visitors, the monks, St Michael and God himself.

Of Michael's presence the chief reminder today is the great image above the lofty spire. Many centuries divide the nave from choir and spire. By the fifteenth century the abbots of the Mount were absentees, great men enabled to maintain their princely state by accumulating the revenues of abbacies and other dignities. One such was the Cardinal d'Estouteville;

123–5, 18

163–6, 18

329
334

349

350

349 An early nineteenth-century drawing of the representation of St Francis, and the inscription dating the cloister 1228, now almost obliterated in the cloister itself. Paris, Bibliothèque Nationale, MS Français 4902, f.226.

350 Mont Saint-Michel, grape picking, from a spandrel in the cloister.

327–8, 351–7 Sant'Ambrogio, Milan

351 St Ambrose, an early fifth-century mosaic from within a generation of Ambrose's death, showing the saint flanked by the martyrs for whom the basilica was first designed, Sts Protasius and Gervasius; in the chapel of S Vittore in Ciel d'Oro.

352 The pulpit, ninth to thirteenth centuries.

353 Oxen climb up and down the door from the atrium to the church.

he was not, however, so neglectful of his abbey but that he helped to rebuild the choir, which had collapsed in 1421. The choir was finished and the spire added in the following century.

At Fountains we saw a world apart: a community as cut off from its neighbours as circumstances and human affairs allowed. At Mont Saint-Michel we see the traces of a community much more intimately linked with the burgesses of its little town and with the pilgrims. This contrast brings us face to face with one of the greatest issues in monastic history: is the life of the monk and of his community inward looking, interior, concerned with its own affairs and its own salvation; or outward looking, concerned to help the world outside in practical ways as well as by prayer? If there were a single

352

351

answer to this question, then either Fountains or the Mount would be unintelligible. Fountains reflects an urgent desire to escape from the world, the Mount to be in it and yet not of it; or rather, to keep one's hands in reach of earth and heaven at once—an awkward acrobatic feat, symbolically represented by this strange pile of buildings precariously perched on a rock jutting out into the English Channel.

III Sant'Ambrogio, Milan

Our third visit is to a house securely placed in one of the world's centres which is a monument not only to the close and permanent links of traditional monasticism with the world, but of the long stretches of time over which these links have been formed. There is indeed no more powerful reminder of the force of tradition in the history of the Church than the Basilica of St Ambrose, Sant'Ambrogio, of Milan.

At first sight, the monasteries which have been formed and the religious life which has flourished in Sant'Ambrogio seem incidental to the Basilica's true significance; and there is a sense in which that is precisely the point of our visit. Here lie the relics of one of the greatest of the church fathers, surrounded by the Milanese martyrs in whose honour

353

354

Ambrose himself first built the church. He began to build it in 379, and the young African rhetorician Augustine was one of those who witnessed its early progress. In 386 Ambrose consecrated his Basilica, and solemnly laid in a group of oratories around it Sts Nabor and Felix, Valeria, Victor and Vitalis; in the Basilica itself Sts Gervasius and Protasius; and beside these martyrs Ambrose himself has lain since he was buried there in 397. It has always been the centre of the cult, or group of cults, which made the Ambrosian Church in a measure rival Rome as the centre of the Church in Italy. Of all the great churches of Italy Milan sat the most lightly in the early Middle Ages in its allegiance to the papacy, and the papacy in return looked with a suspicious eye on the successor of St Ambrose seated on the ancient throne in Sant'Ambrogio and the less ancient throne in the cathedral. As the centuries passed a separate rite distinguished the province of Milan from the rest of Italy and in the end from the rest of western Christendom; Roman in origin, but yet sufficiently independent to symbolise the relations of the Ambrosian to the Petrine Church.

Sant'Ambrogio is a palimpsest on which many different epochs have scored their mark. Some fragments only of the original Basilica survive, though its general shape has been preserved through all the later rebuildings. So deep was the mark of tradition on its later builders that many different estimates have been made of the age of the Basilica as we know it.[14] It seems now fairly clear that the crypt represents the first major reconstruction, that of the eighth century, dating from the years following 789, when Archbishop Peter was attempting to convert the church into a monastery. The monastic community was founded in that year, and rapidly became one of the notable monastic centres of the empire of Charlemagne. There are few more splendid monuments of Carolingian art and wealth than the golden altar, presented 327-8 to the Basilica by Archbishop Angilbert about 835. On it are inscribed scenes from the life of Christ and of St Ambrose; archbishop, abbot and monks celebrated mass in the presence of Christ and the archbishop's eminent predecessor, the saint

who presided over abbey, Basilica, city and province, whose *alter ego* the archbishop claimed to be. Although it sat outside the original limits of the city, surrounded by the ancient cemeteries and the other cemetery churches, the medieval city lapped round it, and it became a busy centre of civic and monastic intercourse.

It had become the home of monks, but not of monks only. This was true in a peculiar sense, for the canons who had lived in Sant'Ambrogio and its precinct before 789, and were expected to fade away as the monks became established, obstinately refused to disappear. The result was that instead of replacing one presence by another, the archbishops had unintentionally established two quite different groups of clergy in one church; and in the eleventh century the canons adopted a regular way of life and became—whatever they had been before—canons regular (see pp. 125 ff.); so that there were in effect two communities following different monastic or quasi-monastic Rules in the Basilica. Hence the great cloisters on either side—that to the north, the cloister of the 357 canons, those to the south (now the Università Cattolica), of the monks. Their present form is the result of a new design by Bramante (c. 1492), and of much later work; but they still reflect this extraordinary passage of history. The presence of two towers reflects these divisions even more vividly. An important part of the income of any monastic community in the early Middle Ages was likely to consist of the offerings of the faithful (see pp. 93-5). From the ninth century on, in the smaller of the two towers, bells rang to summon the faithful to the monks' solemn mass. The canons also celebrated

354-6 Sant'Ambrogio, Milan. The interior, looking east, mainly eleventh/twelfth centuries. The ciborium over the Golden Altar is of the 8th-9th century; the serpent on the left (355) rests on a column of the fourth century.

356 The atrium of the eleventh/twelfth centuries, from which can be seen the monks' tower on the right, ninth century, and the canons' tower on the left, finished in 1144.
All that we see had to undergo elaborate restoration after bombardment in 1943.

355

356

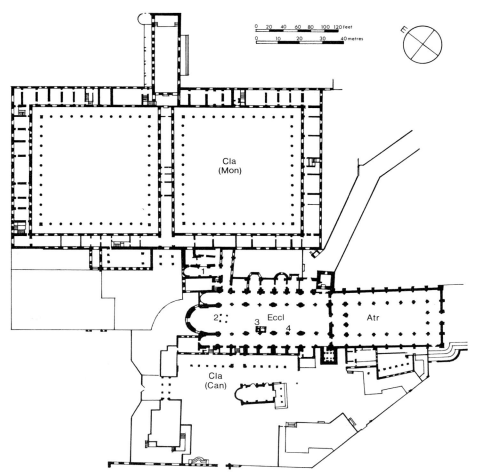

Fig. 27

Fig.27 Plan of Sant'Ambrogio, Milan. The present church and atrium are mainly eleventh to twelfth century, incorporating elements from almost every century since the foundation of the basilica by St Ambrose in the fourth. It lies between two great cloisters of the fifteenth century: the monks' to the north, the canons' to the south. It was severely damaged in 1943 and had to be extensively restored and partly rebuilt. 1. Chapel of S Vittore (St Victor) in Ciel d'Oro, with fifth-century mosaics. 2. Golden Altar and ciborium. 3. Pulpit. 4. Serpent.

mass, but they had no campanile and were not allowed to ring bells.

In the eleventh and twelfth centuries Milan grew in size, population, wealth and political power. The city had long been one of the major centres—and the undisputed ecclesiastical centre—of Lombardy; it now came to play a dominant political role in its region, first under the aegis of St Ambrose and his succeeding archbishops, later under the city fathers, as they came, like those of other Italian cities, to be increasingly independent of the authority of the archbishop. Milan in the eleventh century was the scene of some of the most dramatic incidents in the investiture contest. The Emperor Henry IV (1056-1106) strove to preserve his power in northern Italy by investing and supporting archbishops of the traditional, easy-going clerical dynasties; in response Pope Gregory VII (1073-85: see p. 93) lent his support to a movement among the citizens which strove to oust the old aristocracy, to give rein to the fervent, ascetic, celibate clergy of the movement for ecclesiastical reform. The vicissitudes of the political scene, the political and ecclesiastical complexion of the archbishops, changed many times.

So too changed the fortunes of the monks and canons of

Sant'Ambrogio, who found their own domestic controversy entangled with the affairs of archbishop, emperor, pope and commune. The canons were able to use the political vicissitudes to win a larger share of the offerings; but in 1098 they accused the monks of breaking into the Basilica and taking their offerings by force. Early in the twelfth century the canons mounted a larger counter-attack, and began to build a campanile loftier than the monks'. In the end, a series of uneasy compromises was enforced, which lasted until both communities disappeared in the age of the French Revolution. The culminating moment had come in 1144, when an archbishop at loggerheads with the city commune, but at peace with both pope and emperor, solemnly announced that the splendid new campanile of the canons, which the monks and the commune had sought to destroy, could remain; and it has remained to this day, a symbol of the generations in the eleventh and twelfth centuries when the affairs of pope and emperor, and the future of Milan, were closer than ever before or since to the altars of Sant' Ambrogio.

The great atrium, though itself of the eleventh and twelfth centuries, is in form a link between the world of St Ambrose and St Benedict and the epoch of this book. In form it resembles both the courtyard of a large house and the cloister of a monastery, like the cloisters for the houses of monks and canons raised by Bramante in the same complex of buildings. This kind of atrium, set before the western portal, was commonly attached to great basilicas in the fourth and fifth centuries.[15] It was not in early days monastic; it was essentially the meeting place of the laity, assembled to worship in the church, and it was commonly attached to a cemetery church,

356

where martyrs were buried or commemorated, as at Sant'Ambrogio itself and its neighbour San Lorenzo, where substantial remains of an ancient atrium may still be seen. In due course a number of such churches came to have monasteries associated with them—as did both the Milanese cemetery basilicas, the Santi Quattro Coronati at Rome, and a number more; and they are found as parts of a monastic complex in northern Europe in Carolingian times, at Saint-Riquier and Essen.[16] By *c.* 1080, when the present atrium at Sant'Ambrogio was begun, it was old-fashioned; but not wholly outmoded, since it retained a liturgical use, especially for great processions outside the church and through the western door on Palm Sunday; and these and other festivities explain the common appearance, in many different forms, of western chapels and courtyards, often called Paradises or Galilees.

These were not confined to monastic churches, nor were cloisters set beside the church, for in Italy especially a cloister is commonly found attached to churches never monastic or conventual, and even in England the secular cathedrals acquired fine cloister walks in the later Middle Ages. Yet the cloister in its usual sense, a secluded garth between the church and the domestic buildings of a community, was in a special sense a vital feature of the monastic plan, in contrast to the atrium, a garth open to the laity, between the church and the world. The origin of the cloister is obscure. Although it is unlikely that there was any sort of uniformity in the monastic plan before the central Middle Ages—for the imposition of a common plan in the eleventh and twelfth centuries gives the impression of a uniformity which may well be, for earlier times, deceptive—traces of a cloister or evidence of buildings grouped round a square courtyard of some kind have been found much earlier than this. It is possible that the cloister was modelled on the ancient atrium; or that both grew out of the courtyards common in ancient Roman houses and villas. It is hard not to feel that it was a strange imposition in climates less kind than those of the Mediterranean lands where courtyards and atria were born. It is a nice question when its use became established; but it is essentially a product of the tenth and eleventh centuries. It is an even nicer question when in the cold north it became the practice to fix glass in the open arches of the cloister walk:[17] not perhaps before the thirteenth century. For three or four centuries, that is, the northern monk lived out his day almost in the open. The manner of life of the early Middle Ages makes this less surprising than it seems to us; but only a little. It is striking testimony to the force of tradition and the power of the customs which became associated with the Rule.

The cloister became the heart of the fortress within which monastic life was led, the symbol of separation from the world, of dedication to the life of the spirit, of stability in religion. In the fourth chapter of his Rule, St Benedict listed the qualities and attitudes and virtues of a monk 'the instruments of the craft of the spirit', he calls them. 'And the workshop where we assiduously deploy all these skills are the *claustra* [the enclosure, the 'cloister'] of the monastery, and stability in the communal life'. It is a very characteristic passage in the Rule, since Benedict loved to mingle metaphor and concrete image in a way designed to baffle a translator. In suggesting the rendering *claustra* as cloister we have cheated a little, since he meant simply the enclosure, the complex of buildings of the monastery; what we know as the cloister was devised some centuries later. But every monk of Benedict's obedience

357

357 Sant'Ambrogio, to the north of the basilica, Bramante's cloister for the canons, *c.*1492.

in the mid and late Middle Ages was expected to know this passage—and the whole Rule—by heart; and by the eleventh century the word *claustra* carried the overtone cloister in their minds. Originally it meant the locks which bolted and barred a fortress; and Benedict enjoyed the word because it gave that sense of assurance and security which he wished above all to impart to those who dwelt within. Then it meant too a fortress, *ein' feste Burg*, God's fortress against the devil, man's fortress against the barbarous, lay, sinful world of the early Middle Ages. As time passed, a particular form was established for the buildings of this fortress. Just as the fortified towns of the ninth, tenth and eleventh centuries were receiving a pattern in which the wall round the periphery and the market-place in the centre were the essential features, so in the same epoch the monastic plan was formed and fixed. Its heart lay in a great Church in which God's work, the *opus Dei*, was performed. Next to the church lay the more modest courtyard where man's work was performed, the cloister. It provided the central living and circulating space of a group of communal buildings, and so was reckoned convenient; it was inward looking and so symbolised the monastic ideal and stability; it came to be called the cloister and so was associated for all time with the *claustra* of Benedict's Rule.

360

360 The cloister at Ripoll is full of strange beasts, here a lobster, there a rabbit.

the orders of knights. The brief rule of the kings of Jerusalem had come to an end, and the small posse of monasteries in Palestine had all been withdrawn before 1300 (see p. 165). The Byzantine Empire had been ruled for a space after the Fourth Crusade of 1204 by western princes, and a certain influx of western religious had taken place. By 1300 this was over, and St Benedict's disciples had withdrawn to the traditional areas of papal obedience, leaving St Basil and his successors in command of the field in most of what would now be Greece, Romania, Bulgaria, Jugoslavia and Russia. But in Poland, Bohemia and in parts of Hungary a certain number of monastic houses flourished; in Poland and Silesia especially, as in Ireland, many of these represented the meeting of two peoples and two cultures. Castile and Portugal were the frontier kingdoms par excellence; in Poland, eastern Germany and Ireland colonial governors and governed met in the monastic communities as they also met in the castles and the towns.

The interest of the religious history in Spain and Portugal is out of all proportion to the number of foundations that can be counted there. Before the mid eleventh century only about one quarter of the peninsula was in Christian hands; and although in the early generations of the reconquest (c. 1050-c. 1100) Christian and Moslem coexisted in much of Spain without serious religious acrimony between them, and there were substantial Christian communities in many of the Moslem emirates, monastic houses were confined to the north.

In the eleventh century a certain number of Benedictine and Cluniac houses were revived or founded. In Catalonia they were in the world of the western Mediterranean with central and northern Italy and Provence; the chief influences for reform came from Saint-Victor at Marseilles, a house under Cluniac influence, not direct from Cluny (see p. 54). In Aragon and Old Castile, on the roads that led to Santiago de Compostela, Cluny's influence was greater; especially at the turn of the eleventh and twelfth centuries; and although its direct impact has been somewhat exaggerated, the pilgrims on these roads passed several houses subject to Cluny, or independent centres of Cluniac observance. Thus in the east the old house of Ripoll was reformed from Cuxa and Saint-Victor; further west Cluniac centres of reform appeared in Silos and Sahagún. By 1300 these were independent Benedictine abbeys; but about twenty-five priories dependent on Cluny still remained within the Cluniac province of Spain. 18-22, 138-40 178

In the twelfth century several other orders penetrated into Spain and Portugal; but the most powerful influence was Cistercian. In the regions securely Christian there appeared in the mid twelfth century a scatter of Cistercian houses from Poblet and Santes Creus (1150-1) in Catalonia to the north of 361-80 Portugal; and they spread as far south as Alcobaça (c. 1153) and the outskirts of Lisbon, after the area had been conquered from Islam by a company which detached itself from the Second Crusade in 1147. Poblet was a descendant of Clairvaux, and a proportion of the Castilian and most of the Portuguese houses likewise; Alcobaça was the last foundation direct from Clairvaux before St Bernard's death. In due course some of these houses felt the presence of the Moslem, and

Alcobaça itself had to be restored and largely rebuilt after a serious raid in the thirteenth century. In the north and north-east, a rival to the Catholic religious life appeared in the dualist, Cathar or Albigensian heresy in the second half of the twelfth century. From Poblet the formidable Abbot Arnaud Amaury went to be Archbishop of Narbonne and ecclesiastical director of the Albigensian Crusade (1209). This was one of the first signs of a growing intolerance of differences of race and religion which was to clear the Moslem and the Jew out of Spain in the fifteenth century. The later stages of the reconquest showed a more fanatical spirit than the earlier, and by 1300 most of the peninsula was in Christian hands. Thus it is easy to understand why over much of the peninsula, and especially in the south, the religious orders were most characteristically represented at this time by the orders of knights. As well as fostering Templars and Hospitallers, the Iberian peninsula gave birth to a whole family of new orders, some relatively local and short-lived,[1] and others large enough to survive suppression and amalgamation, like the Order of Santiago and the Order of Calatrava.[2] The Orden de Cristo and the Order of Calatrava were among a group founded under

361-4, 369-73 Alcobaça, Portugal

361 The palatial abbey church, here seen from the apse, looking west; still relatively simple, but fitted to house the tombs of princes as well as a large Cistercian community. It was founded by St Bernard and the first king of Portugal, Afonso Henriques, c.1153; but the church is of the late twelfth and early thirteenth centuries.

362 The apse; note the similarity to Poblet (pl.376).

Cistercian auspices, and some of their houses were indeed Cistercian in origin, but converted from abbeys to castles in the wars and rumours of war of the thirteenth century. Thus by 1300 the religious houses, be they havens of peace or war, often had embattled exteriors. The influence of Cîteaux was very powerful, affecting not only the knights but the ladies, as the great house of Las Huelgas particularly shows; nor were the canons regular negligible in their influence, for the most important Spanish order of the Middle Ages, that of the Friars Preacher, was founded by an Augustinian canon of Osma, St Dominic of Caleruega. 277-84

To the islands and especially to Sicily the Cistercians also spread in the twelfth century; and although Sicily had important Benedictine foundations too, it had lain too long outside the Christian fold—it was only after two centuries of Moslem rule that it was invaded in the 1060s, like England, by a Norman army bearing a papal banner—for the influence of traditional monachism to be deep. From the time of Gregory VII (1073-87), and still more of Urban II, the Cluniac pope who preached the First Crusade (1088-99), papal patronage and intervention, combined with the generosity of the Norman con-querors in the distribution of their own and other people's goods, had fostered the growth of houses formed or reformed from Monte Cassino and La Cava to replace the old Greek houses of the extreme south and of Sicily. At its height the subjects of La Cava included San Paolo fuori le Mura at Rome 71-4 and the great abbey of Monreale in Sicily; and with the houses of La Cava came at first a sprinkling, then a stream of canons regular.

On the eastern frontiers of Europe another pattern of settle-

361

362

363

364

ment and conquest was reflected in a monastic map quite different in some of its lineaments, though also closely dependent on its own story of conquest and settlement. The early stages are obscure, but in Poland and Bohemia, whose monastic history has been most thoroughly investigated, three distinct phases can be distinguished.[3] The conversion of Bohemia had been due to collaboration between the Roman monk St Adalbert and the native dynasty; and the first two foundations were the work of the Princess Mlada-Maria, first abbess of the house at Hradcany in Prague and of Adalbert himself, in founding Brevnov abbey. In Poland another Italian influence, of hermits inspired by St Romuald, played a part in the first formation of Christianity. In both countries, as had been for many centuries traditional, there were monks among the missionaries, and the early cathedral chapters—like that

363-4 Alcobaça. In the church, Don Pedro, King Peter I (1357-67), with detail of his rich and splendid tomb representing the tragic story of Doña Inês de Castro, first his concubine, then claimed to be his wife, who was murdered by order of Pedro's father, King Afonso IV, in 1355, for fear that she should arrange for her own children to usurp the inheritance of Pedro's offspring by his first marriage.

365 A thirteenth-century reliquary of St Francis, now in the Louvre, showing the saint receiving the stigmata. Thus his bones were clothed in the blue and gold of Limoges enamel shrines (see p.197).

366 St Ambrose, an eighth-century stucco tondo in the Museo at Sant'Ambrogio, Milan.

367 The Lamb of God, a fourth-century mosaic in the Museo at Sant'Ambrogio, Milan.

365

366

367

368

at Toledo in the late eleventh century—seem to have contained both monks and canons. Already in the mid eleventh century Brevnov and its offshoots formed an important element in the secular as well as the spiritual life of Bohemia, much on the pattern of the German imperial monasteries. In Poland meanwhile, there was a generation of civil war and confusion in which the monastic life disappeared, followed by new foundations, of which Tyniec near Kraków was the most permanent and powerful. The third epoch in Poland came in the mid and late twelfth century, with the arrival of the Cistercians. By this date Bohemia and eastern Germany had come more generally under western influence; and the Cistercians and Premonstratensians formed major settlements in the frontier lands, as the boundaries of Germany advanced, and more and more German towns and villages were founded in lands traditionally Slav. In these areas monasteries were never so numerous as further west, and ancient houses were exceedingly few. But the Cistercians, the canons regular and the friars flourished in every country in the papal allegiance. The nature of the Cistercian imprint can be gauged from rough figures: in Germany east of the Elbe, by 1300, about fifteen, in Poland, including Silesia, twenty-three, in Czechoslovakia fourteen, in Hungary nine, in Romania and Jugoslavia seven.[4] The most remote were at Falkenau near Dorpat in Esthonia and at Dünamünde in Latvia (both now in the U.S.S.R.), where a community gathered in 1208 and was massacred twenty years later. For the most part the Cistercian settlements were more peaceful than this, though not infrequently involved in local politics. The majority of these houses were descendants of Morimond, whose daughters and grand-daughters had moved across the Rhine, through such centres as Altenberg, and formed huge numbers of communities in Germany—Maulbronn is a characteristic sample of a house in this family of the second generation—and central and eastern Europe. Poland was first colonised in the 1140s; in 1176/7 the cosmopolitan nature of the Cistercian Order was illustrated by the foundation, direct from Morimond, of the abbey of St Mary and St Thomas of Canterbury (canonised in 1173) at Sulejów. The main effort there and elsewhere in Eastern Europe was c. 1175-1250.[5] In these regions, in general, the thirteenth century witnessed the monastic flowering characteristic of the twelfth century further west. Already by 1250 there was strong competition from the friars, and the late entry of the monastic order is doubtless one of the reasons why the monastic houses were in the end so many fewer than the mendicant.

In the Slav lands, as in Ireland, there sometimes appeared within Cistercian communities a barrier in language and culture; in Ireland between Saxon and Celt, in Poland between German and Slav. The Irish case is much the better documented, and it has in the past been too readily assumed that racial conflict was commonly reflected in Cistercian communities east of the Elbe. It is in fact clear that in some cases they formed centres of reconciliation rather than citadels of colonialism, and also that the division between German and Slav speaking folk did not always correspond—perhaps rarely

246, 250-1

239-45,
248-9

369

370

368 Poblet, Spain, the abbey from the east (see pls.374-80).

369 Alcobaça, lavabo in the cloister, early fourteenth century, with sixteenth-century fountain.

370 Alcobaça, refectory and pulpit, thirteenth century.

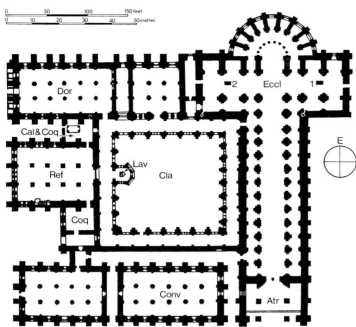

Fig. 28

Fig.28 Plan of Alcobaça before the transformation of the west front in the eighteenth century. The kitchen shown in pls. 371-2 was originally the calefactory. 1. Don Pedro's tomb. 2. Doña Inês's tomb.

Alcobaça. 371 One of the chief workshops, the kitchen, originally the calefactory. Within a medieval framework, chimneys tiled in the eighteenth century to complete 'the most distinguished temple of gluttony in all Europe' in William Beckford's phrase (*Recollections of an Excursion to the Monasteries of Alcobaça and Batalha*, 1835, p.37).

372 'Through the centre of the immense and nobly groined hall . . . ran a brisk rivulet of the clearest water, flowing through pierced wooden reservoirs, containing every sort and size of the finest river-fish . . .' (Beckford, p.38)

373 A chalice of silver gilt, twelfth century, formerly at Alcobaça, now in Lisbon, Museu de Arte Antiga.

372

373

corresponded—with any precision to the division between choir monks and lay brothers in Cistercian cloisters.

If the family of Morimond reigned throughout the land mass of central and eastern Europe, along the Baltic littoral we meet the direct influence of St Bernard and the family of Clairvaux. This family, by 1300, counted five houses near the southern Baltic coast (three of them now in Poland), five in Sweden—and one more on the island of Gotland—five in Denmark and three in Norway. This is not quite the whole count of the order in Scandinavia, but very nearly.[6] The writ of Cluny and Gorze never ran in these lands, which were only converted in the tenth and eleventh centuries. Thus traditional monasticism had very slight influence here. A daughter of the English house of Evesham was established at Odensee in Denmark shortly before 1100,[7] and elsewhere a small number of houses of English and German origin grew up. The crucial step, however, came with the sending of monks from Clairvaux to Alvastra in 1143, in a part of Sweden only recently and superficially converted. 'I have left my father's house— put behind me everything desirable in this world . . . and come to you, father, hoping to enjoy your sweet presence,' cried one of the monks of Clairvaux when enjoined by Bernard to set off for Sweden. '. . . I hoped to await the judgement day among the holy corpses of the brothers in this cemetery. And

today you cast me out. . . .'[8] Bernard promised that he would die at Clairvaux, and the party set off to brave the northern climate, to found both Alvastra and Nydala, from which the order spread to other parts of Sweden. A few years later another party from Clairvaux started the first Danish community at Esrom; and Clairvaux's English daughters Fountains and Kirkstead had meanwhile sent colonies to Lyse and Hovedö in Norway in 1146-7.

In no part of western Europe was the monastic life more ancient or more deeply entrenched than in Ireland; yet the pattern of religious houses there was of the twelfth and thirteenth centuries, and not earlier. A new era had dawned *c.* 1124 when St Malachy became abbot of Bangor, the first ancient house to be reformed; he was later to be bishop of

fig. 15

fig. 14

371

374

375

three different sees and to spend much time in travel. After his death in 1148 his life was written by St Bernard in person, a sign of the impression Malachy himself was able to make at the heart of the monastic world of the day. Malachy was deeply affected by the Cistercian way of life; and also by the practical utility of the canons regular, which he found for himself in the notable French abbey of Arrouaise,[9] whose customs had

368, 374-80 Poblet, Spain. One of the finest medieval monastic houses still in use, and one of the most complete Cistercian complexes to survive.

374 Like many Spanish religious houses, it was also at times a castle; hence the massive Gothic gateway.

375 Behind the towers are the workshops, still showing the character of a medieval Cistercian community.

Fig.29 Plan of Poblet. The buildings range widely in date, from the church, cloister, calefactory, cloister and chapel of St Stephen (twelfth century), lavabo, refectory, kitchen, chapter house (c.1200), to the large sacristy, buildings for older monks, etc. of the eighteenth century. 1.Gardens. 2.Chapel of St Catherine. 3.Royal Apartments. 4.Sacristies (the larger is of the eighteenth century). 5.Eighteenth-century buildings for the older monks. 6,7.Twelfth-century cloister and chapel of St Stephen. 8.Twelfth-century infirmary.

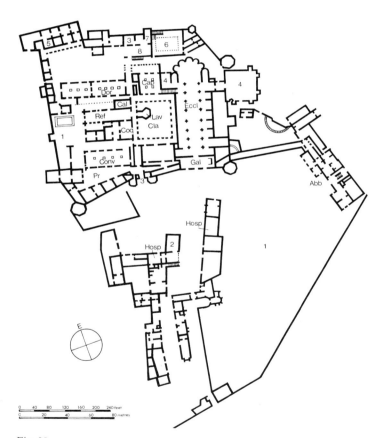

Fig. 29

been influenced by Bernard. In the end some thirty to forty Cistercian houses were founded between 1142 and *c.* 1230 and over a hundred Augustinian. Malachy had laid the foundations for a new Irish Church in which native traditions and the new cosmopolitan fashions of the twelfth century mingled; a tragic misfortune—the English invasion of the 1170s—was to make it in a measure a centre of colonialism. From 1216 to 1228 the monks of the large house of Mellifont were in rebellion against a discipline which had become

376

377

376 The *altar mayor* (high altar) in the church: a late twelfth-century Cistercian apse at odds with a Mannerist reredos.

377 On the cloister roof; to the left, the Gothic windows of the unfinished royal palace (fourteenth to fifteenth centuries)

378 The cloister: Romanesque on the left (twelfth century), Gothic in front.

378

associated with foreign rule. In 1228 a brave English monk, Stephen of Lexington, then abbot of Stanley, later abbot of Clairvaux itself, was sent by the general chapter on visitation. He ended the rebellion, but in the process started a policy of appointing foreign abbots and settling foreign monks in the Irish Cistercian houses. This was not in its origin intended to mean English rule; but it rapidly became associated in Irish eyes with the more general policy of English dominion in their Church; and as the hold of the general chapter weakened, the Cistercian overlords became ever more evidently English. The rebellion at Mellifont was the first of a long series of clashes. But it would be superficial to reckon colonial rule the only legacy of twelfth century monasticism in Ireland; for in later times, when the English dissolved their own monasteries, a small number of Irish communities enjoyed an Indian summer, and final dissolution was delayed till the eighteenth century; no great space of time divides the old monasticism in Ireland from the new foundations of the nineteenth and twentieth centuries.

What Malachy inspired in Ireland on the grand scale—and (one would think) far beyond the economic resources of a poor country—King David (1124-53) attempted more modestly in Scotland. He was the youngest and most civilised of the sons of St Margaret, and thus brother to Matilda, Henry I's queen, as well as earl of Huntingdon and Northampton and a leading English baron. His notable achievement was to spread a network of Norman Scottish baronies in the lowlands of Scotland, with a scatter of religious houses among them, whose nucleus lay near the border, where an anthology of religious orders owed him patronage—the Benedictines of Tiron at Kelso, the Cistercians at Melrose, the Augustinian canons at Jedburgh, 212-13

the Premonstratensians at Dryburgh; a notable group, whose fine remains are the monument to one of the most lavish and imaginative monastic patrons of the age. Wales had no Malachy and no David; but in a country originally as poor as Ireland, there came to be a small group of Benedictine houses, mostly outposts of Norman settlement, a small group of Augustinian houses, and a scatter of Cistercian, where Welsh and English met as genuinely as in the most successful of the houses in the borders of Germany and in the Slav countries. 301-2

None of these lands on the borders of western Christendom had any concentration of monastic houses and population to compare with those in England, France, Germany and Italy. In the current state of research, only for England can figures of any precision be given.[10] Between 1066 and the mid twelfth

380

379 Poblet, chapter house, thirteenth century, with Romanesque arches over the window, but Gothic tracery and vaults.

380 Poblet, the lavabo and fountain in the cloister, twelfth to thirteenth centuries.

century the number of houses increased about ten-fold, from 60 to nearly 600 (of monks alone, from 48 to about 500); and this probably reflects a growth in monastic population from a little over 1,000 to 7-8,000. The grand total by 1300 was 1,000 houses and 17-18,000 religious; but this included the friars, and a considerable part of the expansion consisted in small houses, especially of canons, and dependencies, some of them tiny. None the less, it is clear that the increase was dramatic, and that it was no peculiarity of the English scene. In all these countries the monastic map of 1300 is most obviously a palimpsest, on which the traditional monasticism of Cluny, Gorze, Glastonbury, Fruttuaria, La Cava, Hirsau, *undsoweiter*, scored its mark widely and deeply, and the new movements of the late eleventh, twelfth and thirteenth centuries, have scored theirs everywhere too. A traveller in 1300 would have been hard put to it to find a place in these lands more than thirty kilometres from the nearest religious house; and in the richest areas, in the Low Countries, the Rhineland, in Burgundy, Normandy, Poitou, Provence, Lombardy and Tuscany, more than fifteen—and to this day in many parts of western Europe one can walk from one surviving fragment of a medieval abbey to the next for weeks on end.

Such a traveller in 1300 would have found the friars and the Cistercians everywhere as ubiquitous as the traditional houses. But he would have found some notable changes in the pattern as he moved from region to region. In south Italy, in the kingdom of Naples or of the Two Sicilies, he is in the world of La Cava and Monte Cassino, where old movements still flourished and the Cistercians had a modest but visible foothold. Almost every order had its house in or near Rome; and here the houses under Cassino's influence met those reformed from Fruttuaria in Lombardy; here too were Cistercians at Fossanova, Casamari, Tre Fontane and else-

where. In Umbria and the Marches, in the homeland of St Francis, friars and hermits lived side by side; here and in Tuscany lay most of the houses sprung from Camaldoli and Vallombrosa, on the peaks and in the cities. Further north again, we find traditional centres in Fruttuaria and Sant'Ambrogio in Milan, and Cistercian at Chiaravalle; and presently we pass from the world of Camaldoli to that of the Chartreuse, thinly spread all over the Alpine regions and the north of Europe, but with its centre in the regions of Rhône and Rhine. In Burgundy we are in the homeland of Cluny and Cîteaux, the capitals of the largest of all monastic congregations. Even in its decline, in the late fourteenth and fifteenth centuries, Cluny reckoned it had about seven hundred dependencies, and the number was probably higher in the twelfth and thirteenth centuries.[11] Cîteaux had about the

327-8, 351-7, 366-7

381-3 385, 387-9 Fossanova, Italy. An old Benedictine abbey, adopted by the Cistercians and refounded in St Bernard's lifetime (c. 1135) by French and Italian monks.

381 A thirteenth-century octagonal tower, combining French and Italian features, presides over a characteristic Cistercian church of the late twelfth century, consecrated by Pope Innocent III in 1208.

381

382

383

384

and its offshoots had reigned, and not Cluny—though the houses of traditional monasticism must have looked much alike to the casual visitor both sides of the frontier of France and the Empire. Second, the Elbe formed the old frontier of German Christendom, and the pattern was quite different to its east, where Premonstratensian canons and Cistercian monks played a leading part in the settlement of some areas hardly inhabited before, and where the Cistercians in particular were pioneers in the study of forestry and the techniques of reclamation. Third, the female element was much stronger in Germany and the Low Countries than elsewhere. This is particularly noticeable among the Cistercian nuns. In England and Wales there were about thirty houses of nuns which claimed at one time or another to be Cistercian; most of them were relatively small and poor, and all but a handful founded before 1200. In France the number is said to have been about one hundred and sixty, and a higher proportion were of the thirteenth century. In Germany the figure is over two hundred and fifty, most of them founded after 1200; and although these houses were often quite modest in size, the total number exceeded those of the men. The final total for the whole order throughout Europe was not so disparate: about seven hundred and forty for men and about six hundred and fifty for women.[12]

If we ask, what quality of life would the traveller have found within the cloisters in 1300, we can gather many answers, and of a bewildering variety, from the comments of the day; but in the end, we can only say one of two things: that we cannot

119, 121-2

same number of daughters, no doubt still housing in 1300 a far larger number of monks than Cluny could count—for many Cluniac houses were diminutive and the lay brothers still swelled the Cistercian population. Cluny, Cîteaux and Prémontré are not far apart, and their daughters lay all over France and England. In Dijon, the centre of Burgundy, lies Saint-Bénigne, home of St William, who had inspired the observance of eleventh century Normandy and early Norman England. In Germany and Provence we meet numerous houses influenced by Cluny, especially through St-Victor of Marseille and Hirsau; and Hirsau's influence had spread right through Germany in the late eleventh and twelfth centuries.

But in Germany itself we meet striking differences in the monastic map. First of all, there is the large area where Gorze

Fossanova

382 Interior of the church.

383 A perfect Cistercian refectory, with pulpit of the late twelfth century (or *c.*1200).

384 Gniezno Cathedral, Poland, bronze doors, *c.*1170. St Adalbert (d.997) preaching (see p.228).

385 Fossanova, west front, Italian Gothic of the thirteenth century.

now enter the lives of a hundred thousand or more religious in several thousand houses; or, that what we know shows us that we would have found a cross-section of mankind, in glory and in squalor; much that was humdrum and routine, much that was vicious, much that was devoted, and something that was heroic. One such traveller must speak for all. It was to the year 1300 that Dante assigned his own pilgrimage to hell and purgatory and heaven—and not long after that in truth he composed his *Commedia*. In the seventh heaven, and the 22nd canto of the *Paradiso*,[13] he encountered St Benedict himself, who thus addressed him:

> 'In old days,
> That mountain, at whose side Cassino rests,
> Was, on its height, frequented by a race
> Deceived and ill-disposed: and I it was,
> Who thither carried first the name of Him,
> Who brought the soul-subliming truth to man
> And such a speeding grace shone over me,
> That from their impious worship I reclaim'd
> The dwellers round about, who with the world
> Were in delusion lost. These other flames,
> The spirits of men contemplative, were all
> Enliven'd by that warmth, whose kindly force
> Gives birth to flowers and fruits of holiness.
> Here is Macarius; Romoaldo [Romuald] here;
> And here my brethren, who their steps refrain'd
> Within the cloisters, and held firm their heart.'

Dante asks to see Benedict's face, but is put off; first, like any follower of the Rule, he must climb the ladder of humility (see Rule, chap. 7).

> 'Brother!' he thus rejoin'd, 'in the last sphere
> Expect completion of thy lofty aim:
> For there on each desire completion waits,
> And there on mine; where every aim is found
> Perfect, entire, and for fulfilment ripe.
> There all things are as they have ever been:
> For space is none to bound; nor pole divides.
> Our ladder reaches even to that clime;
> And so, at giddy distance, mocks thy view.
> Thither the patriarch Jacob saw it stretch
> Its topmost round; when it appear'd to him
> With angels laden. But to mount it now
> None lifts his foot from earth: and hence my rule
> Is left a profitless stain upon the leaves;
> The walls, for abbey rear'd, turn'd into dens;
> The cowls, to sacks choak'd up with musty meal.
> Foul usury doth not more lift itself
> Against God's pleasure, than that fruit, which makes
> The hearts of monks so wanton: for whate'er
> Is in the church's keeping, all pertains
> To such, as sue for heaven's sweet sake; and not
> To those, who in respect of kindred claim,
> Or on more vile allowance. Mortal flesh

386 Much Wenlock Priory, England. The church is mainly thirteenth century: a detail shows its fine quality.

Fig.30 Plan of Fossanova showing the original layout, twelfth to fourteenth centuries.

387-8 Fossanova. Most of the cloister arcading is very simple, and of the twelfth century. But the south walk and lavabo (388), more ornate and with twisted columns, are of the fourteenth.

386

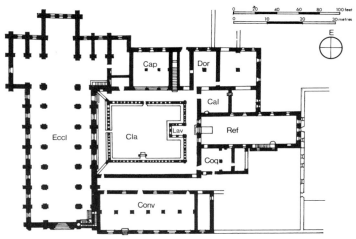

Fig. 30

387

388

389

Is grown so dainty, good beginnings last not
From the oak's birth unto the acorn's setting.
His convent Peter founded without gold
Or silver; I, with prayers and fasting, mine;
And Francis, his in meek humility.
And if thou note the point, whence each proceeds,
Then look what it hath err'd to; thou shalt find
The white grown murky. Jordan was turned back:
And a less wonder, than the refluent sea,
May, at God's pleasure, work amendment here.'

389 Fossanova. Over the west door of the church (see pl.385) are cosmati
inlays.

15 Epilogue

The monastic houses of Europe have passed through many vicissitudes. Some have survived, or been revived; life at the Chartreuse, at Camaldoli, at Vallombrosa, is much the same as it was in the Middle Ages; there are still—or perhaps one should say there are again—thousands of monks and canons scattered over the face of Christendom. A few samples show the kind of changes time has brought. The small Cistercian houses in Provence either survived or faded away; in either event they never commanded the resources or the ambition for great changes; they were never converted into great country houses or made quarries for local towns.[1] In many parts of Germany and Switzerland the Reformation swept the monasteries away as in England; what the Reformation began, the French Revolution and Napoleon carried further, especially

*77,
126-33*

*226-34,
254-8*

in France and Italy; and most of the communities which were left have suffered extinction, for a time at least, in more recent anti-clerical movements. But not quite all, for in Einsiedeln in Switzerland one can visit the centre of one of the longest stretches of continuous history to be found in Europe: a Benedictine house of immense antiquity, still a flourishing monastery; also the centre of a great estate and even one of the chief places of the Canton Schwyz. A visit to Catholic Einsiedeln from nearby Zürich, Zwingli's Zürich, one of the greatest of the Protestant cities and cantons, is like passing

390 Einsiedeln, Switzerland, a great Benedictine house founded in the tenth century, now mainly in Baroque costume. A seventeenth-century engraving by Wenzel Hollar, Hamburg, Kunsthalle, no. 23408.

390

into another world, where the Reformation is no more. But the continuing prosperity of the abbey is above all revealed by the total absence of any medieval buildings: it is an immense and powerful monument to the Baroque.

1300-1500

These were mighty changes of a later date, but let us first glance at one of the subtlest expressions of the course of monastic history in the centuries after 1300, my formal closing date. At Lacock we can see a group of medieval monastic buildings melting into the country house of the sixteenth and eighteenth centuries. For this reason, they are an excellent witness of the nature of late medieval domestic planning and of the approach and habit of mind of the dissolvers. At Much Wenlock the change was slighter still. In the fifteenth century the prior built one of the most charming late medieval manor houses which survives anywhere in western Europe for his lodgement; and the monks, meanwhile, made substantial alterations in the older infirmary alongside. Between the two buildings, domestic quarters of solid comfort and moderate privacy—not luxurious by our standards, but in reasonable accord with the standards of country gentry of moderate means of the fifteenth century—could be found for the senior monks at least, and probably for the greater part of the community. No doubt the monks preserved the fabric, and some semblance of the services, in their tremendous church. No doubt they visited the cloister, and the younger ones may have slept in cubicles in the dormitory and fed in the refectory, after washing their hands ceremonially in the lavabo, still adorned with charming sculptures of the twelfth century. But there seems to have been a tendency and drift towards the more domestic buildings of the convent, to the infirmary, where meat might be eaten and the great silence somewhat relaxed, and to the prior's lodging, which looks as if it were designed to be the centre of their life, and certainly of their hospitality. At the dissolution such buildings needed no conversion to suit the needs of a line of country gentlemen of moderate fortune and large families. We must not unduly diminish the impact of dissolution. The monks departed; St Milburga, who had presided over the little town and the church through many vicissitudes since the seventh century, was violently removed from her shrine. Church and cloister fell into decay. But life was quickly resumed in the prior's lodging and infirmary: and to this day it is a modest country seat.

Behind this story we may detect a world in which priors and monks lived in comparative ease, the lives of country gentlemen of moderate means: a far cry from the spiritual

adventure which had founded and refounded Much Wenlock in earlier centuries, or created the Cistercian complex at neighbouring Buildwas. I use the word detect because we know 235-8 little of the inner life of most monasteries in this age of vegetation. From time to time in the late Middle Ages there were movements for reform: among the friars in particular these enjoyed some spectacular successes, and one or two orders, like the Carthusian, stood in no need of such reforms. But for the most part, so far as we can tell, from 1300 on until the Reformation and Counter Reformation, the religious were not climbing Jacob's ladder, as St Bernard had insisted that they must (see p. 76). For this they fell under severe criticism in the fourteenth and fifteenth centuries and they have often been condemned in recent times, especially by two kinds of

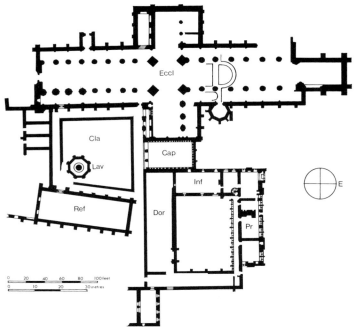

Fig. 31

391 Ottobeuren, the monastic church, now a fine example of German Baroque.

Fig.31 Plan of Much Wenlock showing existing medieval walls and those which can be traced with reasonable confidence, and the line of the apse (perhaps eleventh century) excavated in 1901. Lavabo, infirmary and chapter house are twelfth century; church and refectory, thirteenth; the prior's lodging was built and the infirmary remodelled in the fifteenth.

386, 392-4 Much Wenlock, England

392 In the fifteenth century the charming prior's lodging, right, was added to the twelfth-century infirmary, left, which was adapted to make comfortable quarters for the last generation of monks. At the dissolution, both these wings were taken over as a country house.

critic: from without, by stern Protestant opponents of the medieval Church, like G. G. Coulton, who for all his Protestantism wrote about medieval monks as if he was himself a medieval reformer trouncing contemporary vices; and from within, from historians like Dom David Knowles, who have measured them by the standards of Benedict and Bernard, and found them wanting. Undoubtedly there were many scandals and abuses; but these can be found in the documents of the eleventh and twelfth centuries as well as in the fourteenth and fifteenth. Sometimes an intimate chronicle or the record of a bishop's visitation will show that something had gone drastically wrong. This should cause no surprise. It must also have been common, then as now, for communities to be tolerably well run under a shrewd and sensible direction, and to enjoy a happy sense of community, even though not a power house of spiritual life. But if such a director is removed, or if a spirit of gossip and faction is abroad, a community may rapidly degenerate, even without the sins against chastity, poverty and obedience which broke out from time to time in every age. Sometimes a weak abbot or a bickering council of elder monks demoralised a community; sometimes mismanagement of its affairs and debt led to real hardship, even to the dispersal of the monks or nuns. But much more often, so far as we can tell, communities survived without impressing their neighbours with their special fervour, nor impressing themselves on the historical record by scandal or disgrace. In the long run, somewhere between the extremes of fervour and corruption, innumerable communities lived on through the late Middle Ages to the Reformation—and in many countries far beyond the Reformation—in the humdrum circumstances represented by the prior's lodging at Much Wenlock. For all the criticism to which they were subjected, on the whole they accepted themselves, and were widely accepted, as a normal part of the social scene. Yet this acceptance could be seriously challenged, and there was no age between the eleventh and the nineteenth centuries in which a zealous reformer or a rapacious secular ruler did not suppress a number of houses in the name of reform.

Every age since Dante voiced his hope for a renewal of the religious life has seen something of the decline St Benedict lamented, something of the renewal. All that lies beyond 1300 must be for us an epilogue, a coda; but it would be quite false to see even the last centuries of the Middle Ages as mere decline, still less to end without any word upon the major revival of the sixteenth and seventeenth centuries, and its successor in the nineteenth and twentieth.

The Black Death of 1348-9 and the sharp decline in the population which had supplied the monasteries helped to sharpen a crisis: many communities became a tiny shadow of what they had been; many seemed little more than caretakers for an old heritage whose original purpose was but slightly remembered. Yet at the same time St Bridget in Sweden was founding a new double order, and in the fifteenth century San Bernardino began a renewal among the friars which not only provided numberless houses like the Carceri above Assisi with new life, but stirred revival in the end in all the orders of friars.

306, 316

393 Much Wenlock. The ancient abbey of St Milburga had been revived in the eleventh century for Cluniac monks. Two fine twelfth-century features survive: celestial geometry decorating the chapter house, and the lavabo (see pl.394).

393

Since 1500

Thus the stage was prepared for the drama of the sixteenth century, and with the Reformation came the first major onslaught: it started in Germany with Luther and his associates in the 1520s, then passed on to England in the 1530s, when Henry VIII was in search of marriage and money. When Henry and Thomas Cromwell destroyed the whole monastic fabric in England in the late 1530s innumerable communities were pensioned off with scarcely a murmur. Here and there voices were raised very loudly indeed against so cynical an act of destruction and spoliation; and in a few houses—most notably among the Carthusians of London—there were martyrs for the religious life. In the other parts of Europe in which the Protestant cause succeeded, the religious were taken out of their monasteries and their lands confiscated. There was rarely so sudden and complete a breach as in England—in Scotland, for example there were two generations of slow decay and secularisation, so that lay lords gradually acquired the titles and properties of the abbots, and the last monk might die in his abbey still in possession of some of his ancient rights. But nothing like the monastic life survived in the Protestant communions of the sixteenth century.

Thus by 1600 the religious life had virtually disappeared from the British Isles, save in parts of Ireland, save also for Jesuits and others in hiding and under proscription; and the abbeys of the Low Countries, of Protestant Germany and Scandinavia had gone, and many of those in France had suffered from Huguenot attacks. Elsewhere the sixteenth century was a new golden age of religious observance, when the Jesuits and the Discalced (barefoot) Carmelites—the orders of St Ignatius Loyola, St Teresa and St John of the Cross, and many others—spread ideas of religion undreamed of in earlier ages. Both the contemplative and the active wings received new life and inspiration; and in the seventeenth century many an old abbey or congregation submitted to reform. These included the humane, scholarly, cultured congregation of Saint-Maur, the Benedictine reform unexpectedly founded under the patronage of Cardinal Richelieu. In due course its houses included Mont Saint-Michel and many other great houses, and its monks some of the most eminent theologians and church historians of the seventeenth and eighteenth centuries, above all Dom Jean Mabillon, a pious and humble monk who yet played a notable part in the scientific revolution of the seventeenth century by laying the foundations for the scientific study of medieval history.

Mabillon was a man of peace; but he was from time to time drawn into controversy, and among his most dramatic encounters was his pamphlet war with the most celebrated and puritanical of the reformers of the day, l'abbé tempête, Armand de Rancé, founder of the reformed Cistercian Order which we call Trappist, after his own abbey of La Trappe. The essence of de Rancé's position was that monks should not engage in intellectual pursuits: Mabillon's answer showed how wide and deep a share in the Benedictine tradition learning had enjoyed. De Rancé was in some respects a caricature of St Bernard; yet he gave a genuine impulse to the contemplative life which helped the monastic ideal to survive the French Revolution; and he allowed his battle with Mabillon to end in one of those dramatic personal reconciliations such as Bernard himself greatly loved. But the Trappist was only one way of reform for the Cistercians, and Bernard's ideals, and the contemplative life itself, have followed many apart from those of the tempestuous abbot.

In certain respects the eighteenth century was like the fifteenth in monastic history: the orders survived, the storm was near but hardly heard within the cloister. Between 1780 and 1810 the large majority of the surviving religious communities in Europe were suppressed, their inmates pensioned off, turned away or forced into secular life. First, the 'enlightened' despots showed their despotism in characteristic fashion and Joseph II suppressed a handsome proportion of the religious houses in the Austrian Empire. Next, the French Revolution abolished all those in France: many were understandably hated as the symbols of privilege and caste; and, as in Henry VIII's England, such feelings were exploited to excuse total destruction. As the armies of the Revolution and Napoleon marched about Europe, the abbeys fell in every land that was conquered—throughout Germany, much of Austria and Italy. A few survived, but a reasonable observer in the early or mid nineteenth century might well have supposed that the religious life would soon be persecuted out of existence altogether. True, it was allowed to revive from time to time even in France; but in the nineteenth century such revivals were comparatively short-lived, and anti-clericalism became powerful once again under the Third Republic. Between 1880 and 1903 the monks of Solesmes were expelled four times, only finally to return in 1922.[2] There are a few abbeys, especially in the remoter parts of Switzerland and Austria, whose life has continued almost unhindered; but there is no country which has not witnessed some measure of repression, suppression, control or persecution. Paradoxically, it is in Protestant England that European monasticism has had its least troubled history in the last two centuries.

Under these conditions one might reasonably have supposed that today the religious life would be an antiquarian memory; that a few fragments of religious communities might live on here and there, forgotten or tolerated by complaisant authority. It comes as a surprise, therefore, to learn that there are over a million Roman Catholic religious in the world today, not counting numerous monks in the Orthodox communions, and that phenomenon of the modern world, the Protestant religious.[3] This is at first a staggering figure. Most educated people today, not closely in touch with the religious orders, are inclined to think of the Middle Ages as the epoch when monks were most numerous. No doubt there is a sense in which this is true. For if we guessed that there were in 1300 about 150-200,000 religious in western Christendom, they doubtless included far more than the 20,000 or so Benedictine, Cistercian and Carthusian monks who still follow the rule of St Benedict today; and even if there are probably more friars now than in 1300, it is only by a relatively small margin, whereas the population of Europe has increased many times.

A study of current statistics shows three outstanding differences: first, the orders are now world-wide, and even if persecution has effectively abolished them in some parts of Asia and Eastern Europe, America has been in recent times the home of many of the most flourishing houses of every complexion. Secondly, the greater number of religious belong to orders scarcely or never mentioned in this book. There are many thousand monks following ancient rules, and over 50,000 friars; but there are also about 36,000 Jesuits and numerous members of the new orders which grew in the nineteenth and early twentieth centuries. Many are small, but they include some, like the Christian Brothers (nearly 18,000)

and the Marist Brothers (about 10,000), of substantial size. The third characteristic of the modern orders is that the nuns outnumber the male religious by about three to one—one million to about 300,000. Here is a dramatic change indeed, for in parts of western Europe in the twelfth and thirteenth centuries the men may have outnumbered the women by an even larger multiple, and even in Germany and the Low Countries it is most unlikely that they commanded anything approaching equality.

It would be fascinating to pursue the comparison beyond this point, and inquire below the superficial tale of figures into the inwardness of the religious life today. It is, however, essential to dwell on the contrasts between the Middle Ages and the present for a moment longer, for the differences stir us to question assumptions we might too readily accept as to the relation of society and monasticism in the Middle Ages; and also because the figures serve to remind us that our subject is alive and actual, not a story from a lost world.

Do these figures mean that the religious life is now flourishing, and, in an atmosphere more tolerant than that of the nineteenth century, can look forward to a future as long and as prosperous as its past? No one can tell. The orders are trying to assimilate a wealth of new ideas and inspirations; they are under attack from without and within; not for the most part under persecution, but under a growing fervour of critical inquiry. This in itself is nothing new. Critical inquiry was especially characteristic of the 'crise du monachisme' of the eleventh and twelfth centuries, which accompanied the golden age of monastic expansion in the west; and the same could be said of the revivals of the nineteenth and twentieth when a remarkable revival of the religious orders accompanied the spread of agnostic thought, the denial of the roots of Christian belief on a scale without precedent since the early Middle Ages. It is evident that the growth of agnostic humanism has continued unabated, and in numbers at least the churches have in recent generations suffered an obvious decline. More than that, the religious life has in a fair measure depended on deep traditional attitudes within the Roman Catholic Church. While it is undoubtedly true that this way of life has often been grafted on new stock in the last two centuries, and has come to flourish abundantly in ecumenical centres such as Taizé, the ascetic, celibate ideal has been questioned even among Roman Catholics to a degree unprecedented. In former centuries it was widely accepted that the life of the religious was in some sense, often in a very obvious sense, higher and better than the married. To hint such a thought in the presence of many religious in the 1970s is to invite an instant denial. In the 1970s, within the Roman Catholic communion and in the ecumenical Church at large, there has been a questioning of traditional positions so deep and wide that the notion of the monastic life as a privileged version of the Christian ideal is rapidly declining.

In the ten or twenty years which followed the Second World War, traditional monasticism enjoyed a rapid increase in recruits, in the contemplative as well as the more active orders. In the 1960s, this was sharply reversed; and the more enclosed orders seem to have suffered relatively the most. In part, this reflects the pattern in all the churches: recruitment

394 Much Wenlock. Watery scenes adorn the lavabo: here Christ helps St Peter on the sea.

of clergy and ministers declined sharply in the 1960s; all began to face a crisis of identity; traditional attitudes to the clerical profession at large were subjected to criticism. Some traditionalists blame the new crisis, and the movement which they interpret as decline, on the flow of new ideas; and one cannot but sympathise with their protest against the urge in some quarters to press every type of religious practice into a single mould. Yet the ferment seems to a sympathetic outsider to show, as could no era of peace or quiet, that there is life in the religious orders. Such a comment would raise a smile on the faces of many monks of ancient orders; for a continuous, vivid and effective life is evidently carried on in numerous houses little affected by the hum of the world outside—and the spiritual life is not subject to statistics or quantitative measurement at all.

In the ferment of the eleventh and twelfth centuries controversy accompanied growth, not only in numbers, but in variety and depth of experience; and similarly, when the call to a more active life—not wholly without analogies in the 1960s and 1970s—helped the orders of friars into flourishing life in the thirteenth century, there was clearly a sense in which new life in some orders was balanced by decline in others. The malaise of the 1960s has been in part a call for a more active life, for an end to the barriers between the cloister and the world, and for a new appraisal of the religious life in terms more active even than those of St Francis and St Dominic. It was a tightening of the ancient tension between the inward and the outward view. If this were the whole case, one might feel that it was a tide ebbing and flowing that we are witnessing, not a fundamental questioning of a traditional mode of life. In one respect this seems an inadequate statement of the current dilemma. In the past, Roman Catholic religious have been able to see their vocation against a doctrine of marriage which rarely set the ideal of obedience between husband and wife in the sacrament on a level with celibate obedience in religion. This is no longer the case. For all the dangers which social custom, fashion and law have laid in the way of Christian marriage, it remains obvious enough, even from the most superficial reading of the literature of the 1960s and 1970s, that an ideal of marriage is laid before the modern Christian, of whatever denomination, of a novel profundity; it sets a standard of partnership and common action which strives to make genuine sense of the likening of marriage to the union of Christ and the Church. Theological tides are one cause of this; the social customs of our day are another—for it would be absurd to pretend that it is only among Christians that such ideals now flourish, and contend with their very visible enemies in modern society. One source of these changing customs has been the demand of women for a freer and more equal place in the world; and it is no doubt also one of the reasons why the numbers of nuns grew so rapidly in the last century and is declining now. Modern custom, and the ideals of the new generation of the 1960s, seem to face the religious life with a challenge which is genuinely new.

An intelligent observer of the age of Napoleon might well have thought that the regular life was really defunct. He would look very foolish now. Equally, it would be ridiculous to argue that because there is novelty in the current challenges, the orders will succumb. On the contrary, they have shown themselves in the past remarkably resilient in the face of controversy and shifting fashion. There are still parts of the world where the monasteries are associated with all that is most repellent in social and economic privilege, as they were over much of western Europe before 1789. This is now rare; equally often they are seen to be in sympathy with the varied and genuine aspirations of our day. The ideal of marriage alone is unlikely to destroy them; for man is infinitely various, and there are many for whom total absorption in a single union is meaningless or inadequate. Hitherto it has been the keynote of our civilisation that, whatever its ups and downs, the variety of occupation open to men has tended to increase rather than decline. If this continues, then the spiritual experience whose history has been traced in this book will surely continue to find adherents, and to inspire new generations of postulants—although St Benedict may be even more astonished by the adventures of his children in the third millenium than he was when he met Dante in 1300.

Every monastery whose ruins are substantial carries on its face some stories of change and decay: rebuilding, alteration, destruction or mere neglect. Some carry the scars of war and revolutions; some of peaceful decay; some of long centuries of use, others of rapid and dramatic change. In every case we have to work back in imagination, through the centuries of epilogue to the building and to the community as it was in the eleventh, twelfth or thirteenth century. In this book I have tried to throw a pebble into the centre of a pool of clear water. As the ripples spread we see the life of medieval monks spreading out into the whole history of an epoch. This book is selective and incomplete. But it has aimed to show how the history of a medieval monastery may reveal the history of life and thought, literature, society, economy and culture of the central Middle Ages.

Notes

Abbreviations

Atlas Cist.
F. Van der Meer, *Atlas de l'Ordre Cistercien*, Amsterdam-Brussels, 1965.

Backmund
N. Backmund, *Monasticon Praemonstratense*, 3 vols., Straubing, 1949-56.

Chadwick, *Asceticism*
Owen Chadwick, *Western Asceticism, Selected Translations . . . by Owen Chadwick*, London, 1958.

Chadwick, *Cassian*
O. Chadwick, *John Cassian*, 2nd edn., Cambridge, 1968.

Cottineau
L. H. Cottineau, *Répertoire topo-bibliographique des abbayes et prieurés*, 2 vols., Mâcon, 1939-70.

DHGE
Dictionnaire d'histoire et de géographie ecclésiastiques, Paris, 1912-

Dickinson
J. C. Dickinson, *The Origins of the Austin Canons and their Introduction into England*, London, 1950.

Dimier (1971)
L'art cistercien hors de France, ed. M.-A. Dimier, Zodiaque, 1971.

GB
Germania Benedictina, vol. II only so far, on Bavaria, Ottobeuren, 1970.

GP
Germania Pontificia, ed. A. Brackmann, I-III, Berlin, 1911-35.

Hauck
A. Hauck, *Kirchengeschichte Deutschlands*, I-III, 3rd and 4th edn., Leipzig, 1904-6; IV-V, 1st and 2nd edn., Leipzig, 1903-20.

Hunt (1967)
Noreen Hunt, *Cluny under St Hugh, 1049-1109*, London, 1967.

Hunt (1971)
Cluniac Monasticism in the Central Middle Ages (selected papers, Eng. trans.), ed. N. Hunt, London, 1971.

IP
Italia Pontificia, ed. P. Kehr (*et alii*), I-IX, Berlin, 1906-62.

KH
D. Knowles and R. N. Hadcock, *Medieval Religious Houses, England and Wales*, 2nd edn., London, 1971.

Knowles, *GHE*
D. Knowles, *Great Historical Enterprises: Problems in Monastic History*, London, 1963.

Knowles, *MO*
D. Knowles, *The Monastic Order in England, 940-1216*, Cambridge, 1940; 2nd edn., pagination unaltered, but with additional notes etc., 1963.

Knowles, *RO*
D. Knowles, *The Religious Orders in England*, 3 vols., Cambridge, 1948-59.

Krautheimer
R. Krautheimer, *Studies in Early Christian, Medieval and Renaissance Art*, New York-London, 1969.

La Mendola
Miscellanea del Centro di Studi Medievali, I-VI, Settimane . . . alla Mendola, Milan, 1956-71.

MSA
D. Knowles and J. K. S. St Joseph, *Monastic Sites from the Air*, Cambridge, 1952.

PL
Patrologiae cursus completus, series latina, ed. J. P. Migne, Paris, 1844-64.

Schmitz
P. Schmitz, *Histoire de l'Ordre de S. Benoît*, 7 vols., Maredsous, 1942-56 (quoted from French edn., vols. I, II, 2nd edn., 1949).

VCH
Victoria History of the Counties of England.

Chapter 1, Prelude, pp. 13-32

1. Matthew, 19, 5-29 (cf. Luke, 18, esp. 29). The opening sentence is quoted from the Authorised Version, the rest from the New English Bible.
2. Many critics doubt whether the Epistle was written by St Paul; yet it seems reasonable to accept that even if he was not the author it was evidently the work of a disciple who believed himself wholly faithful to the apostle's teaching.
3. Acts, 4, 32.
4. Matthew, 10, 9 ff.; Mark, 6, 8 ff.; Luke, 9, 3 ff.; 10, 4 ff. See p. 191.
5. See pp. 114-15, 125 ff., 182 ff.
6. Cf. D. J. Chitty, *The Desert a City* (Oxford, 1966), pp. 1 ff. The movement owed much, needless to say, to non-Christian as well as Christian thinkers. It has in the past been much disputed whether Christian monasticism was grafted on pagan stock or essentially original. The answer must in large measure depend on how precisely the question is framed; for it is evident that a large movement of this time was likely to draw on a range of experience both wider and more ancient than the Christian Church; equally, that many of its special features, and its essential inspiration, are unintelligible except in the context of the early Church. Nothing of this is said in the text, since the aim is to introduce the monasticism of the Middle Ages; but it is a topic of great interest.
7. *Collations*, 18, esp. cc. 5 ff., quoted from Chadwick, *Asceticism*, pp. 266-7.
8. Chadwick, *Cassian* (edn. of 1968), pp. 25-6, 86 ff., esp. 89, where Jerome's attack on Evagrius' conception of *apatheia* is explained and refuted.
9. *Collations*, 18, c. 4; Chadwick, *Asceticism*, p. 266. See below,

pp. 35, 252, chap. 2, n. 5.

10. Since the theme of this book is the western monastic tradition, no more can be said of the eastern, Basilian, Orthodox tradition of monastic life. See next note, and A. J. Festugière, *Les moines d'orient*, 4 vols. in 3, Paris, 1961-5 (lives of eastern monks with introduction).

11. W. K. Lowther Clarke, *The Ascetic Works of St Basil*, London, 1925, pp. 163-6 (Longer Rules, c. 7).

12. See pp. 125-6.

13. Matthew, 6, 26.

14. See R. A. Markus in *Work: an Enquiry into Christian Thought and Practice*, London, 1960, pp. 13-26.

15. *Confessions*, bk. viii, cc. 14-15.

16. *Institutes*, bk. iv, *ad fin.*, quoted Chadwick, *Cassian*, p. 93.

17. The use of Cassian in later monastic history has never been fully studied. Manuscripts of the *Collations* are very numerous and catalogues of great monastic libraries from the 9th century on rarely omit all reference to it. Yet in some of the major monastic thinkers of the 11th and 12th centuries (such as St Anselm and St Bernard) his direct influence seems slight. His indirect influence, through St Benedict and Gregory the Great, was constant and immense.

18. *Collations*, 9, c. 6; 1, c. 6; trans. Chadwick, *Asceticism*, pp. 198, 217.

19. *Collations*, 1, cc. 5, 7, trans. Chadwick, *Asceticism*, pp. 197-8.

20. *Collations*, 1, c. 8, trans. Chadwick, *Asceticism*, p. 200.

21. *Collations*, 9, cc. 9-15, trans. Chadwick, *Asceticism*, pp. 219-20; based on I Timothy, 2, 1.

22. *Collations*, 9, c. 31, trans. Chadwick, *Asceticism*, p. 229; and see pp. 143-56.

'Abba' was a term of respect used for senior monks in Cassian and other early writers, etymologically the equivalent of 'abbot' but not necessarily implying authority over a community (cf. Chadwick, *Asceticism*, p. 31).

23. Matthew, 5, 48—echoed in many passages of the *Collations* and the Rule; specifically the theme of *Collations*, 11, 'On Perfection'.

Chapter 2 The Rule of St Benedict, pp. 33-40

1. The view here stated is that of A. de Vogüé in the introduction to his edition. See n. 3.

2. R. W. Southern, *Western Society and the Church in the Middle Ages*, Pelican History of the Church, II, 1970, p. 222.

3. Knowles, *GHE*, p. 146, from his admirable survey of the controversy down to 1962, ib., pp. 139-95.

4. The quotations are my own translation from *Regula Magistri*, ed. A. de Vogüé, prol., Ths. 45, I, 326, from P. Schmitz's edition of the Rule (see p. 256), prol., pp. 5-6.

5. C. 1, p. 7; what follows is from c. 73, pp. 99-100. The analysis of the four types is based on the *Reg. Magistri*, c. 1; both are derived from Cassian, *Collations*, 18, esp. cc. 4 ff. (trans. Chadwick, *Asceticism*, pp. 265 ff.).

6. See pp. 20, 22 ff. On the version of Basil's Rule which was known to Benedict, see Chadwick, *Cassian*, pp. 62-3.

7. The audience of the Rule has been much discussed: see e.g. Knowles, *GHE*, p. 144, indicating the general rejection of Abbot Chapman's thesis that it was officially commissioned by the pope. It seems clear that Benedict had no idea of compiling a manual for general use, or to be followed by any great number of communities; but that he was writing with the idea in mind that the Rule might be studied and pondered elsewhere than at his own houses (i.e. Subiaco and its neighbours, or Monte Cassino).

8. Cf. Rule, c. 2, with *Reg. Magistri*, c. 2.

9. Ecclesiasticus, 32, 24 (v. 19, A.V.).

Chapter 3 The formation of the traditional monasticism, pp. 41-58

1. Gregory the Great, *Dialog.*, ii, 36 (ed. U. Moricca, Fonti per la storia d'Italia, Rome, 1924, p. 131). Echoes and quotations from the Rule are strikingly absent from Gregory's monastic writings, and this has never been satisfactorily explained—save by those writers who maintain the paradoxical view that Gregory did not know it (K. Hallinger in *Studia Anselmiana*, XLII (Rome, 1957), pp. 231-319;

contra, Knowles, *MO*, edn. of 1963, pp. 750-2; P. Meyvaert, *Bede and Gregory the Great*, Jarrow Lecture, 1964, p. 26n). I say 'paradoxical' since most commentators are impressed by the appropriateness of Gregory's reference to the Rule, cited in the text, and assume that the reference, and Gregory's whole attitude to Benedict, presuppose knowledge of the Rule. The question is open.

2. On the earliest MS of the Rule, Oxford, Bodleian Lib., Hatton MS 48, see *Early English MSS in Facsimile*, XV, ed. D. H. Farmer, Copenhagen, 1968, esp. p. 25.

3. What follows is based on K. Hughes, *The Church in Early Irish Society*, London, 1966, esp. chaps. 6-9, 13; q.v. for the rich modern literature on Celtic monasticism.

4. Bede, *Hist. Eccl.*, iii, 5, 14-17, etc. (ed. B. Colgrave and R. A. B. Mynors, Oxford Medieval Texts, 1969, pp. 226-9, 258-67).

5. See pl. 39; see A. de Vogüé's introd. to the Rule.

6. Wolfram von Eschenbach's *Willehalm* was written *c.* 1210-20. The story was derived from earlier French *chansons de geste*. See p. 122.

7. E. Bishop, *Liturgica Historica*, Oxford, 1918, p. 213.

8. See Bishop, pp. 349 ff.; and on the history of Reichenau and St Gall, pp. 261-2.

Chapter 4 Life, work and prayer, pp. 59-74

1. To save confusion, I call the first two offices Mattins and Lauds; the earlier names, still used in the eleventh century customaries, were Nocturns and Mattins. For the literature of Cluny and its customaries, see p. 257.

2. These hours have, of course, a spurious air of precision; I quote them to make the approximate length of the day clear. They are given in Knowles, *MO*, p. 449, on the basis of a wide study of medieval customs.

3. See the historical chapters in the Downside Symposium on *Work* (p. 252, chap. 1, n. 14), (London, 1960).

4. On the library of Cluny, see L. Delisle, *Le Cabinet des manuscrits de la Bibl. Nationale*, II (Paris, 1874), 458 ff.; Delisle, *Inventaire des mss. de la Bibliothèque Nationale: Fonds de Cluni* (Paris, 1884); A. Wilmart in *Revue Mabillon*, XI (1921), 89 ff.—it is in the last that the book-list of the 1040s is dated and analysed.

5. On this and on Cluny's economy see G. Duby in *Petrus Venerabilis* (p. 257), pp. 128-40. The monks of Cluny wore the familiar black habit; the practice arose in the eleventh century for monks in some humbler monastic houses, such as Bec in Normandy, to wear undyed cloth, and this practice was consecrated as part of their constitution by the Cistercian monks. There is some doubt as to what this meant in practice in early days, for Cistercian MSS of the early twelfth century show the monks sometimes in a brown, sometimes a greyish-white habit; in the end, the latter became the norm, hence they were called the 'white monks'.

6. Ulrich, c. 17, col. 760.

7. On poor relief in the Middle Ages, see B. Tierney, *Medieval Poor Law* (Berkeley and Los Angeles, 1959).

8. See Duby, art. cit. (n. 5).

9. See Knowles, *Historian and Character and Other Essays* (Cambridge, 1963), chapter 4, esp. pp. 62-3 for a brilliant summary of the *Apologia*, and pp. 70-1 for Peter's *Statuta* which confess to many abuses; but one cannot help feeling that some of these, such as public use of the cloister and abuse of trust by some of the servants, were a natural concomitant of the traditional monasticism in its heyday, and that both Professor Knowles and Abbot Peter are a little curt with some of their monks, since they cannot forget that Cistercian eyes have been reading the Rule of St Benedict: for what this meant, see pp. 136 ff.

10. Peter the Venerable, *Letters*, ed. G. Constable (Cambridge, Mass., 1967), no. 20, esp. I, 37-8.

Chapter 5 The hermits, pp. 75-84

1. See p. 228. On the work of Adalbert in Bohemia and Poland, see *La Mendola*, IV, 336 ff. (J. Kłoczowski). Contemporaries sometimes distinguished the more stable hermit from the wandering anchorite, and the word hermitage was used of isolated communities as well as of cells for individuals (cf. J. Leclercq in *Cluniac Monasticism*, ed. N.

24-9,
221-2

Hunt, London, 1971, p. 217n). Outstanding examples of itinerant founders, after St Romuald, were St Robert of Molesme and St Bruno (see pp. 135, 79).

2. Bernard, *Epistola* 91, *PL*, CLXXXII, 224 (trans. B. S. James, London, 1953, no. 94).

3. *PL*, CXLV, 246 ff.

4. What follows is an extract from *Magna Vita*, i, 13 (ed. Douie and Farmer, I, 38 ff.).

5. On Peter of Tarentaise, see H. Brultey, *S. Pierre de Tarentaise*, 2nd edn., Besançon, 1945.

6. *Magna Vita*, i, 10, iv, 12 (I, 32-3; II, 55-6).

7. Evidence on the furnishing of dormitories is scanty in early days. But the Rule of St Benedict and many of the customaries clearly presuppose a dormitory without partitions and with the sparsest furniture; and this is consistent with surviving examples down to the period (approximately the late thirteenth and fourteenth centuries) when panelling, wainscotting and partitioning became a regular feature both of domestic and of ecclesiastical architecture.

8. *Magna Vita*, ii, 11 (I, 81); cf. the similar story of the monk of Rievaulx told by Walter Daniel, *Life of Ailred*, pp. 30-1, etc.

9. See D. Knowles and W. F. Grimes, *Charterhouse* (London, 1954); *MSA*, pp. 234-5.

Chapter 6 The cloister and the world, pp. 76-98

1. See C. Brooke, *Medieval Church and Society*, London, 1971, p. 153 and n.

2. For what follows, see H. E. J. Cowdrey, *The Cluniacs and the Gregorian Reform*, Oxford, 1970, pp. 3 ff. and *passim*.

3. The title 'vicar of Christ' was occasionally applied to kings and emperors in the tenth and eleventh centuries; it only became a specifically papal title in the twelfth and thirteenth.

4. See p. 257.

5. G. Constable, *Monastic Tithes*, Cambridge, 1964, p. 145; Schmitz, I, 264-5; cf. also J. Leclercq in *Studia Monastica*, III (1961), 137 ff. On the development of daily mass, see S. J. P. Van Dijk and J. H. Walker, *The Origins of the Modern Roman Liturgy*, London, 1960, p. 51 f.: it was widely assumed to be a normal practice as early as the eleventh century, but was by no means universal even in the thirteenth.

6. From *Epistola* 8 (7) (ed. T. P. McLaughlin, *Mediaeval Studies*, XVIII (1956), 275, trans. C. K. Scott Moncrieff, London, 1925, p. 188).

7. On the urban 'renaissance' of the 11th-13th centuries, see C. Brooke and G. Keir, *London 800-1216*, London, 1974, chap. 3.

8. KH, *passim*, esp. pp. 488 ff.

9. He had certainly been a monk, almost certainly not at Cluny: see references in Cowdrey (n. 2), pp. 148-9n.

10. On pastoral work performed by monks see U. Berlière in *Revue Bénédictine*, XXXIX (1927), 227-50, 340-64; G. Constable, *Monastic Tithes*, esp. pp. 145 ff.; D. J. A. Matthew, *The Norman Monasteries and their English Possessions* (Oxford, 1962), esp. pp. 51-65; M. Chibnall, in *Journal of Eccl. History*, XVIII (1967), 165-72 (cf. Brooke in *Studies in Church History*, VI, Cambridge, 1970, p. 82n). On tithes, see Constable, esp. pt. ii, chaps. 3-6.

11. *Vita Gauzlini* (p. 257), ii, 57 ff., pp. 104 ff.; *Les Miracles de S. Benoît*, ed. E. de Certain (Paris, 1858), viii, 25-7, 30, pp. 317-28. The second fire and the beginning of the new scheme seem to have belonged to the time of Abbot William, *c*. 1069-80 (cf. *DHGE*, XVII, 449, 470).

12. For what follows, see esp. G. Duby in *Annales*, VII (1952), 155-71.

13. *Letters*, ed. G. Constable (p. 257), no. 89, I, 229; cf. Brooke in *La Mendola*, VI, 137 ff.

14. See Brooke, *Medieval Church and Society*, chap. 8. On San Zeno, see p. 262.

Chapter 7 The monastic contribution to the twelfth-century renaissance, pp. 99-122

1. See J. Harvey, in *Antiquaries Journal*, XLVIII (1968), 87-99; cf. Brooke, *Twelfth Century Renaissance*, London, 1969/70, pp. 101 ff.

2. On Suger, see esp. E. Panofsky, *Abbot Suger on the Abbey Church of Saint-Denis*, Princeton, 1946; E. Mâle, *L'art religieux du xiie siècle en France*, 4th edn., Paris, 1940, chap. V.

3. See pls. 24-9, 221-2; C. R. Dodwell, *Painting in Europe 800-1200*, Harmondsworth, 1971, pp. 89 ff.; C. Oursel, *Miniature du xiie siècle à l'abbaye de Cîteaux* and *Miniatures cisterciennes (1109-1134)*, Dijon, 1926, 1960.

4. For a corpus of material, see Joan Evans, *Romanesque Architecture of the Order of Cluny* (Cambridge, 1938); and on the Hirsau congregation W. Hoffmann, *Hirsau und die 'Hirsauer Bauschule'* (Munich, 1950), concluding that Hirsau was not the centre of a specific school of architecture.

5. Theophilus, *De diuersis artibus*, ed. and trans. C. R. Dodwell, Nelson's Medieval Texts, 1961, i, prol., pp. 1-4; on the MS tradition, see Dodwell, pp. xxxiv ff., lvii ff.; B. Bischoff, *Mittelalterlichen Studien*, II, Stuttgart, 1967, pp. 175-82.

6. See R. W. Southern, *St Anselm and His Biographer* (Cambridge, 1963), pp. 209-17 and literature cited.

7. Eadmer, *Vita Anselmi*, ed. and trans. R. W. Southern, Nelson's Medieval Texts, 1962 (repr. Oxford Med. Texts, 1972), pp. 37-8.

8. Orderic Vitalis, ed. Le Prévost, V, 133 ff. (based on my own version in *Europe in the Central Middle Ages*, London, 1964, pp. 13 ff., but slightly adapted). Cf. Mrs M. Chibnall's introduction to vol. II of her edition; R. W. Church, *St Anselm* (London, 1870), chap. VI.

Chapter 8 The Augustinian canons, pp. 125-34

1. See p. 94 and Constable, *Monastic Tithes* (Cambridge, 1964), pp. 165 ff.

2. Essentially because, although both rules were interpreted freely, both could be studied literally; and this lay at the root of many of the distinctively monastic movements, notably those like the Cistercian (see chap. 9), which depended on the literal interpretation of the Rule of St Benedict.

3. Cf. J. F. Rivera in *La Mendola*, III, vol. i, 220-37. Toledo and (apparently) Osma later became secular. The list of Spanish cathedrals at one time or another Augustinian on p. 236 omits these and adds Siguenza (cf. pp. 233-5) and the collegiate church of Soria.

4. The canons of Saint-Trophime at Arles were subjected to a rule *c*. 1060 (J. C. Dickinson, *Origins of the Austin Canons*, London, 1950, p. 43; *Gallia Christiana Novissima*, III, Valence, 1901, pp. 168-9, 176; *Gallia Christ.*, edn. of Paris, 1715-1865, I, Instruments, p. 96); whether they were then, and remained, strictly Augustinian, is not clear. But Arles is not far from Avignon, and it is reasonable to presume a link with the cathedral there and with Saint-Ruf (cf. A. Borg, *Architectural Sculpture in Romanesque Provence*, Oxford, 1972, p. 67 and n. 22). Surviving communal buildings and inscriptions in the cloister (see pl. 209) show them to have been subject to a rule in the mid and late twelfth century; they were presumably Augustinian then.

5. Dickinson, pp. 108 ff., 125-6, etc.; Brooke in *La Mendola*, VI, 136 ff., esp. 141-2.

6. *Libellus de diuersis ordinibus*, ed. G. Constable and B. Smith (Oxford Medieval Texts, 1972), with a full commentary.

7. Canterbury Tales, *Prologue*, slightly modernised. Austin and Benet are the traditional vernacular forms of Augustine and Benedict. 'Maure' was St Maurus, Benedict's companion; he was not in fact the author of a separate Rule.

8. Knowles, *RO*, II, Appendix I, pp. 365-6.

Chapter 9 The Cistercians, pp. 135-62

1. The most famous case is his reconciliation with Abelard, arranged by Peter the Venerable partly, at least, at Bernard's request. Bernard also tried to arrange a reconciliation with Gilbert de la Porrée, the other theologian whom he attacked; but the reconciliation, like the attack, was unsuccessful (John of Salisbury, *Historia Pontificalis*, Nelson's Medieval Texts, 1956, pp. 26-7).

2. Stephen Harding's letter was ed. C. H. Talbot in *Collectanea Ord. Cist. Reformat.*, III (1936), 66-9; D. L. Bethell, *Downside Rev.*, LXXIX (1961), 349-50.

3. Printed in *Statuta Capitulorum Generalium Ordinis Cisterciensis*, ed. J.-M. Canivez, I (Louvain, 1933), with other early Cistercian statutes; but it has been shown in recent years that some of the clauses,

especially those describing the general chapter and system of visitation, belong to the mid twelfth century, not to the time of Stephen Harding. For the original form see the articles by Mgr. J. Turk and C. Noschitzka in *Analecta S. Ordinis Cist.*, I, IV, VI (1945-50); and for the story of its discovery and recent controversies on Cistercian origins, Knowles, *GHE*, pp. 197 ff.

4. Mystical knowledge and experience have been thus defined in D. Knowles, *The English Mystical Tradition* (London, 1961), pp. 2-3. 'This knowledge, this experience, which is never entirely separable from an equally immediate and experimental union with God by love, has three main characteristics. It is recognized by the person concerned as something utterly different from and more real and adequate than all his previous knowledge and love of God. It is experienced as something at once immanent and received, something moving and filling the powers of the mind and soul. It is felt as taking place at a deeper level of the personality and soul than that on which the normal processes of thought and will take place, and the mystic is aware, both in himself and in others, of the soul, its qualities and of the divine presence and action within it, as something wholly distinct from the reasoning mind with its powers. Finally, this experience is wholly incommunicable, save as a bare statement, and in this respect all the utterances of the mystics are entirely inadequate as representations of the mystical experience, but it brings absolute certainty to the mind of the recipient. This is the traditional mystical theology, the mystical knowledge of God, in its purest form.'

5. In several churches, especially Rievaulx, Fountains and Tintern, traces can still be seen of partitions in the nave aisles, doubtless to increase the number of altars; but this seems to be a development of the late thirteenth and fourteenth centuries.

6. *Vita prima S. Bernardi*, ii, 5 (*PL*, CLXXXV, 285; quoted Brooke, *Europe in the Central Middle Ages*, pp. 70-1).

7. As King John mulcted, or taxed, the English Cistercians in the early stages of his dispute with the pope; he was later induced to found the Cistercian abbey of Beaulieu in Hants, partly to compensate for what he had taken from the Cistercians.

8. See Brooke, *Medieval Church and Society*, p. 166 and n.; M. Aubert, *L'architecture cistercienne en France*, I, 317, etc.

9. As has recently been emphasised by Dom Jean Leclercq, in *S. Bernard et l'esprit cistercien*, p. 20.

10. For the plan, see Aubert, op. cit.; and the works of Esser, Dimier and Hahn, cited, n. 11 and p. 258. For the constitution, above, n. 3.

11. 'Über den Kirchenbau des Hl. Bernhard von Clairvaux', *Archiv für mittelrheinische Kirchengeschichte*, V (1953), 195-222, from which pl. 252 is reproduced (with kind permission); cf. F. Bucher, 'Cistercian architectural purism', *Comparative Studies in Society and History*, III (1960-1), 89-105, at pp. 97-8, 105. The history of the square east end, its significance and proportions, are considerably sophisticated in H. Hahn's *Frühe Kirchenbaukunst der Zisterzienser*, Berlin, 1957; but this has not diminished the value of Dr Esser's dramatic presentation of the basic evidence. Hahn's study of proportions etc. has shown e.g. that at Eberbach there was a change of plan while the church was being built.

12. I am informed that extensive tree felling over the centuries has substantially reduced the water supply in the valley.

13. The design of the Sénanque chapter house was evidently altered in course of construction, and the heavy ribs seem to be an afterthought. But the basic layout is characteristic of Cistercian cloisters and must be as originally intended.

14. For what follows, see Walter Daniel's *Life of Ailred of Rievaulx*, ed. F. M. Powicke (Nelson's Medieval Texts, 1950), pp. 12 f.

15. *Life of Ailred*, pp. 11-12.

16. But see Powicke's note, p. 38. The chapter house at Rievaulx was originally of more normal form; it was rebuilt, very likely in Ailred's time, and the new shape is strikingly similar to the twelfth century chapter house at Durham, Ailred's original home.

17. *Life of Ailred*, pp. 36-8.

18. E.g. *Letters*, trans. B. S. James (London, 1953), nos. 95, 146, 204.

19. *Sermones in Canticum*, no. 26 (*Opera*, I, ed. J. Leclercq, C. H. Talbot,

H. M. Rochais, Rome, 1957, p. 172).

Chapter 10 The knights, pp. 163-6

1. See D. W. Lomax, *La Orden de Santiago (1170-1275)*, Madrid, 1965.

2. The most recent study is V. Gervers-Molnár, *A Középkori Magyarország Rotundái* (Budapest, 1972, in Hungarian, with English summary, pp. 84-90).

3. See M. Gervers, 'Rotundae Anglicanae', *Actes du xxiie Congrès Internationale de l'Histoire de l'Art* (1969) (Budapest, 1972), pp. 359-76. On the order of the Holy Sepulchre, see J. C. Dickinson in *Trans. Royal Hist. Soc.*, 5th Series, I (1951), 71 ff., esp. p. 73.

Chapter 11 On abbesses and prioresses, pp. 167-80

1. Edited by Dom Germain Morin, Bonn, 1933.

2. For England. See KH, esp. p. 494 (strictly 48 to 13 *c.* 1066, but the disproportion rapidly increased for a time after the Norman Conquest); for France no comparable statistics have been made: the statement in the text is based on a survey kindly undertaken for me by Miss E. Hallam.

3. See pp. 49-50, 125.

4. A. Schulte, *Der Adel und die deutsche Kirche im Mittelalter*, Kirchenrechtliche Abhandlungen, ed. U. Stutz, 63-4, Stuttgart, 1910, pp. 401 ff. On Matilda of Essen, see pp. 167-8.

5. N. Hunt, *Cluny under St Hugh*, London, 1967, pp. 186 ff.

6. A father who placed a daughter in a nunnery was expected to present the convent with a 'dowry', though the exaction of dowries was forbidden by reforming councils. A good example of a house of very modest origins which rose to tolerable prosperity by enjoying the neighbourhood of rich citizens whose daughters and legacies greatly benefited its endowments was Haliwell, the earliest to be founded of the London convents of nuns (see C. Brooke and G. Keir, *London 800-1216*, London, 1974, chap. 12).

7. See KH, p. 251.

8. Especially by R. R. Bezzola, *Les origines et la formation de la littérature courtoise en occident* (Paris, 1958-60), esp. II, ii, 275-92. The theory of a direct connexion has found little support, but Bezzola's interesting discussion has drawn attention to certain parallels which cannot be due solely to chance.

9. I follow G. Zarnecki (see *The Monastic Achievement*, London, 1972, pp. 93-4) in dating the effigies of the kings to *c.* 1200-4, and the other two to *c.* 1220 or soon after.

10. The correspondence is ed. J. T. Muckle and T. P. McLaughlin in *Mediaeval Studies*, XII, XV, XVII, XVIII (1950-6); translated C. K. Scott Moncrieff, London, 1925. The quotations below are from Scott Moncrieff, pp. 91, 96; *Mediaeval Studies*, XVII, 243, 247. In what follows I accept the authenticity of the correspondence, which is, however, controversial: see the forthcoming study by Professor John Benton.

Chapter 12 St Norbert and St Francis, pp. 181-98

1. See esp. 'Un débat sur le sacerdoce des moines au xie siècle', ed. R. Foreville and J. Leclercq, *Studia Anselmiana*, XLI, 8-118.

2. See Brooke, *Medieval Church and Society* (London, 1971), chap. 7, esp. pp. 147 ff., and books cited, esp. H. Grundmann, *Religiöse Bewegungen im Mittelalter* (2nd ed., Hildesheim, 1961).

3. St Gilbert formed his first convent, at Sempringham in Lincs, in the 1130s, and in 1147 travelled to Cîteaux with the idea of placing the house under Cistercian jurisdiction. The Cistercians refused to accept his plan in the form in which he wished it; but he took much advice from Bernard and the Cistercian pope, Eugenius III (1145-53), in forming his Rule. The Gilbertines never spread outside England. See R. Graham, *S. Gilbert of Sempringham and the Gilbertines* (London, 1901); KH, pp. 194 ff.

4. Though many scholars doubt if Francis influenced Dominic in any crucial way, and some have doubted if they ever met. I have discussed this problem in *Medieval Church and Society*, pp. 222-9.

5. *Opuscula S. Patris Francisci Assisiensis* (Quaracchi, 2nd ed., 1941), pp. 83-4.

6. *Epistola* 3 (*Opuscula*, p. 108); for the reading *non*, 'not', in the text above, see R. B. Brooke, *Early Franciscan Government* (Cambridge,

1959), p. 173n.

7. *Scripta Leonis, Rufini et Angeli*, ed. R. B. Brooke (Oxford Medieval Texts, 1970), no. 98, pp. 260-3.

8. The Franciscan renunciation of property was absolute both in theory and practice, though the relation between possession and ownership led to many difficulties, and they were compelled in the long run to accept that the Holy See could hold property for their use, which in effect meant (contrary to the founder's intention) for their exclusive use. The Dominican renunciation was not so fundamental, nor quite so complete; but in practice both orders lived on alms. On the Franciscan idea and practice, see M. D. Lambert, *Franciscan Poverty* (London, 1961).

Nothing is said in this book about the other orders of Friars, which proliferated in the thirteenth century. Of these the most important—and the only ones to survive in the long run—were the Orders of Carmelite and Austin Friars. See Knowles, *RO*, I, chap. xvii; KH, pp. 232 ff.

Chapter 13 Three visits, pp. 201-23

1. Studley Park was laid out by John Aislabie (Chancellor of the Exchequer, 1718-21; died 1742) and rounded off by his son, William Aislabie, who bought the Fountains estate. Their successors by degrees converted the abbey from a romantic folly into a well-preserved ruin, and it is now in the custody of the Department of the Environment.

2. Walter Map, *De nugis curialium*, i. 25, trans. M. R. James (Cymmrodorion Rec. Soc., 1923), p. 49. Map's quotation is from Ovid, *Heroides*, i. 53.

3. See R. A. Donkin, in *Bulletin of the Inst. of Hist. Research*, XXXIII (1960), 141-65; M. W. Barley, in *Nottingham Mediaeval Studies*, I (1957), 75-89. In practice, even the Cistercians had to accept deviations from their basic rules, and these increased as time went on (see Knowles, *MO*, 2nd edn., pp. 746-7, for articles by R. A. Donkin and C. V. Graves on settlement and economic activities of the Cistercians in England).

4. St Bernard, *Epistola* 106, quoted *MO*, p. 221; Brooke, *Europe in the Central Middle Ages* (London, 1964), p. 302: slightly adapted.

5. Cf. *Brooke, Twelfth-Century Renaissance* (London, 1969), pl. 23.

6. See article by L. G. D. Baker, cited n. 7.

7. See esp. Baker, in *Northern History*, IV (1969), 38 ff.

8. *Millénaire monastique du Mont St-Michel* (p. 258), I, chapter II (M. Lelegard); in chapter I (J. Hourlier) evidence is adduced for an earlier foundation, *c.* 550-75, as an annexe of a monastery at Asteriac. But the effective history of Mont St-Michel begins with St Aubert in 708. For literature on the abbey, see p. 258. On the cult of St Michael, see *Millénaire* III; O. Chadwick in H. M. Chadwick *et al. Studies in Early British History* (Cambridge, 1954), pp. 182-4; cf. W. Levison, *England and the Continent in the Eighth Century* (Oxford, 1946), p. 263.

9. Monastic life was revived for a time in more recent days.

10. This does not mean, as has sometimes been supposed, that the abbey became a naval power; see M. Mollat in *Millénaire*, II, 73 ff.

11. Ed. L. Delisle in his edition of the Chronicle of Robert of Torigny (2 vols., Rouen, 1872-3); omitted in the ed. by R. Howlett, *Chronicles of the Reigns of Stephen*, etc., IV, Rolls Series, 1889.

12. Swaan, *The Gothic Cathedral*, pp. 151-4, 200-7.

13. I.e. cathedrals served by chapters or communities of secular canons (see p. 125) or monks; Durham itself, and Winchester, were monastic cathedrals.

14. For the building I follow the conclusions of F. Reggiori, *La Basilica di Sant'Ambrogio* (1966); a useful and well illustrated brief account is that by A. M. Romanini (Tesori d'Arte Cristiana, 8, 1966). On the history of the two communities, especially in the eleventh and twelfth centuries, I am much indebted to the advice of Mgr Prof. P. Zerbi, and to his articles in *Studi Medievali*, 3 ser., IV (1963), 136-216; *Vescovi e diocesi in Italia nel Medioevo* (Padua, 1964), pp. 245-313; and in *Miscellanea Gilles Gerard Meersseman* (Padua, 1970), I, 107-32.

15. As at the neighbouring Basilica of San Lorenzo, where a fragment of the atrium may still be seen. At Cassian's St Victor, Marseille (if correctly identified) the traces of the original atrium can also be seen.

16. Now destroyed (see pp. 167-8). Cf. *S. Laurent de Liège*, ed.

R. Lejeune (Liège, 1968), p. 39.

17. For Saint-Riquier, see A. W. Clapham, *English Romanesque Architecture before the Conquest*, Oxford, 1930, pp. 78 ff. See pls. 229, 256, 387-8; modern restoration has no doubt often obscured the vestiges of medieval glazing in cloister arcades. Such vestiges are clear, however, in the double arcade at Eberbach (pl. 42).

Chapter 14 1300: the monastic map of Europe, pp. 225-41

1. D. W. Lomax, *La Orden de Santiago (1170-1275)* (Madrid, 1965), p. 50.

2. Ib., *passim*, esp. pp. 41-50.

3. J. Kłoczowski in *La Mendola*, VI, 153-72.

4. These details are based on F. Van der Meer, *Atlas de l'Ordre Cistercien* (Amsterdam-Brussels, 1965); for corrections, see E. Krausen and P. Zakar in *Analecta Cisterciensia*, XXII (1966), 279-90; F. Vongrey and F. Hervay in *Analecta Cisterciensia*, XXIII (1967), 115-27. I have followed modern frontiers in the rough figures quoted.

5. See *Atlas Cist.*, on Poland, there are rich details on history as well as architecture in *Sztuka Polska przedromańska i romańska do schylku XIII wieku*, ed. M. Walicki, 2 vols., Warsaw (1968), with Cistercian family tree on I, 167, by J. Kłoczowski; for lists of Polish religious houses in the 18th century, with copious maps, see L. Bieńkowski, J. Kłoczowski, Z. Sułowski, *Zakony Meskie w Polsce w 1772 Roku*, Lublin, 1972.

6. See *Atlas Cist.*, esp. map VIII: there were two other houses in Denmark, one in Sweden. Surviving remains are illustrated in A. Tuulse, *Scandinavia Romanica* (German trans., Vienna-Munich, 1968).

7. Knowles, *MO*, p. 164 and n.; the date there suggested, 1095-6, depends on Robert, abbot of Evesham, corrected in *Heads of Religious Houses, England and Wales, 940-1216*, ed. D. Knowles, C. N. L. Brooke, and V. C. M. London (Cambridge, 1972), p. 47. But the foundation seems to have occurred before the death of William II in 1100.

8. *Vita Bernardi*, vii, 27, 55 (*PL, CLXXXV*, 445) cited E. Vacandard, *Vie de S. Bernard*, 4th edn., Paris, 1910, II, 416-17.

9. See L. Milis, *L'ordre des Chanoines réguliers d'Arrouaise*, Bruges, 1969. On Malachy and the Irish church, see J. A. Watt, *The Church and the Two Nations in Medieval Ireland* (Cambridge, 1970), chap. 1; and ibid. *passim* for what follows. The figures are based on A. Gwynn and R. N. Hadcock, *Medieval Religious Houses, Ireland* (London, 1970).

10. In KH, on which what follows is based.

11. See the fourteenth-fifteenth century lists printed in M. Marrier, *Bibliotheca Cluniacensis* (Paris, 1614, rep. Mâcon, 1915), cols. 1705-52 and by J. Evans, *Romanesque Architecture of the Order of Cluny* (Cambridge, 1938), pp. 153-76. This has not been subjected to critical scrutiny, nor have comprehensive and reliable lists been compiled for earlier periods—for the difficulties, see N. Hunt, *Cluny under St Hugh* (London, 1967), pp. 5 ff.

12. See Vongrey and Hervay, art. cit. (n. 4), XXIII, 137-8, who give 742 and 654.

13. H. F. Cary's translation of lines 35-50, 61-93. Benedict names, among his fellow monks, Macarius and Romuald: two of the best known early monks in Egypt were called Macarius; for Romuald, see pp. 75-8.

Chapter 15 Epilogue, pp. 243-50

1. In some cases monastic buildings dismantled at or after the French Revolution quickly fell into the hands of owners who were personally interested in preserving and restoring them; this helps to explain, e.g., the fine state of preservation of Sénanque.

2. G. Moorhouse, *Against All Reason* (Penguin Edn., 1972), p. 54.

3. These figures are quoted from Moorhouse, pp. 275-7; but cf. his cautions on pp. 82 ff. on the reliability of the figures. On non-Roman Catholic religious, see ibid., esp. chapter 1, on Taizé.

Bibliographical note

The purpose of this note is to be a guide to further reading and an explanation of the literature on which the text is based. Part I contains general studies covering a wide area of the field; II gives the literature chapter by chapter (some more specific points are dealt with in the footnotes); III gives a brief note of the literature on individual monasteries which figure in text and illustrations.

I

Three scholars who have made an exceptionally rich contribution in recent generations to the historical literature on medieval monasticism are Professor Dom David Knowles, Dom Ursmer Berlière and Dom Jean Leclercq.

D. Knowles, *Monastic Order in England, 940-1216* (Cambridge, 1940; 2nd edn., 1963, cited as *MO*); *Religious Orders in England*, I-III (Cambridge, 1948-59, cited as *RO*): both these great books have much to say on the continental background. Knowles has given a brief general survey in *Christian Monasticism* (London, 1969). A number of his essays are reprinted in *The Historian and Character and Other Essays* (Cambridge, 1963). For lists of English houses, Knowles and R. N. Hadcock, *Medieval Religious Houses, England and Wales* (2nd edn., London, 1971: *KH*). For other countries, see p. 259. Knowles and J. K. S. St Joseph, *Monastic Sites from the Air* (Cambridge, 1952: *MSA*) opened a new era in the study of monastic sites.

U. Berlière, *L'ordre monastique* (Maredsous, 1923), *L'ascèse bénédictine* (Paris, 1927) are clear introductions by an eminent scholar. For Dom Jean Leclercq's books, see pp. 257-8; and especially *L'amour de lettres et le désir de Dieu* (Paris, 1957; English trans., New York, 1962); *Études sur le vocabulaire monastique du moyen âge* and *Otia monastica* (Rome, 1961-3; Studia Anselmiana, fasc. 48, 51). Also useful still is C. Butler, *Benedictine Monachism* (London, 1919; new edn. 1961).

A rich store of learning, often ill-organised and polemical in tone, but on St Benedict and St Bernard (e.g.) sympathetic and penetrating, is to be found in G. G. Coulton's *Five Centuries of Religion* (4 vols., Cambridge, 1923-50), the chief of his many works on the subject (see p. 111).

Collected papers of great scholars on monastic and liturgical history are to be found in E. Bishop, *Liturgica Historica* (Oxford, 1918); A. Wilmart, *Auteurs spirituels et textes dévots du moyen âge latin* (Paris, 1932).

Studies covering many aspects of this book are collected in the publications of the *La Mendola* conferences (*Miscellanea del Centro di Studi Medievali*, of the Università Cattolica del Sacro Cuore. I-VI, Milan, 1956-71: see below).

Other useful general books are: G. Zarnecki, *The Monastic Achievement* (London, 1972); P. Cousin, *Précis d'histoire monastique* (Paris-Tournai, 1959); M. Heimbucher, *Die Orden und Kongregationen der Katholischen Kirche* (2 vols., 3rd edn., Paderborn, 1933-4); P. Schmitz, *Histoire de l'Ordre de S. Benoît* (7 vols., Maredsous, 1942-56). For reference, there are numerous valuable articles in *DHGE*; *Dict. de spiritualité*; *Dict. de théologie catholique*; and the *New Catholic*

Encyclopedia. Of many periodicals, the *Revue Bénédictine* and the *Revue Mabillon* are especially useful (and see below); W. Braunfels, *Monasteries of Western Europe: The Architecture of the Orders* (London, 1972) is an interesting, if not altogether successful, attempt to relate the history and architecture of the religious orders (see review in *History*, forthcoming).

There are bibliographies in most of the general works listed; and running bibliographies published yearly in *Revue d'histoire ecclésiastique*.

II

Chapter 1

On early monasticism, see especially D. J. Chitty, *The Desert a City* (Oxford, 1966); O. Chadwick, *Western Asceticism* (London, 1958); K. Heussi, *Der Ursprung des Mönchtums* (Tübingen, 1936). On St Basil, W. K. L. Clarke, *The Ascetic Works of St Basil*, London, 1925. On Cassian, O. Chadwick, *John Cassian* (Cambridge, 1950, 2nd edn., 1968), *Conferences*, ed. and French trans. E. Pichery (Sources Chrétiennes, 3 vols., Paris, 1955-9), *Institutions Cénobitiques*, ed. and French trans. J.-C. Guy, ibid. 1965.

Chapter 2

On the problem of the *Regula magistri* and the Rule of St Benedict, Knowles, *GHE*, pp. 135-95; A. de Vogüé's introductions to his editions of both (Sources Chrétiennes, Paris, 1964-73). His is the best edition of the Rule; on other editions, see P. Meyvaert in *Scriptorium*, XVII (1963), 83 ff. and D. H. Farmer in *Early English MSS in Facsimile*, XV (1968), pp. 28-9. English translations in Chadwick, *Asceticism*, and by J. McCann (1952). The quotations are my own translation from P. Schmitz's edition of the Sangallensis (Maredsous, 1946). Our knowledge of Benedict apart from the Rule comes almost exclusively from the *Dialogues* of Gregory the Great (ed. U. Moricca, Rome, 1924), bk. II; there is a convenient summary in J. McCann, *St Benedict* (London, 1939). On the history of Rules and obedience, Knowles, *From Pachomius to Ignatius* (Oxford, 1966).

Chapter 3

On Cassiodorus, *DHGE*, XI, 1349-1408 (D. M. Cappuyns); on Celtic and Anglo-Saxon monasticism, K. Hughes, *The Church in Early Irish Society* (London, 1966); J. Ryan, *Irish Monasticism* (London, 1931); H. Mayr-Harting, *The Coming of Christianity to Anglo-Saxon England* (London, 1972). On eighth-ninth centuries, W. Levison, *England and the Continent in the Eighth Century* (Oxford, 1946); D. A. Bullough, *The Age of Charlemagne* (London, 1965). On St Benedict of Aniane, *DHGE*, VIII, 177-88 (P. Schmitz); Knowles in *MO*, pp. 25 ff.; *Vita in PL*, CIII, 353-84 (the decrees are in *Corpus consuetudinum monasticarum* —see below—I, 423 ff.). In general, and for the tenth-century movements, see Schmitz I, and below; for Gorze, K. Hallinger, *Gorze-Kluny* (2 vols., Rome, 1950-1); for England, Knowles, *MO*.

Chapters 4 and 6

On Cluny, see Hunt (1967), and Hunt (1971)—a useful collection of essays showing a cross-section of recent work, with references to the rich continental literature; J. Evans, *Monastic Life at Cluny, 910-1157* (Oxford, 1931); K. J. Conant, *Cluny* (Mâcon, 1968); *Spiritualità Cluniacense* (Todi, 1960); J. Leclercq, *Pierre le Vénérable* (St-Wandrille, 1946); *Petrus Venerabilis*, ed. G. Constable and J. Kritzeck (Studia Anselmiana, 40, Rome, 1956), including G. Duby on Cluny's economy, pp. 128-40; on her budget, Duby in *Annales*, VII (1952), 155-71; *Letters of Peter the Venerable*, ed. G. Constable (2 vols., Cambridge, Mass., 1967). On William of Hirsau and his movement, H. Jakobs, *Die Hirsauer* (Köln-Graz, 1961).

For general historical background, R. W. Southern, *Making of the Middle Ages* (London, 1953) and *Western Society and the Church in the Middle Ages* (Harmondsworth, 1970); books listed in C. Brooke, *Europe in the Central Middle Ages* (London, 1964), esp., on papal reform and monasticism, pp. 237-8, 294; to these should be added *La Mendola* VI (1971); H. E. J. Cowdrey, *The Cluniacs and the Gregorian Reform* (Oxford, 1970).

For social background and relations with patrons, *La Mendola* VI; essays in *Millénaire monastique du Mont St-Michel* (p. 258); D. J. A. Matthew, *The Norman Monasteries and Their English Possessions* (Oxford, 1962). On economic background, G. Duby, *L'économie rurale et la vie des campagnes dans l'occident médiéval* (2 vols., Paris, 1962; Eng. trans. by C. Postan, London, 1968); G. Constable, *Monastic Tithes from Their Origins to the Twelfth Century* (Cambridge, 1964); L. Musset in *L'abbaye bénédictine de Fécamp*, I (Fécamp, 1959), pp. 67-79.

The documents on which these chapters are mainly based are:

1. MONASTIC CUSTOMS. Cluny's are printed in *Consuetudines monasticae*, ed. B. Albers, II (Monte Cassino, 1905), pp. 31-61 and I (Stuttgart and Vienna, 1900), *passim* [Customs of 996-1030 and 1030-48; cf. Hunt (1967), p. 33 and references; Knowles in *Corpus Cons. Monast.* III (1967), p. xviii]; M. Herrgott, *Vetus Disciplina Monastica* (Paris, 1726), pp. 133-364 [Bernard of Cluny, 1067; cf. Knowles, loc. cit.]; *PL*, CXLIX, 635-778 [Ulrich, *c.* 1075].

A *Corpus consuetudinum monasticarum*, ed. K. Hallinger, has been planned, and some volumes published, with the intention of drawing the whole body of literature together. Meanwhile, see selection in Albers, op. cit. (5 vols., 1900-12); the vols. of the Henry Bradshaw Society; the major English customaries of the tenth-eleventh centuries are *Regularis Concordia* (*c.* 970), ed. T. Symons (Nelson's Medieval Texts, 1953) and *The Monastic Constitutions of Lanfranc*, ed. D. Knowles (Nelson's Medieval Texts, 1951, with trans.; reprinted, text only, with revised introd. and notes, *Corpus Cons. Mon.*, III, Siegburg, 1967).

2. LIBRI VITAE, NECROLOGIES ETC. Cf. Wollasch in Hunt (1971), chap. 9; the *Liber Vitae* of New Minster, Winchester, is British Museum, Stowe MS 944; ed. W. de G. Birch, Hants. Rec. Soc., London and Winchester, 1892. For prosopography, the material is extremely scattered: for lists of abbots etc. see Hauck; *Germania Sacra* (Berlin etc, 1929-   ); *GB*; *Gallia Christiana* (edn. of Paris, 1739-1877); *Heads of Religious Houses, England and Wales, 940-1216*, ed. D. Knowles, C. N. L. Brooke and V. C. M. London (Cambridge, 1972).

3. BIOGRAPHIES. See esp. Eadmer's *Life of St Anselm* (ed. and trans. R. W. Southern, Nelson's Medieval Texts, 1962(3), rep. Oxford Med. Texts, 1972); cf. R. W. Southern, *St Anselm and His Biographer* (Cambridge, 1963), and Eadmer's *Historia novorum* (ed. M. Rule, Rolls Series, 1884; Eng. trans. G. Bosanquet, London, 1964); 'Vita Herluini' (founder of Bec) in J. A. Robinson, *Gilbert Crispin* (Cambridge, 1911); the Autobiography of Guibert, abbot of Nogent-sous-Coucy (*PL*, CLVI, 837-962; Eng. trans. C. C. Swinton Bland, London, 1925; also in *Self and Society . . .*, by J. F. Benton, Harper Torchbook, 1970); André de Fleury, *Vie de Gauzlin, abbé de Fleury*, ed. and French trans. R.-H. Bautier and G. Labory (Sources d'Histoire Médiévale, Paris, 1969); *Vita S. Godehardi* (*PL*, CXLI: see pp. 57-8, citing col. 1174); *Vita* of William of Hirsau, *Monumenta Germaniae Hist., Scriptores*,

XII, 209-25.

4. THE MORE REFLECTIVE, OR EXPANSIVE, MONASTIC CHRONICLES. Esp. Orderic Vitalis (quoted on p. 122); a new edn. and Eng. trans. by M. Chibnall is in progress (vols. II-IV, Oxford Medieval Texts, 1968-73); full edn. A. Le Prévost, completed by L. Delisle (5 vols., Paris, 1838-55); see also H. Wolter, *Ordericus Vitalis* (Wiesbaden, 1955); Rodulf Glaber (ed. M. Prou, Paris, 1886; new edn. Eng. with trans. by J. France, in preparation); Hugh Candidus, *Chronicle* (of Peterborough abbey), ed. W. T. Mellows (Oxford 1949; also trans. C. and W. T. Mellows, Peterborough, 1941).

5. PRAYERS, SERMONS ETC. OF LEADING SPIRITUAL DIRECTORS. Crucial guides are A. Wilmart, *Auteurs spirituels*, and the writings of J. Leclercq (pp. 256, 258), esp. Leclercq and J. P. Bonnes, *Un maître de la vie spirituelle du xie siècle, Jean de Fécamp* (Paris, 1946).

Chapter 5

On the 'crisis of monasticism' in the eleventh-twelfth centuries, see esp. C. Dereine in *Revue du moyen âge latin*, IV (1948), 137-54; *Revue d'hist. ecclésiastique*, LIV (1959), 41-65; Leclercq in Hunt (1971), chap. 11 (the phrase, in the form 'crise du cénobitisme', seems to have been coined by Dom G. Morin, in *Revue Bénédictine*, XL (1928), 99).

On the hermits, see *La Mendola* IV: *L'eremitismo* (1965). On the Carthusians, Knowles, *MO*, chap. XXII; *PL*, CLII, CLIII: E. M. Thompson, *The Carthusian Order in England*, London, 1930; Guigo or Guy II (prior of the Chartreuse), *The Scale of the Cloister*, trans. B. S. James (London, 1937); on St Hugh, *Magna vita S. Hugonis*, ed. and trans. D. L. Douie and H. Farmer (2 vols., Nelson's Medieval Texts, 1961-2). On the background of movements in Rome, G. Ferrari, *Early Roman Monasteries* (Rome, 1957); B. Hamilton in *Studia monastica*, IV (1962), 35-68. On Camaldoli and Vallombrosa, pp. 259, 262. On Grandmont, *Corpus Christianorum, Cont. Med.*, VIII, ed. J. Becquet (Turnholti, 1968), and R. Graham, *English Ecclesiastical Studies* (London, 1929), chap. IX.

On St Peter Damian, see J. Leclercq, *S. Pierre Damien* (Rome, 1960); St Peter Damian, *Selected Writings on the Spiritual Life*, trans. with introd. by Patricia McNulty (London, 1959).

Chapter 7

On the general themes of this chapter, C. Brooke, *Twelfth-Century Renaissance* (London, 1969), with bibliog. on pp. 203 ff.; C. H. Haskins, *Renaissance of the Twelfth Century* (Cambridge, Mass., 1927); on Anselm, Eadmer and Orderic, above, note to chaps. 4, 6.

On art and architecture, G. Zarnecki, *Romanesque Art*, London, 1971 (first publ. in German trans., *Romanik*, Stuttgart, 1970); R. Oursel, *Invention de l'architecture romane* (Zodiaque, 1970); *Propyläen Kunstgeschichte*, V, Das Mittelalter, ed. K. Fillitz, 1969, esp. the chapter by G. Zarnecki on Romanesque sculpture; O. Demus, *Romanische Wandmalerei* (Munich, 1968; Eng. trans., London, 1970); C. R. Dodwell, *Painting in Europe, 800-1200* (Harmondsworth, 1971); W. Swaan, *The Gothic Cathedral* (London, 1969); O von Simson, *The Gothic Cathedral* (New York, 1956); P. Frankl, *Gothic Architecture* (Harmondsworth, 1962); and the classic studies of E. Mâle, *L'art religieux du XIIe siècle en France* (6th edn., Paris, 1953) and *L'art religieux du XIIIe siècle . . .* (6th edn., Paris, 1925; Eng. trans. D. Nussey, *The Gothic Image*, new edn., London, 1961).

On the monastic contribution, G. G. Coulton, *Art and the Reformation* (Oxford, 1928; 2nd edn., 1953); R. E. Swartwout, *The Monastic Craftsman* (Cambridge, 1932); C. R. Dodwell, *The Canterbury School of Illumination* (Cambridge, 1954); E. Panofsky, *Abbot Suger on the Abbey Church of Saint-Denis* (Princeton, 1946); O. Pächt, C. R. Dodwell and F. Wormald, *The St Albans Psalter* (London, 1960). On the Cistercians, see below; C. Oursel, *La miniature du xiie siècle à l'abbaye de Cîteaux* and *Miniatures cisterciennes (1109-1134)* (Dijon, 1926, 1960); on the Cluniacs, J. Evans, *Romanesque Architecture of the Order of Cluny* and *Cluniac Art of the Romanesque Period* (Cambridge, 1938, 1949).

On Theophilus, see *De diuersis artibus*, ed. and Eng. trans. C. R.

Dodwell (Nelson's Medieval Texts, 1961; cf. chap. 7, n. 5). On professional artists and craftsmen, V. W. Egbert, *The Mediaeval Artist at Work* (Princeton, 1967); A. Martindale, *The Rise of the Artist* (London, 1972).

Chapter 8
J. C. Dickinson, *The Origins of the Austin Canons*; C. Dereine, esp. 'Chanoines' in *DHGE*, XII, 353-405; also in *Revue d'histoire ecclésiastique*, XLI (1946), 365-406, XLIII (1948), 411-42; *Les chanoines réguliers au diocèse de Liège . . .* (Brussels, 1952); and *La Mendola*, III. The most recent and thorough study of the Rule of St Augustine is L. Verheijen, *La règle de S. Augustin* (2 vols., Paris, 1967). On the *conversi* see C. D. Fonseca in *La Mendola*, V, 262-305.

Chapter 9
On the Cistercians and St Bernard, Knowles, *MO*, chaps. XII-XIV, XXXVII, and *Historian and Character and Other Essays* (Cambridge, 1963), chap. III (on Bernard); J. Leclercq, *St Bernard et l'esprit cistercien* (Paris, 1966)—a brief, penetrating survey with ample quotations and useful short bibliography; the standard life is still E. Vacandard, *Vie de S. Bernard* (2 vols., 4th edn., Paris, 1910); for English readers W. Williams, *St Bernard of Clairvaux* (Manchester, 1935) is useful. Bernard's works, ed. J. Mabillon (Paris, 1690), repr. *PL*, CLXXXII-V, are being re-edited by J. Leclercq and other scholars, 4 vols. so far (Rome, 1957-66). Of many translations in various languages, the most useful are *Letters*, Eng. trans. by B. S. James (London, 1953), and the complete works in French by Ravelet-Laffineur and Dion-Charpentier (Paris, 1867, 1874). An interesting general account is L. J. Lekai, *The White Monks* (Okauchee, 1953). For reference, R. A. Donkin, *Cistercian Bibliography* (Rochefort, 1969).

On St Ailred of Rievaulx, Walter Daniel's *Life*, ed. and trans. F. M. Powicke (Nelson's Medieval Texts, 1950); A. Squire, *Aelred of Rievaulx* (London, 1969); *Opera Omnia*, in progress, *Corpus Christianorum, Cont. Med.*, I, ed. A. Hoste and C. H. Talbot (Turnholti, 1971-   ).

The controversies on Cistercian origins are clarified in Knowles, *GHE*, pp. 197-222, with references to the literature and texts; for these, see esp. *Statuta Capitulorum Generalium Ordinis Cisterciensis*, ed. J.-M. Canivez, I (Louvain, 1933), and pp. 253-4, chap. 9, n. 3. For its organisation, J. B. Mahn, *L'ordre cistercien et son gouvernement . . . 1098-1265* (Paris, 1945). On the Cistercian economy, Knowles, *RO*, I, chap. VII; Constable, *Monastic Tithes* (p. 257); Donkin, art. cit. (p. 255, chap. 13, n. 3; cf. list in *MO*, 2nd edn., p. 746); H. Dubled in *Revue d'histoire ecclésiastique*, LIV (1959), 765-82; C. Platt, *The Monastic Grange in Medieval England* (London, 1969). On work, C. J. Holdsworth in *Studies in Church History*, X (1973), 59-76.

For the spread of the order, and for excellent maps, charts of affiliation, plates, notes on individual houses, etc., *Atlas Cist.*; for England, KH, pp. 110 ff.; for the Low Countries, J.-M. Canivez, *L'ordre de Cîteaux en Belgique . . .* (Forges-lez-Chimay, 1926); and other books, below. For detailed studies, the chief periodicals are *Analecta Cisterciensia* (formerly *Anal. S. Ordinis Cist.*) and *Cîteaux* (formerly *Cîteaux in de Nederlanden*).

On Cistercian architecture, M. Aubert, *L'architecture cistercienne en France* (2nd edn., 2 vols., Paris, 1947); H. P. Eydoux, *L'architecture des églises cisterciennes d'Allemagne* (Paris, 1952); M.-A. Dimier, *Recueil des plans des églises cisterciennes* (Grignan-Paris, 1949; supplement, 1967); supplemented by the series of volumes published by Zodiaque, ed. by Père Dimier and others, on *L'art cistercien*, esp. *L'art cist. hors de France* (1971). There is an excellent survey of 'Cistercian architectural purism' by F. Bucher in *Comparative Studies in Society and History*, III (1960-1), 89-105; the special contribution of St Bernard is discussed by K. H. Esser in *Archiv für mittelrheinische Kirchengeschichte*, V (1953), 195-222 (see p. 254, chap. 9, n. 11); the fullest study of church plans and proportions, and of the relations of Cistercian and local styles, is H. Hahn, *Die frühe Kirchenbaukunst der Zisterzienser* (Berlin, 1957), based on Eberbach.

Chapter 10
On the knights, see esp. J. Riley-Smith, *The Knights of St John in Jerusalem and Cyprus, c. 1050-1310* (London, 1967); *New Catholic Encyclopedia*, arts. Knights of Malta, Templars; B. A. Lees, *Records of the Templars in England in the Twelfth Century* (London, 1935); H. G. Prutz, *Entwicklung und Untergang des Tempelherrenordens* (1888); D. W. Lomax, *La Orden de Santiago, 1170-1275* (Madrid, 1965). See also M. Dessubré, *Bibliographie de l'Ordre des Templiers* (Paris, 1928), H. Neu, *Bibliographie des Templer-Ordens . . ., 1927-65* (1965).

Chapter 11
The nuns have been somewhat neglected in recent literature: the only available general accounts are S. Hilpisch, *Geschichte der Benediktinerinnen* (St Ottilien, 1951; Eng. trans. by M. J. Muggli, *History of Benedictine Nuns*, Collegeville, 1958), and the elderly book of L. Eckenstein, *Women under Monasticism* (Cambridge, 1896); see also Hilpisch, *Die Doppelklöster* (Münster, 1928). Eileen Power's *Medieval English Nunneries* (Cambridge, 1922) remains the best book for the subject of this chapter. On Heloise, see p. 254, chap. 11, n. 10 (the letters); E. Gilson, *Héloïse et Abélard* (2nd edn., Paris, 1948; Eng. trans., London, 1953); R. W. Southern, *Medieval Humanism and Other Studies* (Oxford, 1970), chap. 6; on Hildegarde, see below (Rupertsberg); on the thirteenth-century movements, see section III under Villers, H. Grundmann, *Religiöse Bewegungen im Mittelalter* (2nd edn., Hildesheim, 1961), and B. Bolton in *Studies in Church History*, X (1973), pp. 77-95.

Chapter 12
On the Premonstratensians, see H. M. Colvin, *The White Canons in England* (Oxford, 1951, with good bibliography); Backmund; C. Dereine, 'Les Origines de Prémontré', in *Revue d'histoire ecclésiastique*, XLII (1947), 352-78. The two early lives of St Norbert are in *Monumenta Germaniae Hist., Scriptores*, XII (1856), 663 ff., and *PL*, CLXX, 1253-1344.

On the friars, see *RO*, I; P. Gratien, *Histoire de la Fondation et de l'Évolution de l'Ordre des Frères Mineurs au XIIIe siècle* (Paris-Gembloux, 1928); J. R. H. Moorman, *A History of the Franciscan Order* (to 1517) (Oxford, 1968); R. B. Brooke, *Early Franciscan Government* (Cambridge, 1959); R. F. Bennett, *The Early Dominicans* (Cambridge, 1937). On St Francis, the classic is P. Sabatier, *S. François d'Assise* (Paris, 1893-4; Eng. trans. by L. S. Houghton, 1926 edn.; on Sabatier's *Life*, see C. Brooke, *Medieval Church and Society*, chap. 10); for contemporary lives etc., see R. B. Brooke, in *Latin Biography* (ed. T. A. Dorey, London, 1967), pp. 177-98, and her edn. of *Scripta Leonis . . .* (Oxford, 1970). On St Dominic, M.-H. Vicaire, *Histoire de S. Dominique* (2 vols., Paris, 1957; Eng. trans. K. Pond, London, 1964); for contemporary lives etc., see Vicaire, *S. Dominique de Caleruega d'après les documents du XIIIe siècle* (Paris, 1955); C. Brooke, *Medieval Church and Society*, chap. 11. For both saints there are vivid introductions in L. von Matt's pictorial biographies (*St Francis of Assisi*, with W. Hauser; *St Dominic*, with M.-H. Vicaire; London 1956-7; the text of the former is trans. from German, the latter from French; of both there are editions in German, French, Italian and Dutch, and of *St Dominic* also in Spanish and Portuguese). For detailed studies, there are numerous periodicals, e.g. *Archivum Franciscanum historicum, Franciscan Studies, Collectanea Franciscana* (with annual bibliography), *Archivum Fratrum Praedicatorum*.

Chapter 13
On Fountains see *MSA*, pp. 93-7; W. H. St John Hope in *Yorks Archaeological Journal*, XV (1900), 269-402; P. Gilyard-Beer, *Fountains Abbey* (London, HMSO, 1970); articles by L. G. D. Baker (chap. 13, n. 7).

On Mont Saint-Michel, *Millénaire monastique du Mont Saint-Michel*, ed. J. Laporte, R. Foreville, M. Baudot and M. Nortier, 4 vols., Paris, 1966-71; P. Gout, *Le Mont Saint-Michel*, 2 vols., Paris, 1910; G. Bazin, *Le Mont Saint-Michel*, Paris, 1933; J. J. G. Alexander, *Norman Illumination at Mont Saint-Michel 966-1100*, Oxford, 1970 (esp. p. 4

and n. 3 for bibliog. on early buildings).

On Sant'Ambrogio, F. Reggiori, *La Basilica di Sant' Ambrogio* (see p. 255, chap. 13, n. 14; shorter introduction in A. M. Romanini, *Milano: S. Ambrogio*); see also articles by P. Zerbi (ibid.), and for Milanese society, C. Violante, *La pataria milanese e la riforma ecclesiastica*, I (Rome, 1955).

Chapter 14

Especially helpful for this chapter are *Atlas Cist*; Cottineau (useful, but unreliable in matters of detail); and for individual countries KH and its companion volume by D. E. Easson for Scotland (1957) and A. Gwynn and R. N. Hadcock for Ireland (1970); J. A. Watt, *The Church and the Two Nations in Medieval Ireland* (Cambridge, 1970); Hauck; *Gallia Christiana* (see p. 253); *GB*; and for Poland and Bohemia, J. Kłoczowski in *La Mendola*, III, IV and VI.

Chapter 15

For the late Middle Ages, see esp. Coulton, *Five Centuries* (p. 256); Knowles, *RO*, III. For Much Wenlock, *MSA*, pp. 53-5. The chief sources for the internal life of monasteries from the late twelfth to the fifteenth centuries are the comparatively few chroniclers who tell us the gossip of a community, of whom Jocelin of Brakelond (ed. and trans. H. E. Butler, Nelson's Medieval Texts, 1949) is the most celebrated, and visitation records. On these, see esp. Knowles, *RO*, II, chap. XV; the most substantial early records of visitations are in the fascinating mid thirteenth century diary, alias *Register of Eudes of Rouen*, trans. S. M. Brown, ed. J. F. O'Sullivan (Columbia Records of Civilisation, 1964).

It is impossible to summarise briefly the books on recent monastic history. A readable general survey, from without but based on extensive inquiry, is G. Moorhouse, *Against All Reason* (London, 1969; Penguin edn. 1972). Helpful examples of modern literature are *The Cistercian Spirit: A Symposium*, ed. M. B. Pennington (Shannon, 1970) and H. van Zeller, *The Benedictine Idea* (London, 1959).

III

This section comprises a list of monasteries used as examples in this book, and shown on the map, p. 10; it is intended to give very brief details—country, order, date of foundation—and basic references for each. The selection is aimed to support the text and plates and indicate further reading; it is sometimes slanted towards the history of a house, sometimes towards its physical remains, or some special feature, according to the use of the house as an example in the book.

Abbreviations

Aug.	Augustinian Order (canons regular)
f.	founded
O.Cart.	Carthusian Order
O.Cist.	Cistercian Order
O.F.M.	Order of Friars Minor (Franciscan friars)
O.P.	Order of Preachers (Dominican friars)
O.Praem.	Premonstratensian Order
O.S.B.	Order of St Benedict (Benedictine monks)

For other abbreviations, see p. 251.

Abingdon (England), O.S.B., f. 7th cent., ref. *c*. 954. KH, pp. 52, 58.

Alcobaça (Portugal), O.Cist., f. *c*. 1153. Dimier (1971), pp. 254-98.

Altenberg (Dhüntal, W. Germany), O.Cist., f. 1133. *Germania Sacra*, neue Folge II, Berlin, 1965 (H. Mosler).

Alvastra (Sweden), O.Cist., f. 1143. *Atlas Cist.*, p. 270; see p. 233.

Apt (France), early monastery, f. *c*. 420. Cf. O. Chadwick, *John Cassian*, 2nd edn. (Cambridge, 1968), pp. 37 ff.

Arles (France), Saint-Trophime, Cathedral, Aug. (see p. 253, chap. 8, n. 4). L. H. Labande, *L'église Saint-Trophime d'Arles*, Paris, 1930; A. Borg, *Architectural Sculpture in Romanesque Provence*, Oxford, 1972, chap. 5.

Arrouaise (France), Aug., f. *c*. 1090. L. Milis, *L'ordre de chanoines réguliers d'Arrouaise*, 2 vols., Bruges, 1969; *Constitutiones*, ed. L. Milis and J. Becquet, Turnholti, 1970.

Assisi (Italy), Basilica and Sacro Convento (f. 1228), Carceri, and San Damiano (f. 1213), O.F.M. L. von Matt and W. Hauser, *St Francis of Assisi, a Pictorial Biography*, Eng. trans., London, 1956; B. Kleinschmidt, *Die Basilika San Francesco in Assisi*, 3 vols., Berlin, 1915-28; A. Smart, *The Assisi Problem and the Art of Giotto*, Oxford, 1971.

Bangor (Ireland), early monastery, 6th cent.; O.S.A. 12th (see p. 233). A. Gwynn and R. N. Hadcock, *Medieval Religious Houses, Ireland*, London, 1970, pp. 30, 161.

Bec (France), O.S.B., f. *c*. 1039. A. A. Porée, *Histoire de l'abbaye du Bec*, 2 vols., Évreux, 1901; *Spicilegium Beccense*, I, Congrès international du IXe centénaire de l'arrivée d'Anselme au Bec, Le Bec-Paris, 1959.

Bernay (France), O.S.B., f. -1017. *Gallia Christiana*, XI (edn. of Paris, 1874), coll. 830 ff.; A. W. Clapham, *English Romanesque Architecture after the Conquest* (Oxford, 1934), pp. 4ff.

Bingen, see Rupertsberg.

Blanchland (England), O.Praem., f. 1165. H. M. Colvin, *The White Canons in England* (Oxford, 1951), pp. 97-9, 371.

Bobbio (Italy), f. 613. Schmitz, I, 68 f.; *IP*, VI, ii, 245 ff.

Bologna (Italy), San Domenico, formerly St Nicholas, O.P., f. 1219. M.-H. Vicaire, *St Dominic* (p. 258), pp. 270 ff., 300 ff., 371 ff. (Eng. trans.).

Bologna, Santo Stefano, O.S.B., f. 973 (as monastery; the complex is ?5th cent. in origin). G. Aprato, *Bologna, Complesso di S. Stefano*, Tesori d'Arte Cristiana, 11 (Bologna, 1966); *IP*, V, 264 ff; Krautheimer, pp. 127 ff.

Brevnov, see Prague.

Brogne (France), O.S.B., f. 914. Schmitz, I, 160 ff.; *DHGE*, X, 818-32 (F. Baix).

Buildwas (England), O.Cist., f. 1135 (Savigniac till 1147). *MSA*, pp. 106-7; Dimier (1971), pp. 137-80.

Bury St Edmunds (England), O.S.B., f. 1020-2. KH, pp. 53, 61; *MSA*, pp. 14-15.

Caen (France), Saint-Etienne, O.S.B., and La Sainte-Trinité, O.S.B., nuns, f. *c*. 1066. L. Musset, *Les actes de Guillaume le Conquérant et de la reine Mathilde pour les abbayes caennaises* (Caen, 1967).

Camaldoli (Italy), f. ?*c*. 1000. *DHGE*, XI, 509-12 (on order), 512-36 (on monastery) (A. des Mazis); P. Ciampelli, *Guida storica illustrata di Camaldoli e sacro eremo . . .* (Udine, 1906 and later edns.).

Canterbury (England), Christ Church Cathedral Priory, O.S.B., f. 598, refounded 997. R. W. Southern, *St Anselm and his Biographer* (Cambridge, 1963), chap. VII, and *passim*; Knowles, *MO, passim*; T. S. R. Boase, *English Art 1100-1216* (Oxford, 1953), chaps. II, IX; R. A. L. Smith, *Canterbury Cathedral Priory* (Cambridge, 1943: chiefly economic history, 13th-15th centuries).

Canterbury, St Augustine's, O.S.B., f. 598-605. A. W. Clapham, *St Augustine's Abbey, Canterbury* (London, H.M.S.O., 1955).

Carceri, see Assisi.

Carlisle (England) Cathedral Priory, Aug., f. 1133 (as Cathedral). KH, pp. 139, 152; Dickinson, pp. 245-51; J. Le Neve, *Fasti Ecclesiae Anglic., 1066-1300*, II, ed. D. E. Greenway (London, 1971), pp. 19, 21.

Casamari (Italy), O.S.B., f. -1030; O. Cist., f. 1140. *Atlas Cist.*, p. 275; Dimier (1971), pp. 199-207.

Cava dei Tirreni, La (Italy), O.S.B., f. 1011. Schmitz, I, 185 ff., and bibliog. note, p. 185, n. 39; *DHGE*, XII, 21-5 (P. Schmitz); *IP*, VIII, 309-30.

Cefalù (Sicily), Cathedral, Aug., f. 1131. O. Demus, *The Mosaics of Norman Sicily* (London, 1949 [1950], chap. 1.

Chartreuse, La Grande (France), O.Cart., f. 1084. See p. 257.

Chiaravalle (Italy, near Milan), O.Cist., f. 1135-6. *Atlas Cist.*, p. 275.

Chiusa (Italy), *see* Sagra di S. Michele.

Cîteaux (France), O.Cist., f. 1097-8. *DHGE*, XII, 852 ff. (J.-M. Canivez); Knowles, *GHE*, pp. 197-222.

Clairvaux (France), O.Cist., f. 1115. E. Vacandard, *Vie de S. Bernard* (2 vols., 4th edn., Paris, 1910).

Cluny (France), O.S.B. (Cluniac), f. 910. See p. 257.

Colchester (England), St Botolph, Aug., f. *c.* 1093, completed by 1106. KH, pp. 139, 155; Dickinson, pp. 98 ff.

Conques (France), O.S.B., refounded 8th cent. *Rouergue roman* (Zodiaque, 1963), pp. 27-184.

Cuxa, St-Michel-de- (France), O.S.B., f. -841; revived 10th cent. *DHGE*, XIII, 1121-42 (C.-M. Baraut).

Dijon (France), St-Bénigne, O.S.B., f. 6th cent., refounded 1001. R. Oursel, *Invention de l'architecture romane* (Zodiaque, 1970), pp. 71 ff.; *Bourgogne romane*, ed. R. Oursel (5th edn., Zodiaque, 1968), pp. 47 ff.; Knowles, *MO*, pp. 84 ff.; Hunt (1971), chap. 6, and refs. (the last two on the work and influence of St William of Volpiano and Dijon).

Dryburgh (Scotland), O.Praem., f. 1150-2. J. Bulloch, *Adam of Dryburgh* (London, 1958), esp. chap. 5; J. S. Richardson and M. Wood, *Dryburgh Abbey* (Edinburgh, HMSO, 1948).

Dünamunde (U.S.S.R., formerly Latvia), O.Cist., f. before 1208. *Atlas Cist.*, p. 277.

Durham (England) Cathedral Priory, O.S.B., f. 1083. *MSA*, pp. 2-3; G. H. Cook, *Portrait of Durham Cathedral* (London, 1948); T. S. R. Boase, *English Art 1100-1216* (Oxford, 1953), chaps. I, VIII.

Durrow (Ireland), early monastery, f. ?*c.* 556; Aug., mid 12th cent. A. Gwynn and R. N. Hadcock, *Medieval Religious Houses, Ireland* (London, 1970), pp. 174-5.

Eberbach (Germany), O.Cist., f. *c.* 1135 (previously O.S.B.). Hahn (p. 254, chap. 9, n. 11); Dimier (1971).

Einsiedeln (Switzerland), O.S.B., f. 934. *DHGE*, XV, 95-7 (R. Henggeler); *GP*, II, ii, 65-72.

Esrom (Denmark), O.Cist., f. 1154. *Atlas Cist.*, p. 278.

Essen (Germany), O.S.B., nuns, f. *c.* 850. *DHGE*, XV, 1009-12 (A. Franzen); Dr Sandforth, *Der Essener Münsterschatz* (Essen, n.d.); H. Köhn, *Der Essener Münster* (Essen, 1953).

Essen-Werden (Germany), O.S.B., f. (by St Liudger) 799-801. Hauck, II, 407, 804; Zarnecki; *Romanik* (p. 257), p. 72 and pl. 102; W. Zimmermann *et al.*, *Die Kirchen zu Essen-Werden*, Essen, 1959; R. Wesenberg, *Frühe mittelalterliche Bildwerke*, Düsseldorf, 1972, pp. 101-2.

Evesham (England), O.S.B., f. 8th cent., refounded *c.* 995. KH, pp. 54, 65.

Falkenau (nr Dorpat, U.S.S.R., formerly Esthonia), O.Cist., f. 1233-4. *Atlas Cist.*, p. 278.

Farfa (Italy), ?early monastery, later O.S.B., f. 7th cent. *DHGE*, XVI, 547-53 (I. Tassi); *IP*, II, 55 ff.

Finchale (England), O.S.B., cell of Durham, f. 1170. KH, pp. 65, 66; C. Peers, *Finchale Priory* (London, HMSO, 1933).

Fleury, St-Benoît-sur-Loire (France), O.S.B., f. 672-4. Schmitz, I, 37-8 and n. 76; G. Chenesseau, *L'Abbaye de Fleury à Saint-Benoît-sur-Loire* (Paris, 1931); *S. Benoît-sur-Loire* (Zodiaque, 1962).

Florence (Italy), *see* references under Camaldoli.

Florence, San Miniato, O.S.B., f. ?before 783, refounded early 11th cent. *DHGE*, XVII, 546-8 (C. C. Calzolai).

Fonte Avellana (Italy), O.S.B., f. *c.* 990. *DHGE*, XVII, 888-91 (G. M. Cacciamani); *IP*, IV, 92 ff.

Fontevrault (France), O. Fontevrault, f. 1099. *DHGE*, XVII, 961-71 (J. Daoust); M. Melot, *(L'abbaye de) Fontevrault* (Petites Monographies . . ., Paris, 1971); on the tombs see esp. G. Zarnecki, *The Monastic Achievement* (London, 1972), pp. 93-4.

Fossanova (Italy), O.S.B., f. 8th-9th cent., O.Cist., f. 1135. Dimier (1971), pp. 189-98; C. d'Onofrio e C. Pietrangeli, *Le abbazie del Lazio* (Rome, 1971), pp. 229-44.

Fountains (England), O.Cist., f. 1132-3. See p. 258.

Fruttuaria (Italy), O.S.B., f. *c.* 1003. Schmitz, I, 183; bibliog. in Cottineau, I, 1227-8.

Fulda (Germany), O.S.B., f. 744. Hauck, I, 580 ff., II, *passim*. Krautheimer, pp. 209 ff.

Gandersheim (Germany), nuns, f. 852-6. Hauck, II, 601 ff., 799; A. Schulte, *Der Adel und die deutsche Kirche im Mittelalter* (Stuttgart, 1910), pp. 405 ff.

Gernrode (Germany), nuns, f. 961. Hauck, III, 1017; Schulte, pp. 407 ff.

Glastonbury (England), early monastery (? 6th cent.), then O.S.B., refounded 940. *MSA*, pp. 28-31; KH, pp. 54, 66.

Gloucester, see Llanthony.

Gorze (France, formerly Germany), O.S.B., f. *c.* 933. K. Hallinger, *Gorze-Kluny* (2 vols., Rome, 1950-1).

Grandmont (France), O. Grandmont, f. after 1076. See p. 257.

Heidenheim (Germany), double monastery for monks and nuns, f. 751. Hauck, II, 798, *GP*, II, 10-15; *GB*, II, 114-17.

Heiligenkreuz (Austria), O.Cist., f. *c.* 1135. *Atlas Cist.*, p. 282; *GP*, I, pp. 253-6.

Helmarshausen (Germany), O.S.B., f. 997. Hauck, III, 1022; Theophilus, ed. Dodwell (pp. 257-8), pp. xli ff.

Hexham (England), early monastery, f. 674; later Aug., f. 1113. KH, pp. 140, 159-60.

Hirsau (Germany), O.S.B., f. before 830, refounded by Abbot William in the years following 1069. H. Jakobs, *Die Hirsauer*, Köln-Graz, 1969; W. Hoffmann, *Hirsau und die 'Hirsauer Bauschule'* (Munich, 1950).

Hohenb(o)urg, see St Odilien.

Hovedö (Norway), O.Cist., f. 1147. *Atlas Cist.*, p. 283.

Las Huelgas (nr Burgos, Spain), O.Cist., nuns, f. 1187. *Atlas Cist.*, p. 283.

Iona (Scotland), early monastery, f. late 6th century. A. Gwynn and R. N. Hadcock, *Medieval Religious Houses, Ireland* (London, 1970), p. 38; *Adomnan's Life of Columba*, ed. and trans. A. O. and M. O. Anderson (Edinburgh/London, 1961).

Jarrow (England), early monastery, then O.S.B., f. 681, refounded 1074. Early mon. joint with Monkwearmouth, and the home of Bede. KH, pp. 68, 71; *Medieval Archaeology*, X (1966), 169 f., XI (1967), 263 f.; XII (1968), 155-6, XVI (1972), 148-52 (reports of R. Cramp's excavations).

Jedburgh (Scotland), Aug., f. *c.* 1138. *MSA*, pp. 188-9; *Royal Commission on Ancient Monts., Scotland, Roxburghshire* (1956), I, 194-207.

Jumièges (France), O.S.B., f. *c.* 654. *Jumièges, Congrès scientifique du xiiie centénaire* (2 vols., Rouen, 1955); R. Martin du Gard, *L'abbaye de Jumièges* (Montdidier, 1909); L. Jouen, *Jumièges, Histoire et légendes . . .* (edn. of Rouen, 1954); E. Remnant in *Journal of the Brit. Arch. Association*, 3rd Series, XX-XXI (1957-8), 107-38 and bibliog. on p. 138.

Kelso (Scotland), O.S.B. Tironian, f. 1113-28. *MSA*, pp. 60-1; *Roxburghshire* (see Jedburgh), I, 240-6.

Kingswood (England), O.Cist., f. 1139. KH, pp. 113, 121; *Letters and Charters of Gilbert Foliot*, ed. A. Morey and C. N. L. Brooke (Cambridge, 1967), pp. 510-13.

Kirkstead (England), O.Cist., f. 1139. KH, pp. 113, 121; *MSA*, pp. 126-7.

Lacock (England), Aug. nuns, f. 1230-2. *VCH Wiltshire*, III, 303-16 (H. M. Chew); H. Brakespear in *Archaeologia*, LVII (1901), 125-48; C. H. Talbot in *Journ. of the Brit. Archaeol. Assoc.*, New Series, XI (1905), 175-210; *MSA*, pp. 264-5.

Laon (France), Templars, f. before 1160 (later Hospitallers), now in the Musée municipal garden. *Guide Bleu, Flandre, Hainaut, Artois, Picardie* (edn. of 1966), p. 531.

Leicester (England), Aug., f. 1143. *VCH Leics.*, II, 13-19 (R. A. McKinley).

Lézat (France), O.S.B., f. 940. Hunt (1971), pp. 100 ff. (article by A. M. Mundó).

Llanthony (Monmouthshire and England), two houses closely linked, O.S.A., I, f. 1103-8, II (in Gloucester), f. 1136. *MSA*, pp. 208-9, 210-11, and references.

London (England), Charterhouse, O.Cart., f. 1371. M. D. Knowles and W. F. Grimes, *Charterhouse* (London, 1954).

London, Holy Trinity Priory, Aldgate, Aug., f. 1107-8. Dickinson, pp. 109 ff.; *Cartulary of Holy Trinity Aldgate*, ed. G. A. J. Hodgett (London Red. Soc., 1971); C. Brooke and G. Keir, *Saxon and Norman London* (forthcoming).

London, Clerkenwell, Hospital of St John of Jerusalem, Hospitallers, f. *c.* 1144; *Royal Commission on Hist. Monuments, London*, II, 16 ff.

London, Temple Church, Templars, f. *c.* 1128, moved to present site 1161; suppressed 1308-12. *Records of the Templars in England in the 12th century*, ed. B. A. Lees (London, 1935).

Lucca (Italy), San Frediano, Aug., f. before 1046, but probably not Aug. till 12th cent. M. Giusti in *La Mendola*, III, i, 447-8, and references.

Luxeuil (France), early monastery, then O.S.B., f. *c.* 590. Schmitz, I, 59 ff.

Lyse (Norway), O. Cist., f. 1146-7. *Atlas Cist.*, p. 286.

Marcigny (France), Cluniac, nuns, f. *c.* 1055. Hunt (1967), chap.5.

Maria Laach (Germany), O.S.B., f. 1093. A. Schippers, *Das Laacher Münster* (ed. T. Bogler, Köln, 1967); T. Bogler, *Maria Laach* (6th edn., Munich-Zürich, 1968).

Markyate (England), O.S.B., nuns, f. 1145. *The Life of Christina of Markyate*, ed. and trans. C. H. Talbot (Oxford, 1959); O. Pächt, C. R. Dodwell and F. Wormald, *The St Albans Psalter* (London, 1960).

Marseille (France), St Victor, early monastery (John Cassian's), later O.S.B. On early history, Chadwick, *Cassian*, esp. pp. 32 ff.

Maulbronn (Germany), O.Cist., f. 1138-47. *Atlas Cist.*, p. 287; *GP*, III, pp. 124-8.

Mazan (France), O.Cist., f. 1120. *Atlas Cist.*, p. 287.

Mellifont (Ireland), O.Cist., f. 1142. J. A. Watt, *The Church and the Two Nations in Medieval Ireland* (Cambridge, 1970), chap. 4.

Melrose (Scotland), O.Cist., f. 1136. *MSA*, pp. 64-5; J. S. Richardson and M. Wood, *Melrose Abbey* (2nd edn., Edinburgh, HMSO, 1949); *Roxburghshire* (see Jedburgh), II, 265-91.

Milan (Italy), Sant'Ambrogio, O.S.B., f. 789. See pp. 219 ff., 255, chap. 13, n. 14, 259.

Moissac (France), O.S.B. (for a time Cluniac), f. mid 7th cent. E. Rupin, *L'abbaye et les cloîtres de Moissac* (Paris, 1897); A. Anglès, *L'abbaye de Moissac* (Petites Monographies . . ., Paris, n.d.), *Quercy Roman*, ed. M. Vidal, J. Maury, J. Porcher (2nd edn., Zodiaque, 1969), pp. 33 ff.; E. Mâle, *L'art religieux du xiie siècle . . .* (edn. of 1940), pp. 4 ff.

Molesme (France), O.S.B., f. *c.* 1075. Knowles, *MO*, pp. 198-9, 752-3 and references.

Monkwearmouth (England), early monastery, then O.S.B., f. 674, refounded 1075. See Jarrow.

Monreale (Sicily), Cathedral, O.S.B., f. 1174. O. Demus (see Cefalù), chap. 4.

Mont St-Michel, Le (France), O.S.B., f. *c.* 708, refounded 966. See p. 258.

Monte Cassino (Italy), O.S.B., St Benedict's abbey, f. *c.* 530. Schmitz, I, 20 ff., 72 f., 179 f.

Montserrat (Spain), O.S.B., f. 1022-3. Hunt (1971), pp. 106 ff.; A.

Albareda, *L'abat Oliva, fundador de Montserrat* (Montserrat, 1931).

Morimond (France), O. Cist., f. 1115. *Atlas Cist.*, p. 289.

Mount Grace (England), O. Cart., f. 1398. *MSA*, pp. 234-5; W. Brown and W. H. St John Hope in *Yorks. Archaeol. Journ.*, XVIII (1905), 252-309; A. W. Clapham in *VCH North Riding of Yorks.*, II, 24-7.

Much Wenlock, see Wenlock.

Niederaltaich (Germany), O.S.B., f. 8th cent., ?741. Hauck, I, 508, II, 809; *GP*, I, 178-82; *GB*, II, 188-97.

Nonnberg, see Salzburg.

Northampton (England), St Andrew, Cluniac, f. 1093-1100. *VCH Northants.*, II, 102-9.

Nydala (Sweden), O.Cist., f. 1143. *Atlas Cist.*, p. 290.

Odensee (Denmark), O.S.B., f. *c.* 1095-1100. Knowles, *MO*, p. 164; see p. 255, chap. 14, n. 7.

Odilienberg, see St-Odilien.

Osma (Spain), Cathedral priory, Aug., f. (as Aug.) 1128-40. *La Mendola*, III, i, 233 (J. F. Rivera).

Ottobeuren (Germany), O.S.B., f. before 826, ?764. Hauck, II, 568, 798; *GP*, II, 78-81; *GB*, II, 209-20.

Paraclet(e) (France), O.S.B., nuns; the home of Heloise, f. 1129-31, see pp. 172, 254, chap. 11, n. 10.

Paris, see St-Denis.

Pisa (Italy), *see* references under Camaldoli.

Poblet (Spain), O.Cist., f. 1150-1. Dimier (1971), pp. 125-36; *Scriptorium Populeti* (Poblet, 1966-   ).

Pontefract (England), Cluniac, f. *c.* 1090. KH, pp. 97, 102.

Prague (Czechoslovakia), Hradcany and Brevnov, O.S.B., nuns and monks, f. after 967 and *c.* 993. J. Kłoczowski in *La Mendola*, VI, 159 f.

Prémontré (France), O.Praem., f. *c.* 1121. See p. 258.

Quedlinburg (Germany), nuns, f. 936. Hauck, III, 1016; Schulte (*see* Gandersheim), pp. 401 ff.

Ratzeburg (Germany), O.Praem. Cathedral, f. 1154. Backmund, I, 241-3, with bibliog.; A. Kamphausen, *Der Dom zu Ratzeburg*, 2nd edn., 1966.

Reading (England), O.S.B., f. 1121. Knowles, *MO*, pp. 281-2; *La Mendola*, VI, 138 and references.

Reichenau (Germany), O.S.B., f. 724. *Die Kultur der Abtei Reichenau*, ed. K. Beyerle (2 vols., Munich, 1925); *GP*, II, i, 147-58; C. R. Dodwell and D. H. Turner, *Reichenau Reconsidered* (London, 1965).

Reichersberg (Germany), Aug., f. 1080-4. P. Classen in *La Mendola*, III, i, 304-41; Classen, *Gerhoch von Reichersberg* (Wiesbaden, 1960).

Rievaulx (England), O.Cist., f. 1131-2. *MSA*, pp. 82-5; C. Peers, *Rievaulx Abbey* (London, HMSO, 1967); on Ailred, pp. 156-60.

Ripoll (Spain), O.S.B., f. late 9th cent. Hunt (1971), chap. 7 (by A. M. Mundó); F. Rahlves, *Kathedralen und Klöster in Spanien* (Eng. trans., London, 1966, pp. 118-21); G. Sanoner in *Bulletin Monumental*, LXXXII (1923), 352-99 (on the portal).

Ripon (England), early monastery, f. *c.* 654-60, later secular minster. KH, pp. 417, 435.

Rome (Italy), Santi Quattro Coronati, early Basilica, O.S.B. from early 12th cent. (Camaldol. 16th cent.; now nuns). A. Carletti, *Basilica dei SS. Quattro Coronati* (Rome, n.d.); *IP*, I, 40-2.

Rome, San Paolo fuori le Mura, early Basilica, O.S.B. from 8th cent., refounded mid 10th cent. *IP*, I, 164 ff.; W. Oakeshott, *Mosaics of Rome* (London, 1967), pp. 295 ff., 383.

Rupertsberg, nr. Bingen (Germany), O.S.B., nuns, home of St Hildegarde, f. 1147-8. Hauck, IV, 398 ff., 934-5; H. Liebeschütz, *Das allegorische Weltbild der heiligen Hildegard von Bingen* (2nd edn., Darmstadt, 1964).

Sagra di San Michele (Chiusa), nr Turin (Italy), O.S.B., f. 966 or 999-1002. *IP*, VI, ii, 120 ff.; V. Moccagatta, *Torino: Sagra di S. Michele*, Tesori d'Arte Cristiana, Bologna, 1966; G. Gaddo, *La Sacra di S. Michele . . .*, Genoa, 1958; C. Verzár, *Die romanischen Skulpturen der Abtei Sagra di San Michele*, Bern, 1968.

Sahagún (Spain), O.S.B., f. before 1000, Cluniac from 1080. J. Perez and R. Escalona, *Historia del real monasterio de Sahagún* (Madrid, 1782); H. E. J. Cowdrey, *The Cluniacs and the Gregorian Reform* (Oxford, 1970), pp. 230-44.

St Albans (England), O.S.B., f. *c.* 793, refounded *c.* 970. *MSA*, pp. 6-7; *Royal Commission on Hist. Monuments, Herts.* (London, HMSO, 1910), pp. 177-87.

St-Denis, nr Paris (France), O.S.B., f. 7th cent. *Abbot Suger on the Abbey Church of St-Denis* (Princeton, 1946).

St-Évroult (France), O.S.B., f. mid 7th cent., refounded shortly before 1050. *Ecclesiastical History of Orderic Vitalis*, ed. and trans. M. Chibnall, esp. III (Oxford, 1972), pp. xv ff. and *passim*.

St Gallen (St Gall) (Switzerland), early monastery, later O.S.B., f. by St Gall, disciple of St Columbanus, *c.* 613. J. M. Clark, *The Abbey of St Gall* (Cambridge, 1926); H. Reinhart, *Der St Galler Klosterplan* (St Gallen, 1952).

St-Gilles (France), O.S.B., f. 8th cent. R. Hamann, *Die Abteikirche von St Gilles und ihre künstlerische Nachfolge* (3 vols., Berlin, 1955); E. Goiffon, *St-Gilles* (Nîmes, 1882).

St-Guilhem-le-Desert (France), O.S.B., f. early 9th cent. *Gallia Christiana*, VI (Paris, 1739), 580 ff.

St-Martin-du-Canigou (France), O.S.B., f. 1001. *Roussillon roman*, ed. M. Durliat (2nd edn., Zodiaque, 1964), pp. 115 ff.; Hunt (1971), pp. 105 ff.; M. Durliat in *Bulletin Monumental*, CXXX (1972), 353.

St-Odilien, Odilienberg (Hohenb(o)urg) (France, formerly Germany), nuns, f. 7th cent. Home of Herrad(e), mid-late 12th cent. abbess and author of the *Hortus deliciarum* (ed. A. Straub and G. Keller, Strasbourg, 1879-99); cf. E. Mâle, *L'art religieux du xiie siècle* (4th edn., Paris, 1940), pp. 317-18.

St-Riquier (France), O.S.B., f. mid 7th cent. Cottineau, II, 2868-9; *Gallia Christiana*, X, 1241-63; G. Durand, *L'église de S. Riquier* (Petites Monographies . . ., Paris, 1933); A. W. Clapham, *English Romanesque Architecture before the Conquest* (Oxford, 1930), pp. 78 ff.

St-Ruf (nr Avignon, France), Aug., f. *c.* 1039. Dickinson, p. 42; C. Dereine in *Revue Bénédictine*, LIX (1949), 161-82; A. H. Duparc in *La Mendola*, III, 114-28.

St-Savin-sur-Gartempe (France), O.S.B., f. early 9th cent. R. Crozet in *Dict. des églises de France*, III, C, pp. 188-93; O. Demus, *Romanesque Mural Painting* (Eng. trans., London, 1970), pp. 420-3; *La Bible de S. Savin*, ed. R. Oursel (Zodiaque, 1971).

San Juan de la Peña (Spain), O.S.B., f. early 11th cent. *Aragon roman*, ed. A. Canellas-Lopez and A. San Vicente (Zodiaque, 1971), pp. 69 ff.

Santes Creus (Spain), O.Cist., f. 1150. Dimier (1971), pp. 245-53.

Santo Domingo, see Silos.

Salzburg, Nonnberg (Austria), nuns, *c.* 700. Hauck, I, 376, II, 808.

Savigny (France), O.S.B., f. 1112; from 1147, with its whole order, O.Cist. *Atlas Cist.*, p. 296; Cottineau, II, 2965-7; lives of early abbots and monks ed. E. P. Sauvage in *Analecta Bollandiana*, I (1882), 355-410, II (1883), 475-560 (and see Tiron).

Séez (France), Cathedral, Aug. from 1131. Dickinson, p. 29; *Letters of Arnulf of Lisieux*, ed. F. Barlow (London, 1939), pp. xvii f., 55 ff.

Sempringham (England), Gilbertine Order, f. *c.* 1131. KH, pp. 194 ff.; R. Graham, *S. Gilbert of Sempringham and the Gilbertines* (London, 1901); *MSA*, pp. 242-5.

Sénanque (France), O.Cist., f. 1148. *Atlas Cist.*, p. 297; *Abbaye de Sénanque* (Lyon, n.d.).

Sherborne (England), O.S.B., f. *c.* 993. KH, pp. 57, 76.

Silos, Santo Domingo de (Spain), O.S.B., f. early 10th cent., home of S. Domingo, abbot 1041-73. *DHGE*, XIV, 623-7 (A. Ruiz on S. Domingo); M. Férotin, *Histoire de l'abbaye de Silos* (Paris, 1897); J. Perez de Urbel, *El Claustro de Silos* (Burgos, 1930); *Castille romane*, II, ed. L.-M. de Lojendio and A. Rodriguez (Zodiaque, 1966).

Silvacane (France), O.Cist., f. 1147. *Atlas Cist.*, p. 297; P. Pontus, *L'abbaye de Silvacane* (Caisse Nat. des Monuments Hist., Paris, 1966).

Solesmes (France), O.S.B., f. 1010; refounded 1664 (Maurist), 1833-7. Cottineau, II, 3055-7.

Subiaco (Italy), f. early 6th cent., home of St Benedict (before Monte Cassino). *IP*, II, 83 ff.

Sulejów (Poland), O.Cist., f. 1177. *Atlas Cist.*, p. 298; *Sztuka polska przeromanska i romanska . . .*, ed. M. Walickiego (2 vols., Warsaw, 1971), I, 176, pls. 227, 230-2, 240, II, 826.

Taizé (France), Protestant Community, f. 1940-9. See pp. 248, 255, chap. 15, n. 3.

Tegernsee (Germany), O.S.B., 8th cent. Schmitz, II, 128 ff.; *GP*, I, 360-70; *GB*, II, 297-304.

Le Thoronet (France), O.Cist., f. *c.* 1146. R. Berenguier, *L'abbaye du Thoronet* (Caisse Nat. des Monts. Historiques, Paris, 1971); P. Colas in *Monts. Historiques de la France*, nouv. sér., IV (1958), 32-41, XV (1969), 50-1.

Tiron (France), O.S.B. (Tironian), f. *c.* 1105. Knowles, *MO*, pp. 200-1; H. Grundmann, *Religiöse Bewegungen im Mittelalter* (2nd edn., Hildesheim, 1961), pp. 40 ff., 489 (on Tiron, Savigny etc.).

Toledo (Spain), Cathedral and S. Leocadia, Aug., f. early 12th cent., 1156-62. *La Mendola*, III, i, 221-8.

Tomar (Portugal), Templars, f. *c.* 1160, after suppression of Templars Orden de Cristo, *Guia de Portugal*, II (Lisbon, 1927), 456-83.

Toulouse (France), S. Sernin, early monastery O.S.B., from 9th cent.; Cottineau, II, 3183-5.

La Trappe (France), O.Cist., f. 1122 (Savigniac, 1140, Cist. 1147), refounded 1664. *Atlas Cist.*, p. 299; H. Brémond, *L'abbé tempête* (Paris, 1929, Eng. trans., London, 1930).

Tre Fontane (Italy), O.Cist., f. 7th cent., Cist. 1140. *Atlas Cist.*, p. 299.

Trier, S. Maximin (Germany), O.S.B., f. ? (cf. Hauck, I, 255), refounded 934. Hauck, III, 364 ff., 372 ff.; K. Hallinger, *Gorze-Kluny* (Rome, 1950-1), I, 59 f., 96 ff.

Turin, see Sagra di S. Michele.

Tyniec (nr Kraków, Poland), O.S.B., f. *c.* 1060. J. Kłoczowski in *La Mendola*, VI, 163.

Vallombrosa (Italy), f. *c.* 1039. Cottineau, II, 3286-7; *IP*, III, 834 ff. D. F. Tarani, *L'ordine Vallombrosano* (Florence, 1921).

Verona (Italy), San Zeno Maggiore, O.S.B., f. *c.* 800. *IP*, VII, i, 267-71; L. Puppi, *Chiesa di S. Zeno, Verona* (Tesori d'Arte Cristiana, Bologna, 1967); *Verona e il suo Territorio*, II (Verona, 1964), pp. 670-86, 693-744 etc.

Vézelay (France), O.S.B., f. *c.* 863-8 (Cluniac, 11th-12th cents.). F. Salet, *La Madeleine de Vézelay* (Melun, 1948); H. E. J. Cowdrey, *The Cluniacs and the Gregorian Reform* (Oxford, 1970), pp. 13-14, 85-7.

Villers-la-Ville (Belgium), O.Cist., f. 1146. *Atlas Cist.*, pp. 301-2; E. de Moreau, *L'abbaye de Villers en Brabant aux xiie et xiiie siècles* (Brussels, 1909); S. Roisin, 'L'efflorescence cistercienne et le courant féminin de piété au xiiie siècle', *Revue d'Histoire Ecclésiastique*, XXXIX (1943), 342-78.

Vivarium (Italy), early monastery, home of Cassiodorus, f. *c.* 555. *DHGE*, XI, 1357 ff. (D. M. Cappuyns).

Vreden (Germany), nuns, f. *c.* 839. Hauck, II, 806; Schulte (see Gandersheim), pp. 55 ff.

Wenlock, Much (England), nuns, f. 7th cent., refounded as Cluniac 1080-1. *MSA*, pp. 53-5; R. Graham, *The History of the Alien Priory of Wenlock* (London, HMSO, 1965).

Werden, see Essen-Werden.

Whitby (England), double house under St Hilda, 7th cent. (*c.* 657), refounded O.S.B., before 1077. Bede, *Eccl. History*, esp. bk. iv, c. 23 (21); H. Mayr-Harting, *Coming of Christianity to Anglo-Saxon England* (London, 1972), pp. 149 ff., 297-8; *MSA*, pp. 18-19.

Winchester (England), Cathedral Priory of St Swithun, and New Minster, later Hyde Abbey, O.S.B., f. 964. R. Willis, *Architectural Hist. of Winchester Cathedral* (London, Archaeol. Inst., 1845-6); M. Biddle, archaeol. reports in *Archaeol. Journal*, CXIX (1961), 150 ff. (with R. N. Quirk) and *Antiquaries Journal* from XLIV (1964), esp. LII (1972), 115 ff., summarised in *The Old Minster . . .* (Winchester, 1970).

Witham (England), O.Cart., f. 1178-9. *Magna Vita S. Hugonis*, ed. and trans. D. L. Douie and H. Farmer (2 vols., Nelson's Medieval Texts, 1961-2), esp. I, pp. xxii ff.

Worcester (England) Cathedral Priory, O.S.B., f. ?969. *MSA*, pp. 10-11; Knowles, *MO*, pp. 74 ff.

Xanten (Germany) Cathedral, unsuccessful attempt at regular reform by St Norbert, 1115 (H. M. Colvin, *White Canons in England*, Oxford, 1951, pp. 1-2).

York (England), St Mary, O.S.B., f. -1086. *MSA*, pp. 20-1; *Heads of Religious Houses, England and Wales*, ed. D. Knowles, C. N. L. Brooke, V.C.M. London (Cambridge, 1972), p. 84; *The Noble City of York*, ed. A. Stacpoole (York, 1972).

List of illustrations

Maps and plans

Index

Roman figures refer to the text by page, italic to the illustrations by number. For the abbreviations used for religious orders, see page 259.